5495
65B

Muscular Christianity was an important religious, literary, and social movement of the mid-nineteenth century. This volume draws on recent developments in cultural and gender theory to reveal ideological links between muscular Christianity and the work of novelists and essayists, including Kingsley, Emerson, Dickens, Hughes, MacDonald, and Pater, and to explore the use of images of hyper-masculinized male bodies to represent social as well as physical ideals. *Muscular Christianity* argues that the ideologies of the movement were extreme versions of common cultural conceptions, and that anxieties evident in muscular Christian texts, often manifested through images of the body as a site of socio-political conflict, were pervasive throughout society. Throughout, muscular Christianity is shown to be at the heart of issues of gender, class, and national identity in the Victorian age.

CAMBRIDGE STUDIES IN NINETEENTH-CENTURY
LITERATURE AND CULTURE 2

MUSCULAR CHRISTIANITY

CAMBRIDGE STUDIES IN NINETEENTH-CENTURY
LITERATURE AND CULTURE

General editors
Gillian Beer, *Girton College, Cambridge*
Catherine Gallagher, *Department of English,*
University of California, Berkeley

Editorial board
Isobel Armstrong, *Birkbeck College, London*
Terry Eagleton, *St Catherine's College, Oxford*
Leonore Davidoff, *University of Essex*
D. A. Miller, *Harvard University*
J. Hillis Miller, *University of California, Irvine*
Mary Poovey, *The Johns Hopkins University*
Elaine Showalter, *Princeton University*

Nineteenth-century British literature and culture have been a rich field for
interdisciplinary studies. Since the turn of the twentieth century, scholars
and critics have tracked the intersections and tensions between Victorian
literature and the visual arts, politics, social organization, economic life,
technical innovations, scientific thought – in short, culture in its broadest
sense. In recent years, theoretical challenges and historiographical shifts
have unsettled the assumptions of previous scholarly syntheses and called
into question the terms of older debates. Whereas the tendency in much
past literary critical interpretation was to use the metaphor of culture as
"background", feminist, Foucauldian, and other analyses have employed
more dynamic models that raise questions of power and of circulation.
Such developments have re-animated the field.

This new series aims to accommodate and promote the most interesting
work being undertaken on the frontiers of the field of nineteenth-century
literary studies: work which intersects fruitfully with other fields of study
such as history, or literary theory, or the history of science. Comparative as
well as interdisciplinary approaches are welcomed.

Titles published
The Sickroom in Victorian Fiction
The Art of Being Ill
by Miriam Bailin, *Washington University*

Muscular Christianity
Embodying the Victorian Age
edited by Donald E. Hall, *California State University, Northridge*

MUSCULAR CHRISTIANITY

Embodying the Victorian Age

EDITED BY

DONALD E. HALL

California State University, Northridge

CAMBRIDGE
UNIVERSITY PRESS

Published by the Press Syndicate of the University of Cambridge
The Pitt Building, Trumpington Street, Cambridge CB2 1RP
40 West 20th Street, New York, NY 10011–4211, USA
10 Stamford Road, Oakleigh, Melbourne 3166, Australia

First published 1994

Printed in Great Britain at the University Press, Cambridge

A catalogue record for this book is available from the British Library

Library of Congress cataloguing in publication data
Muscular Christianity: embodying the Victorian age / edited by Donald E. Hall.
p.   cm. – (Cambridge studies in nineteenth-century literature and culture : 2)
Includes bibliographical references and index.
ISBN 0 521 45318 6 (hardback)
1. English prose literature – 19th century – History and criticism.
2. Masculinity (Psychology) in literature.
3. Christianity and literature – Great Britain – History – 19th century.
4. Men in literature.   5. Sex role in literature.
6. Body, Human, in literature.
7. Literature and society – Great Britain – History – 19th century.
8. Great Britain – Intellectual life – 19th century.
I. Hall, Donald E. (Donald Eugene), 1960–   .   II. Series.
PR788.M36M87   1994
823'.809352041–dc20   93–21276CIP

ISBN 0 521 45318 6 hardback

CE

For Carolyn,
for everything

Contents

Contributors

JAMES ELI ADAMS is Assistant Professor of English and Victorian Studies at Indiana University, and Associate Editor of the journal *Victorian Studies*. His essays on Victorian literature and culture have appeared in *ELH*, *Dickens Studies Annual*, *Victorian Studies*, and *Journal of the History of Ideas*. He is currently working on a volume entitled "Bold Against Himself: The Disciplines of Victorian Manhood."

DENNIS W. ALLEN is Associate Professor of English at West Virginia University. He is the author of *Sexuality in Victorian Fiction* (1993). His essays have appeared in *Modern Fiction Studies*, *SEL*, *Cercles*, and other journals and collections.

LAURA FASICK is Assistant Professor of English at Moorhead State University, Minnesota. She has articles published or forthcoming in *Nineteenth-Century Literature*, *South Atlantic Review*, *Essays in Literature*, *Victorian Newsletter*, and *English Literature in Transition 1880–1920*. Her current project is a study of the female body in English fiction from Samuel Richardson to D. H. Lawrence.

DAVID FAULKNER has studied at Northwestern University and Princeton University. His articles have appeared in *Victorian Newsletter* and *Theatre Journal*. He is currently completing a study of global space in works by Dickens, Kipling, Conrad, and Woolf.

DONALD E. HALL is Assistant Professor of English at California State University, Northridge. His essays on Victorian culture have appeared in *Modern Language Studies*, *Victorian Literature and Culture*, and *The Children's Literature Association Quarterly*. He is currently completing work on a book on the responses of Victorian male novelists to the mid-nineteenth-century women's rights movement.

xi

JOHN PENNINGTON is Assistant Professor of English at St. Norber College, Wisconsin. He has published essays on George Mac-Donald, Lewis Carroll, Richard Adams, and Robert Louis Stevenson. He is currently working on a full-length study of MacDonald, Carroll, and John Ruskin.

SUSAN L. ROBERSON teaches at Auburn University, Alabama. Her articles have appeared in *Midwest Quarterly*, *ESQ*, *ATQ*, and *Journal of the American Studies Association of Texas*. She is currently completing a work entitled "Emerson in his Sermons: A Man-Made Self."

DAVID ROSEN is Associate Professor of English and Drama at the University of Maine at Machias. He teaches and writes in the Men's Studies area. His recent works include *The Changing Fictions of Masculinity* (1993).

PATRICIA THOMAS SREBRNIK is Associate Professor of English at the University of Calgary. She is the author of *Alexander Strahan: Victorian Publisher* (1986) and of several articles on Victorian fiction. Her current project is a study of Victorian women authors and their reading publics.

C. J. W.-L. WEE studied in Singapore and at the University of Chicago. He has been a visiting member of the Committee for Cultural Choices and Global Futures and an honorary visiting fellow at the Centre for the Study of Developing Societies, both in Delhi, India. He currently teaches English literature and cultural history at the School of the Arts of the Nanyang Technological University, Singapore.

Acknowledgments

First and foremost, the contributors to this volume deserve special recognition and thanks. It has been a great pleasure working with all of them.

I would also like to express gratitude to my resilient colleagues in the English Department of California State University, Northridge (CSUN), especially the Chair, William Walsh, and my friends, Joel Athey, Melanie Eckford-Prossor, Jan Ramjerdi, Jack Solomon, and Sandra Stanley, all of whom helped make this volume possible, even in the midst of tragedy.

I gratefully acknowledge the support of the School of Humanities at CSUN, including that of Dean Jorge Garcia and then Acting Associate Dean Linda Lam-Easton. I also received a grant for research leave from the Office of Graduate Studies, Research and International Programs at CSUN, of which I am very appreciative.

This study would not have been possible without the support and mentoring of numerous scholars, including (but certainly not limited to) Deirdre David, Martha Nell Smith, Susan Lanser, Neil Fraistat, and R. Baird Shuman. Thanks also go to Cambridge University Press and my amazingly efficient editor there, Kevin Taylor.

Dover Publications kindly granted me permission to use the illustration by Edward Burne-Jones on the jacket of this book; it first appeared in *Pre-Raphaelite Drawings by Burne-Jones* (New York, Dover Publications Inc., 1981, p. 5).

Finally, I wish to express my profound gratitude to Carolyn Francis for her years of friendship and support, as well as her careful editing and proofreading of this work.

Introduction

Muscular Christianity: reading and writing the male social body

Donald E. Hall

The process of planning, building, and publishing this collection of essays has brought into dialogue a group of scholars from extraordinarily diverse critical and personal backgrounds. While chatting with contributors at a recent professional conference, I fielded questions ranging from a mildly, even sweetly, expressed, "So how long have you been interested in Christianity and literature?" to a much more archly inflected "So what exactly is it that *you* get out of Kingsley's novels?" Such is the body of fiction and nonfiction that serves as the focus of this collection. It elicits both reverence and ridicule, provides both "pure" and "perverse" forms of satisfaction, divergent reactions that exist not only *among* readers whose responses to texts depend upon unique interactions between critical, religious, political, and philosophical belief systems, but also, and just as commonly, *within* individual readers. How does an essay or novel provide what might be termed "guilty" pleasure? By pushing those buttons within our own psyches that we as intellectuals often deny possessing. In lives dominated by rigid teaching and writing schedules and consisting of hyper-conscious attention to our own thought processes, as well as those of our students and colleagues, we may find ourselves surprised, even embarrassed, by our racing heartbeat or smile of contentment when a brawny, self-confident hero triumphs handily over a menacing opponent.

My own engagement with Christian manliness or "muscular Christianity" (I will say more on terminology later) dates from the darkest days of graduate school when I was feeling particularly besieged by professional and financial worries and was hard at work on a project examining male anxiety in the novels of George Eliot. My mentor, the feminist critic Deirdre David, suggested that I read Thomas Hughes's *Tom Brown's Schooldays* as a reference point in my critique of Maggie Tulliver's painful struggles against incarnations

3

of brutal masculinity. Tom Brown profoundly influenced my understanding of Tom Tulliver, for in Hughes's smug sexism and glorification of violence, I found a point of entrance into a masculine,
masculinist worldview shaped by mid-Victorian social forces. Tom
Brown represented all that Tom Tulliver wished to be, all that
Hughes celebrated with warmth and nostalgia, and much of what
Eliot revealed as hollow and oppressive.

Yet the novel was morally compelling as well as repugnant. Its
celebration of resiliency, determination, comradeship, and hard-
fought, successful struggles against overwhelming odds struck chords
deep inside me. I could not help but wish that pluck and hard work
would lead always to earthly and heavenly rewards, that social
harmony was finally attainable by living in accordance with
broadly defined, simply stated rules. As Dennis W. Allen suggests in
his own essay on *Tom Brown's Schooldays* in this volume, Hughes's
novel represents both the best and the worst aspects of Victorian
society, its ideals and its very real shortfalls. For those included in
Hughes's social vision, life can be full of hope, joy and accomplishment; those excluded are simply never heard from and only
occasionally glimpsed. Indeed, the works of Kingsley, Hughes, and
the other writers examined here, embody their age, for they capture
the dreams and disappointments of a patriarchal society, the profound silences of which are as revealing as its explicit vocalizations.
The hyperbole of the muscular Christians brings into relief the
frictions and fractures of an era, while their vision of social harmony
and religious salvation represents the unattainable "reach" that lay
well outside of their "grasp."

In its ten essays reflecting on these issues, this collection seeks to
accomplish three related goals: (1) to provide a thorough overview
of an important but all-too-often-neglected Victorian religious,
social, and literary movement. It seeks to augment such influential
studies as Norman Vance's *The Sinews of the Spirit* and Mangan and
Walvin's *Manliness and Morality* by bringing to bear some of the most
recent work in cultural and gender studies on texts that evince not
only admirable agendas for moral and social salvation, but also
sexist, classist, and imperialist ideological underpinnings; (2) to
explore Victorian culture beyond the narrow confines of the muscular Christian movement by tracing the complex ways in which the
movement both reflected and reinforced common cultural conceptions. The essays that make up this collection attempt to provide a

psychological portrait of a patriarchal era; and finally (3), to intervene both explicitly and implicitly in current theoretical debates on
processes of "writing the body" and on the use of the body as a site
for the contestation and resolution of socio-political conflicts. In
striving for these goals, the essayists involved were not required to
toe a single party line; in fact, I actively encouraged rather than
suppressed dialogue, even debate. Thus individual critics read texts
very differently, arriving at often divergent conclusions concerning
the relative progressiveness or regressiveness of individual authors'
social programs. In doing so, we continue and build upon debates
that began in the last century and that reflect participants' differing
positions within and in relation to social, national, economic, religious, and gender power structures.

However, this collection takes as one common point of departure
the acknowledgment that ruling-class, white, male power is reproduced in and by most texts written by privileged men, that male
control of the political process, the medical community, the
publishing industry, and of discourse itself has produced a body of
work that actively inscribes patriarchy. Hélène Cixous proclaims
confidently that "there is such a thing as *marked* writing" (283). But
where and how is male writing marked? How is the process by which
men have constructed exclusionary versions of contemporary and
historical "realities" related to male self-perception and the physical
contours of the male body? In "Male Feminism," Stephen Heath
argues that "men's writing, male discourse, will simply be the same
again; there is no politically progressive project that can work
through that idea [of writing the male body] (unless perhaps in and
from areas of gay men's experience, in a literature for that)" (25).
Perhaps Heath is justified in his despair over the possibility that any
active project to write and thereby celebrate the heterosexual male
social body might still produce "progressive" work, but surely the
acknowledgment that the male body has been written throughout
history, coupled with an active critique of when and how that
writing was produced, can itself serve to further a gender studies
project through which the numerous forces limiting human expression and constraining human freedom are uncovered. Heath quotes
Tillie Olsen: "Telling the truth about one's body [is] a necessary
freeing subject for the woman writer" (25). He continues by
remarking that it "seems unlikely ... that that sentence could also
be written for the male writer" (25). Few would disagree. But

critiquing others' claims of "truth-telling" may also represent a freeing process for both women and men, one that can begin with a recognition that, throughout history, certain groups of men have shaped the truth to ensure their own freedom (as well as argue for, comment upon, resist, and/or deny that of others) by referring back to, making use of, and extrapolating from the male body, or more precisely, diverse and often competing versions of the male body.

It is not enough to say, as Ann Rosalind Jones does, that "white, European, and ruling-class" men have summarily claimed, "I am the unified, self-controlled center of the universe ... The rest of the world, which I define as Other, has meaning only in relation to men, as man/father, possessor of the phallus" (362). For while it is true that men throughout history have implicitly (even explicitly) made this claim, it has been a *claim* only, hiding a more complex dynamic by which such assertions are always contested, both externally and internally. While the male body has often served as a paradigm and metaphor for male-dominated culture and society, it has also served as a site for struggle. Constructions of differing political, regional, national, and more recently, sexual identities among men have always worked to undermine any sense of a unified phallic front. Witness, for example, the tensions foregrounded in media representations of the AIDS crisis. Simon Watney and other gay activists have called repeated attention to the battleground represented by the gay male body, its heavily politicized, disease-threatened terrain serving as a field for the play of homophobic and sexist social policies and discourses. I submit that during and around the period covered by this collection, the caricatured bodies of lower-class, Irish, and non-European men provided remarkably similar sites for the play of classist, racist, and imperialist beliefs. *Plus ça change, plus c'est la même chose.*

Thus critics and theorists from many different fields and perspectives have been effectively, if not always consciously, collaborating to map the many murky terrains of the social body and trace the functions and struggles of those individual bodies that comprise it. Peter Stallybrass and Allon White provided pioneering and thoughtful analysis of body-determined cultural perimeters and breaches in *The Politics and Poetics of Transgression*. Klaus Theweleit's critique of fascist literature in *Male Fantasies* traces violence against women, the underprivileged, and leftist organizations during the early twentieth century; it provides chilling evidence of how easily psychological conflicts can be externalized and at least temporarily resolved through degrading, maiming, and killing perceived embodiments of qualities that fascists fear within themselves. His analysis is reinforced in Elaine Scarry's *The Body in Pain* and, more recently, in Judith Butler's *Gender Trouble*, where Butler suggests that a poststructuralist analysis of the body "might well understand the boundaries of the body as the limits of the socially *hegemonic*" (131).

But while Butler builds upon the work of theorists such as Julia Kristeva and Mary Douglas in order to trace the contours of the late-twentieth-century body politic, her assertion above has implications for nineteenth-century studies as well. Her specific focus on "hegemony," the imperfect wielding and reinforcement of social power, and its relationship to male self-perception raises compelling questions about the popular mid-Victorian movement that defined itself and its agenda through direct references to the male body, namely the muscular Christian movement. While several of the essays that follow will explore the historical and philosophical foundations of muscular Christianity at length, a brief examination of some of its more telling parameters will demonstrate its enormous, but generally untapped, potential as a source of insight into Victorian and post-Victorian cultural structures and strictures.

The tag "muscular Christianity" originated in a review of Charles Kingsley's *Two Years Ago* (1857) written by T. C. Sandars for the *Saturday Review*. Kingsley, whose numerous and influential writings are at the center of many of the essays appearing in the present collection, was recognized immediately as the most popular and visible advocate of a new movement:

We all know by this time what is the task that Mr. Kingsley has made specially his own – it is that of spreading the knowledge and fostering the love of a muscular Christianity. His ideal is a man who fears God and can walk a thousand miles in a thousand hours – who, in the language which Mr. Kingsley has made popular, breathes God's free air on God's rich earth, and at the same time can hit a woodcock, doctor a horse, and twist a poker around his fingers. (Bevington 188)

In his generally laudatory assessment of Kingsley's purpose and abilities, Sandars highlights a central, even defining, characteristic of muscular Christianity: an association between physical strength, religious certainty, and the ability to shape and control the world around oneself. Acts such as hunting, doctoring, and twisting were inextricably linked with "self"-construction and a physical armor-plating to withstand various potential threats to religious belief, bodily health, and social stability. Kingsley, his younger friend Hughes, and others such as J. M. Ludlow and F. D. Maurice, use the male body as a canvas upon which they portray both social and psychological dramas. Kingsley's early novel, *Yeast* (1848), concerns the acquisition of a social conscience by its hero Lancelot Smith after a hunting accident and through a lengthy convalescence. The boundaries of the male body in this novel are quite clearly the limits of the socially hegemonic, for as Smith's bodily strength grows, so too does his moral strength. Kingsley even represents the potentially volcanic violence of class conflict in the dying body of an old poacher: "his lungs pumped great jets of blood out over the still heather-flowers as they slept in the moonshine, and dabbled them with smoking gore" (139). Throughout works written by the muscular Christians, the male body appears as a metaphor for social, national, and religious bodies, while at the same time it attempts to enforce a particular construction of those bodies. I place considerable emphasis here on the word "attempts," for as several of the essays in this collection suggest, conflict both characterized and surrounded the muscular Christian movement.

Fitzjames Stephen, one contemporary critic of the movement, argues cogently in an 1858 *Edinburgh Review* essay on *Tom Brown's Schooldays*, that muscular Christianity

consists of writing novels, the hero of which is almost always drawn in the most glowing colours, and intended to display the excellence of a simple massive understanding united with the almost unconscious instinct to do good, and adorned, generally speaking, with every sort of athletic accomplishment. (191)

Stephen takes issue with the muscular Christians because "The facts of life are far too complex to be embraced by an understanding which only recognizes a few broad divisions. Many most essential distinctions are to the last degree refined" (191). As Stephen well recognized, the broad divisions and broadly defined programs of the muscular Christians were their responses to complex contemporary questions on issues of class, nationality, and gender, responses that have provided grist for critical mills for almost 150 years. Walter Houghton, in *The Victorian Frame of Mind* (1957), provides incisive commentary on muscular Christianity when he relates the fears of many Victorian men to the profound insecurity of an age that was "deeply troubled with religious doubt, acutely aware of weakness and frustration" (216). The broad strokes in the discourse of the muscular Christians were reactions to the threats posed by a world growing ever more confusing and fragmented. Houghton ties the anxieties of the age to scientific discoveries that called into question Biblical accounts of creation, to technological advances that rendered the world increasingly complex and hostile, and to industrial processes that isolated individuals from each other and the past. Muscular Christianity was an attempt to assert control over a world that had seemingly gone mad: "In such a mood, not of cynicism but of bitter exasperation, the objective correlative is the destructive force of a conquering hero" (216). Houghton demonstrates convincingly that Victorian anxieties propelled diverse and often violent projects for controlling the unknown, the threatening, and the potentially disruptive.

Such a recognition is fundamental to Norman Vance's respected overview of muscular Christianity, *The Sinews of the Spirit* (1985). Vance's work, to which most of the essays in this volume will refer often, traces the movement from its roots in the thoughts of Coleridge and Maurice to its manifestations in the public schools and the discourse of empire. It is necessary to note, however, that Vance consistently uses the term "Christian manliness" rather than muscular Christianity, arguing that the former was more commonly accepted by clergymen of the era and that the latter "draws attention more to muscularity than to Christianity" (2). The essays that follow generally adopt the phrase "muscular Christianity" for precisely that reason. For Kingsley, Hughes, and others of the period, "manliness" was synonymous with strength, both physical and moral, and the term "muscular Christianity" highlights these writers' consistent, even insistent, use of the ideologically charged and aggressively poised male body as a point of reference in and determiner of a masculinist economy of signification and (all too often) degradation. While Vance does a superb and thorough job critiquing the "Christianity" of the muscular Christians, the following essays address the muscularity of the same men, while they attempt never to lose sight of the other half of the phrase.

Thus *Muscular Christianity: embodying the Victorian age* builds upon almost a century and a half of analysis; yet it also fills a certain void, for it focuses on issues raised not infrequently, but often only tangentially, in preceding examinations of the muscular Christians. Indeed, this movement, which was so thoroughly grounded in male experience and the male body, had gender-related impetuses and implications that have never received adequate attention. How was the armored male body both a reaction to and an intensification of a gender power struggle that was well underway by the mid-nineteenth century? How did the male body provide a canvas upon which real and imagined threats to male power were portrayed and what do the specific contours of those portrayals tell us about the psychologies of the men who produced them? Finally, what can these texts tell us about the way patriarchal, phallocentric metaphors become entrenched and thereby help determine the very parameters of both male and female responses to personal quandaries and questions of social justice? Such problematics provide a starting point for much of the analysis that follows.

But of equal interest is the question of how representations of class hierarchies reflect and respond to the contours of the male body. As materialist feminists and Marxist critics have long noted, Victorian patriarchy encompassed not only women but also the underprivileged of both sexes. The Victorian ruling-class male reserved for himself social decision-making power that silenced the voices of other men as well as women. How is class conflict metaphorized and fictionally resolved in works by muscular Christians? How are body anxieties intensified by and how do they intensify class anxieties? How are questions of land ownership and labor resolved metaphorically on the canvas of the male body?

Finally, several of the contributors to this volume ask, "What are the connections between British male self-perception and the imperial project that was well underway in Africa and Asia by mid-century?" How do processes of colonization depend upon and solidify perceptions of a national, masculine "self"? How is that "self" constructed and maintained in the face of clear challenges at home and abroad? How are male insecurities and domestic political problems projected onto the bodies and lands of the colonized, and how do processes of "civilization" intersect with gender, class, and religious ideologies?

I asked the writers who collaborated on this project to ground their analysis of these issues in concrete historical data and textual evidence. While addressing diverse theoretical issues and intervening in sometimes heated critical debates, the essays that follow are rooted firmly in a tradition of close reading. At the same time, most move from textual to cultural analysis and actively critique the historical specificity of constructions of reality, as well as the effects on writing and reading of a particular positioning within a social network of classes, genders, and national identities. While I believe that the success of a volume such as this depends partially upon a sense of shared purpose and a common political awareness, I have encouraged the contributors to explore new approaches to old problems, to find better (or at least usefully different) answers to perhaps insolvable questions, and to draw on whichever critical tradition (or even combination of traditions) that best suits the needs of an individual reading. In response, I received the diverse and exciting pieces that follow.

And here I must say a few words about their order of appearance, for *Muscular Christianity: embodying the Victorian age* is divided into three parts that often overlap in focus and chronology – literary and social history does not neatly partition itself. Part I is entitled "Foundations of muscular Christianity" and includes three essays that examine Victorian social debates on gender, class, and imperial identity, controversies that elicited "muscular" responses at mid-century. David Rosen explores Charles Kingsley's use of the Platonic conception of *thumos*, a deep, central force from which manly action flows and through which virtue, sexuality, and masculine primacy are reconciled and reiterated. My own essay examines the Christian Socialists' response to the Chartist movement and critiques the manner in which they and later the muscular Christians portrayed the "lower" body threat posed by the rebellious underclasses. C. J. W.-L. Wee, in his examination of *Alton Locke* and *Westward Ho!*, finds in Kingsley's fiction a quest for a source of primitive racial energy needed to rejuvenate the sick body of an ailing nation. All three essays look to the socio-historical and biographical contexts surrounding the beginnings of the muscular Christian movement and look forward in time to some of its later consequences and reverberations.

Part II, "Varieties of muscular Christianity," examines specific manifestations of muscularity, critiquing individual writers' politics, policies, and religious purposes. Laura Fasick places Kingsley's representations of women in the context of nineteenth-century scientific theory, finding in Kingsley's fictional use of disease and torture an attempt to reiterate rigid gender constructs. Dennis W. Allen examines Hughes's portrayal of both corporeal and corporate bodies in *Tom Brown's Schooldays*, uncovering a vaguely defined conceptualization of "work" that serves to reconcile the physical and the metaphysical and that invokes a democratic vision while insisting on middle-class privilege. John Pennington finds muscular resonances in the fairy tales of George MacDonald, a Christian Darwinist who used children's bodies as a canvas upon which to portray his own vision for social and religious salvation. Susan Roberson concludes this section by looking to the other side of the Atlantic at Ralph Waldo Emerson's muscular spirituality, a masculine, American religion of self-construction and self-reliance.

Part III, "Responses to muscular Christianity," charts reactions to, and some surprising reiterations of, the movement after mid-century. David Faulkner explores Dickens's careful deconstruction of the transparency, honesty, and self-possession epitomized by the muscular Septimus Crisparkle in *The Mystery of Edwin Drood*. Patricia Srebrnik traces Mary Kingsley Harrison's life-long struggle against the oppressive social currents supported by her own father; Srebrnik thus contextualizes and accounts for the writer's seemingly unlikely conversion to Catholicism in 1902. Finally, James Adams finds telling conjunctions between works by Kingsley and Walter Pater, as he argues that the twin figures of the muscular Christian and the Paterian aesthete arise out of a common project: the reclamation of the body from the antagonisms of an orthodox, ascetic morality. His essay explores the volatility, indeed inadequacy, of the familiar gender norms articulated in Victorian and post-Victorian discourse on masculinity.

And, of course, it is a volatility that is reflected throughout the pages of this collection, in essays that catalogue the mechanisms used not only to liberate souls, but also to oppress women, peoples of colonized lands, and men from marginalized groups. Piety, pomposity, and patriarchal posturing are all found within the same body of work, often within the same male body. And these covergences are not unique to Victorian life and literature, for the ten essays that follow hold up for scrutiny aspects of Anglo-American culture that continue in modified forms to affect the lived experiences of individuals today. In doing so, I hope they will be of interest to readers from a wide range of disciplines, for *Muscular Christianity: embodying the Victorian age* attempts to add critical muscle to what has been termed "men's studies," even as it embodies the diverse critical perspectives of our own day.

WORKS CITED

Bevington, Merle Mowbray, *The Saturday Review 1855–1868*. New York: Columbia University Press, 1941.

Butler, Judith, *Gender Trouble: Feminism and the Subversion of Identity*. New York: Routledge, 1990.

Cixous, Hélène, "The Laugh of the Medusa," trs. Keith Cohen and Paula Cohen, in *The Signs Reader: Women, Gender & Scholarship*, eds. Elizabeth Abel and Emily K. Abel. University of Chicago Press, 1983, pp. 279–97.

Heath, Stephen, "Male Feminism" in *Men in Feminism*, eds. Alice Jardine and Paul Smith. New York: Methuen, 1987, pp. 1–32.

Houghton, Walter E., *The Victorian Frame of Mind: 1830–1870*. New Haven: Yale University Press, 1957.

Jones, Ann Rosalind, "Writing the Body: Toward an Understanding of *l'Ecriture Féminine*" in *The New Feminist Criticism: Essays on Women, Literature & Theory*, ed. Elaine Showalter. New York: Pantheon, 1985, pp. 361–77.

Kingsley, Charles, *Yeast* (1848) in *Charles Kingsley: The Works*, vol. II. London, 1882. Reprinted Hildesheim, Germany: Georg Olms, 1968.

Mangan, J. A. and James Walvin, eds., *Manliness and Morality: Middle-class Masculinity in Britain and America 1800–1940*. Manchester University Press, 1987.

Stephen, Fitzjames, review of *Tom Brown's Schooldays*, *Edinburgh Review* 107 (January 1858): 172–93.

Vance, Norman, *The Sinews of the Spirit: The Ideal of Christian Manliness in Victorian Literature and Religious Thought*. Cambridge University Press, 1985.

PART I

Foundations of muscular Christianity

The volcano and the cathedral: muscular Christianity and the origins of primal manliness

David Rosen

The movement labeled by its derogators as "muscular Christianity" arose, paradoxically perhaps, among notably liberal men, the Christian Socialists, who had fought for the Chartists, for improvements in living conditions, and even for limited rights for women. These men alternately rejected (Kingsley, *Letters* II 83) and embraced the term "muscular Christian" (*Letters* II 54; Hughes, *Oxford* 98–100), as did Victorian society. In Charles Kingsley's Cambridge sermons on King David in 1866, every mention of "muscular Christianity" produced loud cheers of approval, although the iterations were intended to deride the term. While some may have seen in the movement a gentle, liberal but realistic, and hard-working social activism (see Vance *passim*), for many in Victorian England muscular Christianity meant macho: Tom Brown boxing bullies at Rugby and bloodying townies at Oxford, Amyas Leigh heroically hacking wily Spaniards, and Guy Heavystone dismembering menacing Irish peasants:

Suddenly the window opened. With the rapidity of lightning, Guy Heavystone cast the net over the head of the ringleader, ejaculated "Habet!" and with a back stroke of the cavalry sabre severed the member from its trunk, and drawing the net back again, cast the gory head upon the floor, saying quietly: "One."
... "Do you remember what Pliny says of the gladiator?" said Guy, calmly wiping his sabre. "How graphic is the passage commencing: 'Inter nos,' etc." The sport continued until the heads of twenty desperadoes had been gathered. The rest seemed inclined to disperse. Guy cautiously showed himself at the door; a ringing shot was heard, and he staggered back pierced through the heart. Grasping the door-post in the last unconscious throes of his mighty frame, the whole side of the house yielded to that earthquake tremor, and we had barely time to escape before the whole building fell in ruins. I thought of Samson, the Giant Judge, etc., etc.; but all was over.

Guy Heavystone had died as he had lived – hard. (Harte, "Guy Heavy-stone," 128–9)

As *Guy Heavystone*, Bret Harte's parody of genteel rowdyism, suggests, certain educated Englishmen in the mid-nineteenth century found toughness and violence physically exhilarating, intellectually justified, and morally acceptable. Although Harte targets George Alfred Lawrence, the inventor of the "Doctrine of Force," also known as "muscular Blackguardism," the satire glances at muscular Christianity and at Lawrence's unwilling mentor, Charles Kingsley, whose own works often conferred the status of "manly" on men of force.

Manliness preoccupied Kingsley, and his concern underlay most of his varied activities. Not only did Kingsley frequently write of manliness, he himself became a text for his manly ideal. In commenting on a Kingsley lecture, a friend underlined Kingsley's manly display: "[N]o other man in England could have done what he did; I say *man* emphatically, because if I were to seek a word to express my opinion of it, I would say it was the *manliest* thing I had ever heard. Such a right bold honest way of turning from side to side, looking everything straight in the face, and speaking out all the good and all the ill that could be said of it, in the plainest way, was surely never seen before" (*Letters* 1 249). A few days later, on June 22, 1851, Kingsley's Great Exhibition sermon on equality, freedom, and brotherhood turned into a demonstration of manliness when the vicar of the church declared Kingsley's sermon dangerous, untrue, and contrary to church teaching. Kingsley passed stoically from pulpit to vestry while the attending congregation tried to chair him out of the door (*Letters* 1 250). Such occasions, when the "manliness" of Kingsley became more meaningful than his speech, led John Addington Symonds to write of "Kingsleiolatreia." At the Social Science Association meeting in October, 1869, Symonds, whose own sexuality undoubtedly sensitized him to Kingsley's display, noted that Kingsley was "ranting and raging and foaming and swelling himself to twice his natural dimensions." He concluded that "because of all this [Kingsley seemed] to be the right man in the right place. He made an impression on the masses" (37–8). In Symonds's words, Kingsley had become a god in England, his worship replacing the "Mariolatreia" or Mary-worship that Kingsley despised and thought the bane of true manliness. The public demeanor of Kingsley, insofar as his contemporaries used it to define masculinity, suggested that manliness required "boldness," "honesty," and "plainness"; defiance of authority; stoic patience; and violent energy. In these features it closely resembled the masculinity parodied by Harte.

But Kingsley's masculinity had a less public dimension. One month after the Great Exhibition sermon, prostrated by his many exertions, Kingsley sought refuge in a trip to Germany with his brother Henry and his parents. Embarking from London Bridge on a small steamer, alone in his cabin, Kingsley opened his travel desk to take up the writing that occupied him daily until the last two days of his life in 1875. Before he began, he fondled, as he often did, twin locks of hair from Fanny, his wife of seven and a half years. "Oh that I were with you, or rather you with me here," he writes on July 24, 1851. "The beds are so small that we should be forced to lie inside each other, and the weather is so hot that you might walk about naked all day, as night – *cela va sans dire*! Oh, those naked nights at Chelsea! When will they come again? I kiss both locks of hair every time I open my desk – but the little curly one seems to bring me nearer to you" (quoted in Chitty, 148). This fantasy of "naked nights" and sexual union may seem to corroborate the public picture of fierce honesty and boldness. Yet Kingsley's relish for both the head hairs and pubic hairs of his wife presents a problem. In preferring the pubic hair because of its apparent association with a more authentic self, Kingsley not only sanctions sexual appetite as the center of humanness but also makes the private self, which here is identified with the sexual self, more "real" than the public self. The public displays of "masculinity," this image argues, only give presence to a limited aspect of Kingsley's "masculine" self.

Kingsley eventually reconstructed masculinity as a private, partially disclosed, substructure of self. As Symonds's description of him itself implies, Kingsley's masculinity came to be viewed as a deep, volcanic force which found only a limited but enticing public display. Both the suggestion that manliness had a "deep" structure and the suggestion as to what shape that structure took found original expression in Kingsley. While many have criticized the cruel and brutal heritage of muscular Christianity, most have failed to recognize the deep structure that sustains both the rougher and gentler aspects of muscular Christianity's version of masculinity.

I

What propelled Kingsley to begin so self-consciously reconstructing manliness? Kingsley was not the first to attempt to forge a new masculinity, nor was he the first to attempt to give it a deep structure. The path to Kingsley lies intellectually through Rousseau and Carlyle (Houghton 267, Baker 88, and Stone 26–7) and socially through the heart of the century. In December of 1750, the Academy of Belles Lettres of Corsica, responding perhaps to unsettled issues of gender in pre-revolutionary France, sponsored an essay competition on the question: "What is the virtue most necessary to the hero?" In an essay, which he never entered and which appeared in an unauthorized version in 1768, Rousseau answered: "Manliness!" In Rousseau's version of manliness, moral principles created emotions that precipitated courage, the masculine "executive virtue" which carried out the promptings of the emotions (Jackson 441–3). Rousseau's innovation lay in his attempt to overcome class inequalities that the classical concept of *Andreia* encoded. For Rousseau, being a warrior and being fearless were not heroic in themselves – the hero must have social utility. And even more importantly, unlike the ancients, the hero could be a common person, a legislator, or a sage.

In Britain, writers like Carlyle and Crabbe became preoccupied with the issue of what constituted masculinity, a re-examination prompted by the growing displacement of rural laborers to factory settings and non-agricultural occupations. For instance, Henry Mayhew found that tailors conceptualized their mistreatment as a loss of manliness and complained that in their jobs they could not be men. The connection between masculine potency and social and economic power seems to have been alive in the minds of many marginalized men (Williams 124). Simultaneously, Britain began to feel the subcurrent of women's unhappiness with their allotted roles. The diaries of women of the 1830s and 1840s show a growing unhappiness with received roles and a desire to share in the dignity of work (Blease 98–100). While men on the bottom expressed increasing impatience with problems they conceptualized in terms of gender, and women quietly rebelled against what they saw as repression of their natural abilities (Strachey 46–7), the men of the gentry and lower aristocracy were feeling the encroachment of the middle classes. The result was an attack on both social and gender conditions and an attempt to fix some boundary or definition for both. From about 1830 on, one finds writing inundated with concerns about what is a manly man, as well as what is a womanly woman (Blease 96ff.; Strachey 46–8). The Reform Bill of 1832, by giving power to the wealthier middle classes, may in part have released a further upsurge in rhetorical outpourings on the subject of gender and masculinity, for the debate over who should rule often devolved into a debate over who belonged to that privileged group called "men" (see Gilmore; Tiger). The destabilizing of gender by the various social forces of the day, and the pressure to recoup some notion of masculinity, can be seen most strikingly in the one tangible result of Disraeli's speech in favor of women's suffrage in 1848: the insertion of the word "male" into "the voting clauses of all subsequent Poor Law and Local Government Bills" (Strachey 43).

The wedding of social change and changes in the concept of masculinity had been consummated by mid-century when Thomas Carlyle borrowed Rousseau's notion of heroic manliness to try to deal with problems of the social authority of men. In *On Heroes, Hero-Worship, and The Heroic in History*, Carlyle attempted to preserve "manliness" as the quality most conferring leadership, and to define that concept by recourse to various historical and mythological figures, from Odin to the present; various cultures, from Arabia to Norway; and various occupations, from warriors to poets. Yet in Carlyle's book the concept of "man" – the concept from which all power arises – remains obscure: "A man shall and must be valiant; he must march forward, and quit himself like a man." In his tautological formulation ("A man ... must ... quit himself like a man"), Carlyle shies away from allowing specific behaviors to confer manliness (for example, if one behaves valiantly, one is manly). Instead, the action turns into a demonstration of manliness (for example, if one is manly, one will act valiantly). Carlyle adds other qualifications by suggesting that manliness consists not so much of fighting valiantly, but of "trusting imperturbably in ... the upper Power" which will allow one to fight valiantly (44–5). Thus Carlyle places "manliness" at two removes from behavior. "Manliness" is not valor, nor is it even valorous belief in a higher being. "Manliness" *produces* the belief in a higher being that produces the valor. Thus Carlyle creates a category of "manliness" that one cannot enter simply by behaving in a "manly" fashion, positing the notion of a "deeper" manliness – already implicit in Rousseau's idea – a notion of manliness that detaches itself from surface behavior.

Carlyle's definition of masculinity serves his attempts to conceptualize the convulsive social conditions of his time. As with Kingsley later on, masculinity seems to have a crucial place in this consideration (see Donald E. Hall's essay in this volume). But Carlyle always invokes "manliness" in ways that serve his particular political ideology. For instance, Carlyle includes a greater number of men in his conception of manliness, but he also reserves for their leader a special title to manliness. As a result, one test of manliness becomes the acknowledgment of the hero as the true exemplar of manliness. For Carlyle, masculinity was the hook to pull men into a social order that was both egalitarian and stratified. Masculinity itself was not the center of that order.

In turn, Kingsley, responding to his perception of the ambiguity of social and gender roles, as well as the restraints that made both oppressive, incorporated various features from Carlyle: the idea that masculinity holds the key to solving social problems; the idea that men naturally belong in groups (the team, the army, even the classroom); the idea that men are violent and even at bottom bestial; and, most important, the idea that no particular behavior but something *in* men makes them "manly." "Masculinity" became the expression and perfection of this something.

II

Kingsley's own definition of masculinity, caught up in concerns like Carlyle's, evolved as he tried to solve the first great problem of his life: his sexual longing for his future wife, Frances Eliza Grenfell, and his lack of means to gratify that longing. Biographers, critics and Kingsley himself frequently state that this constituted the major turning point in his life. He and Fanny Grenfell had shared an immediate, strong sexual attraction for each other, but her upper-class and religious background, and Kingsley's own lack of religious, occupational, and class qualifications, according to Grenfell standards, placed obstacles in the path of any relationship. Being mindful of these obstacles, Kingsley used their mutual sexual longings to question the requirements of social and religious conformity. This tension became his means of seduction. We see this pattern as early as Kingsley's sketch of their first kiss. The sketch, which he sent to Fanny, clearly represents a young man with modest clothes and an ill-concealed erection (Chitty 59). In the sketch, Kingsley used the restraint of clothing and the force of the body to symbolize a struggle that he would later conceptualize in the images of the volcano and the church. The kiss becomes a compromise between the demands of the penis and the demands of propriety. Kingsley encouraged Fanny to view this type of compromise – a compromise that co-opts desire – as a figure for aspects of his own life: his erotic desires and the social and religious pressures to curb them; his social desires and the disdain of Fanny's family for him; his desire for fame and the permissible occupational outlet of the clergy. For Kingsley, the need to locate value in erotic release becomes synonymous with the need to validate social position and occupational potency. In a bizarre masterstroke of rhetorical daring, Kingsley decided to collapse the sides of his antithesis – his desire for sexual intercourse, he began to argue to Fanny, was not irreligious, it was the most highly religious stance one could take. In fact, this idea allowed him to enter the clergy with a clear conscience, thus gaining religion, occupation, class status, and Fanny.

Kingsley's letters to Fanny chart the increasing spiritualization of erotic longings that becomes the enabler of their mutual sexual fantasies: "When you go to bed tonight," he writes to her on October 2, 1843, "forget that you ever wore a garment, and open your lips for my kisses that I may lie between your breasts all night" (Canticles 1 13, quoted in Chitty, 80). In another he tells her, "At a quarter past eleven lie down, clasp your arms and every limb around me, and with me repeat the *Te Deum*" (quoted in Chitty, 79). He tells her in his next letter that their married bedroom "shall be our chapel and our study and our heaven on earth" (quoted in Chitty, 85). Their bed was to be "our altar" where "you should be the victim and I the priest, in the bliss of full communion" (quoted in Chitty, 91). The imperfectly realized sadistic fantasy of mutilation in the act of copulation becomes sanctioned by a religious rhetoric that seeks Fanny's complicity. During an ordeal of separation, from August 1842, "a period of misery" that Kingsley recalled as "the most priceless passage of my whole existence" (*Letters* 1 71), certain sexual-religious rituals were observed in unison: On "Festival Nights," each Thursday at eleven, Fanny read a sexually stimulating letter that Charles had written and afterwards imagined that they lay in bed together, as he imagined the same. On "Fast

Nights," each Friday at ten, she read from a guilt-ridden letter and they each did penance. "[A]t that time each week, he stripped himself naked in his cottage bedroom and scourged himself. 'Oh, how I long to kiss away those stripes,' she confided in her diary" (Chitty 74). He wrote to Fanny in 1843 that on All Saints Day, 1842, "I went into the woods at night and lay naked upon thorns" (quoted in Chitty, 75). As a result of these experiences, Kingsley wrote a detailed account of why he found celibacy impossible, which he treasured in a small leather deed box with other precious objects, such as Fanny's gloves and letters from royalty (Chitty 59). He also proposed to Fanny that they preserve their correspondence, so that when their child should begin to struggle with sexual longing, Charles could "open that sacred box and read him some of those letters and say, 'My son, see how I felt when in thy place and age!'" (quoted in Chitty, 87). Sexual texts became a Torah that Charles/ Moses would hand down to his children.

Over the next ten years, sexual union as spiritual fulfillment became a crucial message in Kingsley's works, such as *The Saint's Tragedy* (1848), *Yeast* (1848), *Andromeda* and *Santa Maura* (1852), and *Hypatia* (1853). In the "preface" to *The Saint's Tragedy* he writes: "Is human love unholy – inconsistent with the perfect worship of the Creator? ... Is nature a holy type or a foul prison of our spirits?" Lancelot Smith, the protagonist of Kingsley's autobiographical *Bildungsroman, Yeast*, writes to his Tractarian cousin that he finds within himself "certain appetites": "I suppose that the God whom you say made me, made those appetites as part of me. Why are they to be crushed any more than any other part of me?" (33).

Kingsley later wrote to a friend: "Man is not a mere animal – he is *the* spirit-animal; a spirit manifesting itself in an animal form, as the heathens themselves hold ... and in communion with God's spirit has the right to believe that his affections are under that spirit's guidance, and that when he finds in himself such an affection to any single woman ... to give himself up to his love in child-like simplicity and self-abandonment, and, at the same time, with solemn awe and self-humiliation at being thus readmitted into the very garden of the Lord" (*Letters* 1 161–4). A new masculinity had begun to emerge from Kingsley's early wrestling with his sexuality, a new masculinity that seems far removed from both Rousseau and Carlyle. The key is man as a spirit-animal with divinity conferred on his bestiality. Of course, the idea of bestial manhood occurs throughout English literature: in *Beowulf* one finds bestial rage and passion; in *Hamlet* and *Othello*, bestial sexuality; in *Paradise Lost*, bestial sensation and curiosity. What the beast was, what man's bestial nature was, even what those particular beasts meant, changed. Insofar as each generation envisioned wild and dangerous nature, men recognized that nature in themselves (see Rosen *passim*), but hitherto masculinity had usually been linked to quelling those beasts. Bestiality in Kingsley's formulation is primarily sexual and one can abandon one's self to that bestiality with perfect equanimity since sexual desire, when righteous, falls under divine guidance; it is the divine spirit moving within. This genital/spiritual organization leads to all of Kingsley's later moral positions.

III

From the days of his courtship of Fanny on, Kingsley's writings increasingly stress the theme of the sacredness of the animal aspect of humanity. He contrasted this view to "Manichaeism," an "adoration for a fictitious 'angelic nature'" that was "prone to despise all by which man is brought in contact with this earth" ("Poetry of Sacred and Legendary Art" 214). In *Yeast*, Lancelot had stated that "the finest of us are animals after all, and live by eating and sleeping" (32). "Let us never use those words *animal* and *brutal* in a degrading sense," Kingsley had urged Fanny during their courtship (quoted in Chitty, 80). The next step in the new construction of manliness was to bring men back into "contact with the earth," with the essential underlying truth that men are animals.

For Kingsley, contact with the earth extended not merely to sexuality. Even before Charles Darwin's *On the Origin of Species by Means of Natural Selection* (1859), a large part of the nineteenth-century conception of the animal world involved fighting and competition. As Kingsley put it in a letter to F. D. Maurice in 1856, this is "a universe in which everything is eternally *eating* everything else" (*Letters* II 22). As God's most glorious beast, man fights and competes. In 1843, in a book that Fanny had given Charles and that greatly influenced him, Carlyle described the evolution of "glorious Chivalry" from "two men with clenched teeth, and hell-fire eyes hacking one another's flesh; concerting precious living bodies ... into nameless masses of putrescence":

Man is created to fight; he is perhaps best of all definable as a born soldier; his life "a battle and a march," under the right General. It is forever indispensable for a man to fight: now with Necessity, with Barrenness,

Scarcity, with Puddles, Bogs, tangled Forests, unkempt Cotton; – now also
with hallucinations of his poor fellow man ... mak[ing] him claim over me
rights which are not his. (*Past and Present* 219–20)

Carlyle argues that the vile animal inclination of males has not only
the sanction of nature but a noble application in the current political turmoil about labor and rights.

In 1857 Thomas Hughes took over this passage from Carlyle in his
immensely popular *Tom Brown's Schooldays*, when he wrote that
"from the cradle to the grave, fighting, rightly understood, is ... the
real, highest, honestest business, of every son of man ... It is no good
for Quakers, or any other body of men, to uplift their voices against
fighting. Human nature is too strong." But he also changed
Carlyle's message: "I am as sorry as any man to see folk fighting the
wrong people and the wrong things, but I'd a deal sooner see them
doing that than that they should have no fight in them" (315–16).
Hughes here follows Kingsley: the morality of a masculine action lies
in the sacredness of nature; the goodness of fighting does not come
simply from its being for a good cause. Fighting, for Kingsley, not
only has divine sanction, but Christ's model to assure its goodness.
In *Brave Words for Brave Soldiers and Sailors*, Kingsley writes that the
Prince of Peace was also the Prince of War: "He is the Lord of Hosts,
the God of armies ... Be sure of it; for the Bible tells you so" (quoted
in Thorp, 119). Thus violence, like sex, becomes a sanctified force of
male behavior, a definitive quality of "real" men. His dedication to
Westward Ho!, linking a man of the cloth and an adventurer, comes
from this idea. Rajah Sir James Brooke and George Augustus
Selwyn, Bishop of New Zealand, are equally "manful and godly"
types who represent real-life Elizabethan heroic virtue exemplified
by the fictional hero, Amyas Leigh, for whom life is not "a mere
spiritual fight, but one of flesh and blood, wherein simple men ...
help God's cause not merely with prayer and pen, but with sharp
shot and cold steel" (610).

IV

With increasing frequency, Kingsley used the lens of an innate,
animalistic masculinity through which to view and criticize society.
For instance, he linked the denial of rights in mid-nineteenth-
century English society with the denial of "maturity," especially of
manhood. Poets and clergymen alike considered childhood and

early death beautiful and blessed, noted Kingsley. He complained about this, saying that as for "escaping sin by an early death, one feels sad at hearing Christians talk so. Who has made him what he is but God, and is He not able to perfect His work, and keep that committed to Him?" (*Letters* II 111). God created both manhood and childhood. In *Yeast*, artist Claude Mellot explains that he wears his beard "for a testimony and a sign that a man has no right to be ashamed of the mark of manhood" (52). Kingsley argued that men had every right to declare their maleness and not to be ashamed of it. Kingsley often contrasted the smooth Jacob and the hairy Esau, declaring that God had made both and that both reflected God's image (*Letters* II 85). The fashion of whiskers in the Crimean and American Civil wars may stem from this sentiment. It would seem that, like Kingsley, other men had come to identify their loss of power in a rising tide of expectations with the dissonance they felt between their experience of their mature bodies and the socially prescribed roles that tried to repress that maturity. What men thought of as the repressive restrictions of religion, law, and social policy they identified with the hampering of their manhood, pushed perhaps by the example of women liberating themselves and at the same time by the desire to locate some new, indelible mark of masculinity that could differentiate men from women and create a foundation for masculine power.

Over time, Kingsley became "convinced of one thing ... by experience, that the whole question [of morality] is an anthropological one. 'Define a human being,' ought to be the first query. It is thence that the point of departure, perhaps unconsciously takes place" (*Letters* I 221–8). In *Yeast*, Lancelot Smith expresses the need to re-examine the concept of human "being," pushing this examination beyond the bounds of the strictly animal: "I am the whole of what I find in myself – am I to pick and choose myself out of myself?" (33). Later he elaborates: "My body, and brain, and faculties, and appetites must be [God's] will ... Whatsoever I can do with them in accordance with the constitution of them and nature must be His will ... Those laws of Nature must reveal Him" (86–7). Human nature itself, and whatever it entailed, is God's nature. Kingsley states his argument most succinctly in his letter to Reverend George Henslowe on September 11, 1857: "*Hominis est = Ergo Christi = Ergo Dei est*" (*Letters* II 73). In 1872, while offering suggestions to the Reverend S. B. Monsell on a new Anglican hymnary,

Kingsley argued that the line "Sacred heart of Jesus, heart of God in man" should be "Heart of man in God," asserting that the union of man and God transpired "not by conversion of the Godhead to flesh, but by the taking of manhood into God" (*Letters* II 327). Kingsley had come to believe that, through the incarnation, humanity had achieved divinity. "I have to preach the divineness of the whole manhood, and am content to be called a Muscular Christian, or any other impertinent name," he writes to Maurice in 1857 (*Letters* II 54).

While these passages suggest that Kingsley came to see the whole of man – intellectual, aesthetic, and animal – as spiritual, we can see some subtle shifts in his thinking. For one thing, Kingsley's letters to Fanny had argued about the sanctity of all human nature, while these later writings stress the "whole of manhood," the emphasis lying on *man*. This did not mean that Kingsley was uninterested in examining the restrictions placed on women as well. In 1847 he gave the first lectures at what was to become Queen's College, England's first women's college; in 1857 he became a founder of the National Association for the Promotion of Social Science, an organization that included paper-giving women members such as Florence Nightingale; and in 1875 he helped Emma Patterson launch the Women's Protective and Provident League, the first step towards the Women's Trade Union movement (Strachey 87, 118, 241). Although Kingsley certainly espoused a notion of equality that was limited and in conformity with his prejudices as to "feminine nature" (for example, women should be allowed to practice medicine because they are nurturing), his views were still much more liberal than many other Victorians, such as Froude, Arnold, Tennyson, and even Maurice (Strachey 168–9; Banks, *Faces* 40), and were not out of conformity with the thought of many leading feminists of the era (Fawcett, "Home and Politics" 422–3; Banks, *Becoming a Feminist* – see the section on Contagious Diseases Acts, 46–72 *passim*). Millicent Fawcett not only sat next to Kingsley on the platform of the first public meeting of the women's suffrage movement in July 1869, but in a lecture in March 1871 she praised Kingsley as one of those "men occupying the highest ranks of philosophy, science, and literature," such as Mill, Darwin, and Huxley, who are "warm advocates of women's suffrage" (Fawcett, "Electoral Disabilities of Women" 116). Such associations led the anti-feminist E. Lynn Linton to deride Kingsley in her 1860s' articles for the *Saturday*

Review. The Learned Ladies "adore Mr. Kingsley because he is earnest," she writes (quoted in Cunnington, 177). Linton's "Gushing Man," whose feminine sensibilities become more monstrous when expressed with masculine force, who loves Viking heroes and mystical philosophies, and who is not a "Womanly Woman's Ideal of a Manly Man," surely pokes fun at Kingsley ("Gushing Man" in *The Girl of the Period*).

Thus the popular press not only enjoyed questioning the femininity of feminists, but also argued with the masculinity of their male supporters. This, coupled with the fact that the feminist movement upset earlier gender boundaries, helped drive Kingsley not only to explore new gender definitions for men, but also to concentrate on devising a definition of masculinity that protected men against the possible intrusion of the new evolving femininity (see Laura Fasick's essay in this volume). In addition, while Kingsley subtly shifted his concern about *humans* to a concern about *men*, he also shifted his idea of "human nature." Though a liberated expression of "human nature" – usually synonymous with those aspects previously labeled "animal" – became fundamental to his ideas of manhood, Kingsley shifted away from a generic nature to a personal, individual nature. In *Yeast* he writes of the sanctity of "*My* body, and brain, and faculties, and appetites" and "Whatsoever *I* can do with *them* in accordance with the constitution of *them*" (86–7, my emphasis). That is, while God's nature is revealed in human nature, human nature stands revealed in the individual. "Man" has not only become "male," but has become "a male." Of course Kingsley's substitution of the individual for the group assumes an underlying generic masculinity among individual variations – an assumption that we find in both Rousseau and Carlyle. But another implication surfaces: expressing individual nature to its fullest becomes the ground of virtue and morality. As Kingsley writes in *Yeast*: "I am the whole of what I find *in* myself" (33, my emphasis) – the surface of behavior does not constitute the self. The self is the whole of what is *inside* oneself. Through these permutations Kingsley has made self-actualization the authorizing principle of masculinity.

Kingsley blamed the most powerful intellectual, cultural, and economic forces in England – the Oxford Movement, certain evangelical sects, and the middle class – for repressing both generic and personal areas of human existence. To begin the famous quarrel of pamphlets that led to the *Apologia pro Vita Sua*, Kingsley accused the now-Catholic Cardinal J. H. Newman of recommending lying as a sanctified means "to withstand the brute male force of the world." This fabricated charge, which Kingsley aired in his January 1864 review of *Froude's History of England* in *Macmillan's*, fits with his notion of the Tractarian repression of nature and, more particularly, of innate masculine force (Vance 31–41; Thorp 153ff.). Striking, too, is his accusation that such groups as Catholics, Evangelicals, and Puseyites made aspects of nature "a *terra incognita*" (*Letters* I 103), for as Kingsley developed his idea of the sanctity of the whole man, he appealed implicitly and explicitly to a dark, inner place, such as the uncharted African continent as it appeared through the lens of imperialism, a "primitive" place where men like Speke and Burton proved their manhood by penetrating the continent's secrets. (On the connection between constructions of the primitive and imperialism, see C. J. W.-L. Wee's essay in this volume.) The idea of some deep, dark, central force, some "heart" or "appetite," some inner source from which manly action flows, haunts Kingsley's writings. The idea of exploring taboo terrain that had seduced Fanny was now put to work in his writing to men.

Writing to Tom Hughes on June 12, 1857, his thirty-eighth birthday, Kingsley identified the fiery source of manhood, from which sanctified, fierce male behavior arises, as like lava from primitive volcanic roots: "*Thumos* 'rage' or 'pluck,' which Plato averreth (for why, he'd have been a wrazling man, and therefore was a philospher, and king of 'em) to be the root of all virtue" (*Letters* II 60). In another letter to Hughes, Kingsley again refers to "manly *thumos*, which Plato saith is the root of all virtue" (*Letters* II 62). "Animal passion," a hot rage, becomes the primal stuff of virtue that stamps male nature and seeks expression through sex, fighting, and morality. Manliness can only be achieved by allowing this primal force to flow.

Of course, the idea of a core of human power that needs expression pervades mid-nineteenth-century thought and imagery. Dickens depicts the city as a place where such force has been blocked, where "killing airs and gases were bricked in; ... pressing one another to death; ... chimneys ... built in an immense variety of stunted and crooked shapes, as though every house put out a sign of the kind of people who might be expected to be born in it" (*Hard Times* 70; cf. Kingsley, *Alton Locke* 369). Throughout the period, the notion of an informing power of will, pressing the character into

action, impressing itself on the objective world, structures notions of
the individual. As Samuel Smiles writes: "[E]nergy of will may be
defined to be the very central power of character in a man – in a
word, it is the man himself" (quoted in Houghton, 117). In part,
men like Smiles try to combat the deadening power of machines over
men's lives by making men biological machines, creatures driven by
explosive internal combustions that seek constructive, moral release.
In the realm of moral philosophy, this view of men as harboring,
indeed, incarnating pent energy finds expression in what has been
called the cult of enthusiasm: "[T]he ethic of enthusiasm assumes
that human nature is good; . . . and that moral life depends . . . on the
vitality of the noble emotions, inspiring the delighted service of a
high ideal" (Houghton 264). This view of life powered and guided
by some internal force, of course, finds manifestations throughout
the culture, in psychology, natural history, and theology.

The force of *thumos*, as Kingsley imagines it, is spiritual, primal,
animal, potent, and potentially destructive. As indicated above,
Kingsley used the volcano to figure unrepressed *thumos*. We glimpse
this pattern in Alton Locke's dream, with its twin volcanic images.
In the first, the life force released from the volcano's root commences
an upward evolution from protozoa to imparadised Adamic form
(*Alton Locke* 376–83). In the second, the civilizing spread of human
society begins as Teutonic tribes pour "like lava-streams from the
crater of th[e] great soul-volcano" (384). In the Kingsley myth of
masculinity, manhood consists of the specifically gendered elements
of this sacred primal fire. At first, civilization ameliorated this fire,
but then quenched it. Now only this fire can purge the world, saving
men, souls, and civilization.

In the mystical ending of *Yeast* the volcano becomes the image of a
saving sacred primitivism, as Barnakill describes the ideal society on
the volcanic rim:

"No, you shall rather come to Asia, the oldest and yet the youngest
continent, – to our volcanic mountain ranges, where her bosom still heaves
with the creative energy of youth, around the primeval cradle of the most
ancient race of men. Then . . . I will lead you to a land where you shall see
the highest spiritual cultivation in triumphant contact with the fiercest
energies of matter; where men have learnt to tame and use alike the
volcano and the human heart, where the body and the spirit, the beautiful
and the useful, the human and the divine, are no longer separate, and men
have embodied themselves on earth an image of the 'city not made with
hands, eternal in the heavens.'" (319)

In 1853, Kingsley asked Dean Stanley to check for volcanic sites that Kingsley believed existed in the Holy Land (*Letters* II 159). For Kingsley, the primitive, natural, and purgative informing force that gathered its energy from instinct and animal nature was resolutely male: "*You* cannot understand the excitement of animal exercise from the mere act of cutting wood or playing cricket to the manias of hunting or shooting or fishing," he wrote to Fanny. "[E]ven those who have calmed from age, or from necessity of attention to a profession, which has become custom, have the same feelings flowing as an undercurrent in their minds; and, if they had not, they would neither think nor act like men" (*Letters* I 35–6).

v

According to Kingsley, to block the flow of "manly *thumos*" was to "effeminate" male nature. However, it would be incorrect to assert that the hot core of manhood precluded tender and even "womanly" behavior. For Kingsley, men had diverse qualities that sought expression – for instance, because all men learned love at their mother's breast, Kingsley considered tenderness a natural capacity of masculinity. In *Yeast*, for example, Colonel Bracebridge, the "small wiry American" (12) who has "experience of all society, from the prairie Indian to Crockford's, from the prize-ring to the continental courts" (11) and tells "stories of grizzly bear and buffalo hunts" (20), nurses the injured Lancelot Smith with "almost womanish tenderness" (20). So, too, the tall, raw-boned under-keeper, Paul Tregarva, is said to tend the sick and destitute "as tenderly as any woman" (63). In his memoir, John Martineau writes about Kingsley's own "deep vein of *woman* ... a nervous sensitiveness, an intensity of sympathy, which made him suffer when others suffered; a tender, delicate, soothing touch, which gave him power to understand and reach the heart; to call out ... the inmost confidences of men and women alike in all classes of life" (*Letters* I 261). The term "effeminate," in contrast, implied for Kingsley and others the corruption of a manly trait. Again in *Yeast*, he writes of the cultural process by which men became "effeminate": "at first, your ideal man is an angel. But your angel is merely an unsexed woman; and so you are forced to go back to humanity after all – but to a woman, not to a man!" (282). Because, in Kingsley's view, human notions of the spiritual derived from God working through nature, all models of spiritual perfection had earthly prototypes. According to Kingsley, current ideas of human perfection had derived from female nature, so that to be virtuous, a man had to imitate a woman and so repress parts of his natural force that sought expression.

Much of Kingsley's social criticism focuses on people and institutions that repress "manly *thumos*," denying its divine origins and, hence, its virtue. In "Plays and Puritans," Kingsley complains that men have become "deboshed, insincere, decrepit," repressed by the conditions of peace, lacking an outlet for a nature that comprises "kindliness, wit, spirit and courage": "How many a Monsieur Thomas of our own days, whom two years ago, one had rashly fancied capable of nothing higher than coulisses and cigars, private theatricals and white kid-gloves, has been not only fighting and working like a man, but meditating and writing home like a Christian, through the dull misery of those trenches at Sebastopol" (96). But an even more dangerous block to the expression of innate masculine nature comes from the growing middle class, whose artificial equation of money and power has stifled the more natural masculine sources of power. The middle class threatens to abolish hereditary privilege, for instance, with its foundation in nature and innate worth (*Letters* II 224). Middle-class men do not fight or farm or sew – they buy the labor of others. Prestige comes from their money, not their manly labor: "[M]oney-making is an effeminate pursuit, therefore all sedentary and spooney sins, like covetousness, slander, bigotry, and self-conceit, are to be cockered and plastered over, while the more masculine vices, and the no-vices also, are mercilessly hunted down by your cold-blooded, soft-handed religionists" (*Yeast* 35). In a letter to Sir Henry Taylor of December 26, 1868, Kingsley complains of "[t]he effeminacy of the middle class ... I find that even in the prime of youth they shrink from (and are often unable to bear, from physical neglect of training) fatigue, danger, pain" (*Letters* II242). He writes to Hughes in 1857: "I have good hopes of our class [upper], and better than those of the class below [middle]. They are effeminate." He goes on to allege that they seek to control society "by keeping down manly *thumos*" (*Letters* II 62).

For Kingsley, theological orthodoxy most oppressed manly inner forces. In many cases the cathedral came to symbolize this idea. In *Alton Locke*, a novel dominated by towers, mountains, and volcanoes, the cathedral at D***, like the impassable mountain tops in Alton's mystic vision (389), represents for Alton the repression by past dogmatic theologies that superficially seemed to promise release: "[T]hese cathedrals may be true symbols of the superstitions which created them – on the outside, offering to enfranchise the soul and raise it up to heaven; but when the dupes had entered, giving them only a dark prison, and a crushing bondage" (190). Alton's attitude reflected Kingsley's own, he saw in the cathedral at Salisbury a symbol of what happened to men when theology tried to pen the fiery force of *thumos* in the stone of its system:

The first thing which strikes you in it (spiritually, I mean) is its severe and studied calm, even to "primness" – nothing luscious, very little or no variation ... And then from the center of all this, that glorious spire rises – the work of a slightly later hand – too huge, I believe, for the rest of the cathedral, its weight having split and crushed its supporters. Fit emblem of the result of curbing systems. The moment the tower escapes above the level of the roof, it bursts into the wildest luxuriance, retaining the general character of the building below, but disguising it in a thousand fantastic excrescences – like the mind of man, crushed by human systems, and then suddenly asserting its own will in some burst of extravagance, yet unconsciously retaining the harsh and severe lineaments of the school in which it had been bred. (*Letters* I 93–4)

Here, as in *Alton Locke*, the cathedral spire parodies the volcanic cone. Kingsley takes obvious advantage of the structure of the cathedral as displaced and disfigured sexuality, a trope for all distorted animal passions. The cathedral freezes, crusts over, and crushes passion, robbing humans of their God-given shape and distorting good activity, making it monstrous and sinful.

VI

As has already been suggested, after about 1855 Kingsley associated "manliness" with self-actualization, fully expressing the *thumos* within the individual man to the extent he found possible. Occasionally Kingsley's writings suggest that moral action and manliness come from checking the flow of energy: "a young man['s] ... superfluous excitement has to be broken in like that of a dog or a horse – for it is utterly animal" (*Letters* I 35–6). More often Kingsley seems to accept that "where a man acts from impulse ... his flesh is at harmony with, and obeys, his spirit." Such impulse he finds in the example of being driven to put out a fire, "through blazing rafters and under falling roofs, by an awful energy which must be obeyed." The energy does not always flow, however. Only in "the highest state of harmony and health, the rare moments of life, in which our life is not manifold, but one – body and soul and spirit [work] together!" (*Letters* I 79). If one can achieve "harmony and health," then, Kingsley implies, one can liberate instinct and the unimpeded flow of energy will result in moral action. Education thus becomes the process of conditioning oneself to let this energy flow. For instance, a man "put[s] his animal health into that soundness which shall enable him completely to employ his mental vigour" (*Letters* I 41).

Kingsley's advocacy of sound body and sound mind implies that mind and body have personal limits and that fulfilling one's potential ("enable him completely to employ *his* mental vigour") should be one's goal. "Is not a man's real level not what he is," he asks, "but what he can be, and therefore ought to be?" ("Sir Walter" 2). For Kingsley, the ideal of self-actualization, the fulfilling of manly potential, becomes a moral imperative: "[M]en can and do resist God's will, and break the law, which is appointed for them, and so punish themselves by getting into disharmony with their own constitution and that of the universe" (*Letters* II 64–5). But, as he warns one writer, the self has limits: "Self is not evil, because self is you, whom God made, and each man's self is different from his neighbour's. Now God does not make evil things, therefore He has not made self evil or wrong; but you, or self, are only wrong in proportion as you try to be something in and for yourself, and not the child of a father" (*Letters* I 279). In the last distinction he makes in this letter, being "the child of a father," Kingsley derides the idea of a remaking of one's self in whatever fashion one chooses. Such shaping results in misshapen distortions that pervert society, he claims. Rather, one should follow the "innate" shape of the self. Thus he uses the "liberating" masculine ideal of self-fulfillment as a conservative buffer against those who wish to "rise" beyond their station or to "get on."

While, on one side, Kingsley worried that his notion of masculinity might licence all sorts of socially and politically egalitarian movements, he also worried that it could lead to the type of brutal self-indulgence with which his name had sometimes been linked. After all, a self theoretically comprising bestial impulses and vol-

canic passions could easily justify a most dangerous kind of "actuali-
zation." A reviewer in the *Guardian*, in fact, charged Kingsley with
preaching "that the existence of the passions is a proof that they are
to be gratified" (*Letters* 1 245). Others agreed: "What unspeakable
relief and joy for a Christian, like Mr. Kingsley, whom God had
made boiling over with animal eagerness and fierce aggressive
instincts, to feel that he is not called upon to control these instincts,
but only to direct them; and that once having, or fancying he has, in
view a man or an institution that is God's enemy as well as his, may
hate it with perfect hatred, and go at it *en sabreur!*" (quoted in
Chitty, 171). Similar strains are found in Tennyson's *Maud* (1855),
Charles Reade's *Hard Cash* (1863), Bulwer-Lytton's *Kenelm Chillingly*
(1873), and, of course, in the works of George Alfred Lawrence, who
claimed in the preface to his wildly popular *Guy Livingstone* (1857)
that Amyas Leigh had been the model for his pugnacious and
seductive hero (Baker, *History* 151ff.). In these popular productions,
writers seized the doctrine that men ought to be strong, that
impulse, force, nature, and sexuality are sacred and must be
followed.

Such *confrères* led Thomas Hughes, in his continuation of Tom
Brown's education, to attempt to rein in the idea of promiscuous
force with which he and Kingsley had become identified. After
reaffirming his alliance with Kingsley in the preface – he claimed
Tom Brown's name "stood first in the trio of Brown, Jones, and
Robinson" (the firm to which Lancelot Smith belonged) – Hughes
sought to distinguish "muscular Christians" from "musclemen":

[T]he only point in common between the two being, that both hold it to be
a good thing to have strong and well-exercised bodies, ready to be put at
the shortest notice to any work of which bodies are capable, and to do it
well. Here all likeness ends; for the "muscleman" seems to have no belief
whatever as to the purposes for which his body has been given him, except
some hazy idea that it is to go up and down the world with him, belabour-
ing men and captivating women for his benefit or pleasure, at once the
servant and fomenter of those fierce and brutal passions which he seems to
think it a necessity, rather a fine thing than otherwise, to indulge and obey.
Whereas, so far as I know, the least of the muscular Christians has hold of
the old chivalrous and Christian belief, that a man's body is given him to be
trained and brought into subjection and then used for the protection of the
weak, the advancement of all righteous causes, and the subduing of the
earth which God has given to the children of men. He does not hold that
mere strength or activity are in themselves worthy of any respect or

worship, or that one man is a bit better than another because he can knock him down, or carry a bigger sack of potatoes than he. (*Oxford* 99)

More radically still, Hughes retreated on his claims for fighting, stating that while fighting is a natural disposition, the urge to fight indiscriminately, rather than signaling health, signals disease:

I know that [Tom], and other youngsters of his kidney, will have fits of fighting, or desiring to fight with their poorer brethren, just as children have the measles. But the shorter the fit, the better the patient, for like the measles it is a great mistake, and a most unsatisfactory complaint. If they can escape it altogether so much the better. But instead of treating the fit as a disease, "musclemen" professors are wont to represent it as a state of health, and let their disciples run about in middle age with the measles on them as strong as ever. (*Oxford* 100; see also Worth *passim*)

Kingsley also attempted to rein in those who used his philosophy as a licence for violence, but he wished to do so while keeping within the principles of an essentialist notion of masculinity that is both innate and sacred. As he writes to a nineteen-year-old:

[W]e are of ourselves, and in ourselves, nothing better than – as you see in the savage – a sort of magnified beast of prey, all the more terrible for its wondrous faculties; that . . . may be just as powerful for evil as for good; and that what we want to make us true *men*, over and above that which we bring into the world with us, is some sort of God-given instinct, motive, and new principle of life in us, which shall make us not only see the right, and the true, and the noble, but love it, and give up our wills and hearts to it. (*Letters* I 285)

At first Kingsley seems to suggest that the evil lies "in ourselves," at the very brutal core of manhood that he has posited. But then he withdraws that criticism, for we "true *men*," he argues, have a "God-given [moral] instinct . . . in us." Unlike Hughes, who subjects the body and its instincts to moral authority outside of and larger than the self, Kingsley places moral restraint in the self, in the same place that he puts violent impulses: the police and bully, saint and sinner are all on the same payroll, as it were.

In the above "adjustment" that Kingsley makes to his first principles, one can perceive the slipperiness of the deep structure of masculinity that he has created. *Thumos* as an innate, moral, natural, and primal principle can find expression in a wide number of ways – from G. A. Lawrence's "muscular blackguardism," to a kind of egalitarianism, to a justification for stratification of society, even to cooperation and tenderness. In fact, the power of his formulation comes from the protean manifestations that the structure allows. At a Christmas lecture for the Winchester Scientific Society in 1871, for instance, after speaking of the "internecine competition" and "ruthless selfishness" of living things, Kingsley added that life also requires of its members "universal mutual help," which it is part of their nature to provide. Nature teaches that "self-sacrifice, and not selfishness, is at bottom the law of Nature, as it is the law of grace, and the law of bio-geology, as it is the law of all religion and virtue" (*Letters* II, 318–20). As in the earlier writings, the source of brutality becomes the source of nurture and morality. Under the hand of Kingsley, self-actualization would appear to conduce to any conclusion.

Clearly, the malleability of Kingsley's concept of masculinity arises from the positing of a deep structure rather than from the suggestion that particular behaviors and traits might serve as a masculine code. The clearest declaration of this idea may come in *Alton Locke* when Dean Winnstay tries to explain how one may resolve the superficial contradictions of science and nature by recourse to "deep" laws:

Nature's deepest laws, her only true laws, are her invisible ones. All analyses ... whether of appearances, or causes, or of elements, only lead us down to fresh appearances – we cannot see a law, let the power of our lens be ever so immense. The true causes remain impalpable, as unfathomable as ever, eluding equally our microscope, and our induction – ever tending towards some great primal law ... manifesting itself, according to circumstances, in countless diverse and unexpected forms. (411)

Such a regression to a deep, primal law with diverse manifestations allows Kingsley, as similar constructs did Carlyle, to posit diverse forms of masculinity. It also allows him, as it did Rousseau, to criticize certain forms of violence with which he disagrees on the grounds that they are not truly manly.

Moreover, it is precisely the mobility of such an underlying concept that allowed Kingsley to influence so much of his society and so many institutional forms of nineteenth- and twentieth-century masculinity. While overt forms of muscular Christianity have been institutionalized on both sides of the Atlantic in attitudes towards war (Sassoon 103, 138, 142, 146, 155 and *passim*), in sports (Park 18–19), in youth organizations like the Boys' Brigade and Boy Scouts (Hantover *passim*), and in charitable organizations like the

YMCA (Springhall *passim*), the underlying concept of masculinity has also exerted a great influence on those who claimed no affiliation with such activities. A Cambridge student writes to Kingsley of such an influence: "We are learning above all, I think, to esteem more highly this human nature we have, seeing, as you show us in books and words, how it has been consecrated and raised by union with the God-made Man" (*Letters* II, 163). Leslie Stephen, himself raised in a muscular Christian household, a well-known anti-feminist father of a great feminist, recalls that though not great art, Kingsley's works had resonated with youth, like himself, coming of age between 1848 and 1855, leaving an indelible impression (312–13). Perhaps Harriet Martineau's cousin, John Martineau, Kingsley's admiring pupil, put it best: "[A]nother generation will not fully realise the wide-spread influence, the great power, he exercised through his writings ... [T]hey will *not* live, except as seed lives in the corn which grows, or water in the plant which it has revived. For their power often lay mainly in the direction of their aim at the special need of the hour, the memory of which has passed, or will pass away" (*Letters* I 268–9).

We would find it difficult to overestimate the power of Kingsley's ideas (Houghton 203; Mangan and Walvin 2). Many men, like Symonds and Stephen, found that influence embarrassing. A. C. Benson writes with both repugnance and awe of Kingsley's "deep ancient instinct of which we are half-ashamed, and which we do not and cannot resist" (325). The fear of democratization and the growing voice of women, a desire for conquest, the muscular sciences of evolution and geology, and the later Freudian and Jungian psychologies perhaps reinforced aspects of Kingsley's idea of masculinity and allowed his idea of deep structure to inhabit even the most unlikely sectors of culture. Matthew Arnold, writing against Kingsleyan ideas in his fourth essay in *Culture and Anarchy*, "Hebraism and Hellenism," finally seeks the marriage of Kingsley's ideology and his own. Like so many others who sought a ground for authority, he finds it in prehistoric and eternal core-truth, turning, as his title suggests, to racial identity as one ground. We should not be surprised, therefore, to find a Kingsleyan primitive "driving force" as the final foundation on which he rests his idea of culture. "[W]e want a clue to some sound order and authority," writes Arnold. "This we can only get by going back upon the actual instincts and forces which rule our life, seeing them as they really are, connecting

them with other instincts and forces, and enlarging our whole view
and rule of life" (103). From R. S. S. Baden-Powell to Matthew
Arnold, Kingsley's masculinity produced odd alliances in Britain,
alliances that, while superficially diverse, evinced similar underlying
ideas about manhood and power.

VII

Kingsleyan masculinity has had a pervasive presence in Anglo-
American culture for the last 100 years and we can still hear its
polyphonic voices today – in athletics, in religion, in men's movements. Some of the voices are crude, with screaming titles like "Jesus
was no Wimp" and biblical arguments to prove Jesus could "kick
ass" (Phillips *passim*; see also Springhall 66). In baseball parks,
players mix macho and Bible-thumping: "If Jesus were on the field,
he'd be pitching inside and breaking up double plays" ("Overheard"). But even in less obvious ways, masculinity seems driven by
Kingsley's ideas. If, as Richard Sennett has argued, a corrupting
obsession with "self-actualization" pervades America, the most
macho of male institutions, the US Army, makes that idea the
ground for its appeals: be all that you can be, it urges American
teenage boys. From the blue-collar gun club to the yuppie health
club, the idea of an expressive underlying essence of masculinity
inheres; the idea of reaching some fulfilling, primitive, pristine,
moral notion of masculinity innate in men continues to find shape.
The groups who identify with this idea may be, in accordance with
the apparently schizophrenic dualism of Kingsley's masculinity,
either brutal or gentle, but each finds a common ground that
authorizes the other.

A good example of the longevity of Kingsleyan "deep structure"
can be found in certain "new" men's movements that seek to rid
men of the problems of pre-sixties' macho and post-sixties' sensitiv-
ity. Yet the solution simply reiterates the existence of an essential
masculinity that has primitive, mythic roots, a more pristine, powerful, and holistic concept of manhood. In his 1970s' interviews,
Robert Bly, a founder of this movement, recounted mythologies of
masculine and feminine energies, gods and goddesses that were
rooted in nineteenth-century conceptions of cultural origins
(*Talking* 207–12). More recently, his selection of "Iron John" as the
ur-story of masculinity made this debt even clearer: "Though it was

first set down by the Grimm brothers around 1820, this story could be ten or twenty thousand years old" (*Iron John* 5). Kingsley's ghost hangs over Bly's project: "In every relationship something *fierce* is needed once in a while ... One man, a kind of incarnation of certain spiritual attitudes of the sixties, ... found himself unable to extend his arm when it held a sword" (*Iron John* 3–4). Masculinity, for Bly, contains innately primitive, chivalric elements. Any man, he claims, should be able to flash a sword in the sunlight. He argues that while the man who can fully actualize his masculinity will have both womanly and manly qualities, he will not be soft. On the other hand, he argues that to repress one's deep natural-spiritual core of manhood is to disease one's self and one's society. From Robert Bly to the Army recruiter, the underlying foundation remains the one that Kingsley began to piece together in 1838: be all that you can be, or else suffer grave consequences.

Are today's overt ideological revivals of Victorian masculinity simply the death rattles of a concept no longer functional? In 1838, upper-class men fortified themselves against the democratization, the feminization, and the "middle-classification" of society by using essentialist notions of privileged self-actualization. They appealed to ideas of deep structure that undermined any notion that correct social form was itself a guarantor of legitimate political, gender, or racial power. This was supported by appeals to the natural sciences and to a primal nature of masculinity that began to be moralized and spiritualized. Today, science has changed our notion of humanness. Essentialist theories of human nature and behavior have been challenged by theories that nature and behavior are elastic and adaptive. Human potentials are activated by diverse cultural, social, and physical environments; different traits are expressed under different circumstances, so that "self-actualization," or being all you can be, has become meaningless. Cross-cultural studies, historical reconstructions, and scientific theories have all suggested that human society can exist successfully through a variety of religious, moral, and gender arrangements. Whereas the mid-nineteenth-century men's movement used the natural history and the anthropology of the day to reach its goal of laying an eternal foundation for manliness, the late-twentieth-century men's movement often relies on outmoded nineteenth-century mythology for its notions of the natural and primitive. Men today, like those before, may fear feminization, democratization, and the erosion of their power. Thus they may also feel a need to create a new and lasting foundation for manhood. But the foundation they are creating is neither new nor eternal. Anglo-American masculinity has been building on it since the mid-nineteenth century, at the very latest.

WORKS CITED

Arnold, Matthew, *Culture and Anarchy* (1869). New York: Viking, 1949.

Baker, Ernest A., *The History of the English Novel*, vol. VIII. New York: Barnes & Noble, 1960.

Baker, Joseph Ellis, *The Novel and the Oxford Movement*. New York: Russell & Russell, 1965.

Banks, Olive, *The Faces of Feminism: A Study of Feminism as a Social Movement*. New York: St. Martin's, 1981.

  Becoming a Feminist: The Social Origins of "First Wave" Feminism. Brighton: Wheatsheaf Books, 1986.

Benson, Arthur Christopher, *The Leaves of the Tree: Studies in Biography*. New York: Putnam's, 1911.

Blease, W. Lyon, *The Emancipation of Women* (1910). New York: Arno, 1977.

Bly, Robert, *Talking All Morning*. Ann Arbor: University of Michigan Press, 1980.

  Iron John: A Book About Men. Reading, MA: Addison-Wesley, 1990.

Carlyle, Thomas, *On Heroes, Hero-Worship, and The Heroic in History* (1841). New York: Thomas Crowell, n.d.

  Past and Present (1843). New York: Scribner's, 1918.

Chitty, Susan, *The Beast and the Monk: A Life of Charles Kingsley*. New York: Mason/Charter, 1975.

Cunnington, C. Willett, *Feminine Attitudes in the Nineteenth Century*. New York: Macmillan, 1936.

Dickens, Charles, *Hard Times* (1854). New York: New American Library, 1961.

Fawcett, Millicent Garrett, *Before the Vote was Won: Arguments For and Against Women's Suffrage*, ed. Jane Lewis. London: Routledge & Kegan Paul, 1987.

  "Electoral Disabilities of Women" in *Before the Vote was Won*, pp. 100–17.

  "Home and Politics" in *Before the Vote was Won*, pp. 418–23.

Gilmore, David D., *Manhood in the Making: Cultural Concepts of Masculinity*. New Haven: Yale University Press, 1990.

Gay, Peter, *The Bourgeois Experience: Victoria to Freud*. New York: Oxford University Press, 1984.

Hantover, Jeffrey P., "The Boy Scouts and the Validation of Masculinity," *Journal of Social Issues: Male Roles and the Male Experience* (winter 1978): 184–95.

Harte, Bret, "Guy Heavystone; or, 'Entire': A Muscular Novel by the Author of 'Sword and Gun'" in *Condensed Novels in The Writings of Bret Harte*, vol. I. Boston: Houghton, Mifflin, 1899.

Houghton, Walter E., *The Victorian Frame of Mind, 1830–1870*. New Haven: Yale University Press, 1957.

Hughes, Thomas, *Tom Brown's Schooldays* (1857). Chicago: Belford, Clark & Co., n.d.

Tom Brown at Oxford (1861). London: Macmillan, 1929.

Jackson, M. W., "Rousseau's Discourse on Heroes and Heroism," *Proceedings of the American Philosophical Society*, 133.3 (1989): 434–46.

Kingsley, Charles, *Alton Locke, Tailor and Poet* (1850). New York: Macmillan, 1893.

Letters and Memoirs (2 vols.) in *The Works of Charles Kingsley*, vol. VII.

Miscellanies. Reprinted in America as *Sir Walter Raleigh and his Time, with Other Papers*. Boston: Ticknor and Fields, 1852.

"Plays and Puritans" in *Miscellanies*.

"The Poetry of Sacred and Legendary Art" in *Miscellanies*.

"Sir Walter Raleigh and his Time" in *Miscellanies*.

"Tennyson" in *Miscellanies*.

Westward Ho! (1855). New York: Dodd, Mead & Co., 1941.

Yeast (1848) in *The Works of Charles Kingsley*, vol. IV.

Linton, E. Lynn, *The Girl of the Period and Other Social Essays*. 2 vols. London: Richard Bartley, 1883.

Mangan, J. A. and James Walvin, eds., *Manliness and Morality: Middle-class Masculinity in Britain and America 1800–1940*. Manchester University Press, 1987.

"Overheard," *Newsweek* (May 13, 1991): 17.

Park, Roberta J., "Biological Thought, Athletics and the Formation of a 'Man of Character': 1830–1900" in Mangan and Walvin, *Manliness and Morality*, pp. 7–34.

Phillips, J. B., "Jesus was no Wimp," *Signs of the Times* (February 1991): 30–32.

Rosen, David, *The Changing Fictions of Masculinity*. Urbana, IL: Illinois University Press, 1993.

Sassoon, Siegfried, *Memoirs of an Infantry Officer*. New York: Collier, 1969.

Sennett, Richard, *The Fall of Public Man: On the Social Psychology of Capitalism*. New York: Vintage, 1978.

Springhall, John, "Building Character in the British Boy; the Attempt to Extend Christian Manliness to Working-Class Adolescents, 1880–1914" in Mangan and Walvin, *Manliness and Morality*, pp. 51–74.

Stearns, Peter, *Be a Man! Males in Modern Society*, 2nd edn. New York: Holmes & Meier, 1990.

Stephen, Leslie, *Hours in a Library*, vol III. New York: Putnam, 1904.

Stone, Donald D., *The Romantic Impulse in Victorian Fiction*. Cambridge, MA: Harvard University Press, 1980.

Strachey, Ray, *The Cause: A Short History of the Women's Movement in Great Britain*. London: Bell & Sons, 1928. Reprinted London: Virago, 1978.

Symonds, John Addington, *The Letters and Papers of John Addington Symonds*, ed. Horatio F. Brown. New York: Scribner's, 1923.

Thorp, Margaret Farrand, *Charles Kingsley, 1819–1875*. New York: Octagon Books, 1969.

Tiger, Lionel, *Men in Groups*. New York: Random House, 1969.

Vance, Norman, *The Sinews of the Spirit: The Ideal of Christian Manliness in Victorian Literature and Religious Thought*. Cambridge University Press, 1985.

Williams, David M., "Henry Mayhew and the British Seaman" in *Lisbon as a Port Town, the British Seaman & Other Maritime Themes*, ed. Stephen Fisher. University of Exeter Press, 1988, pp. 111–27.

Worth, George J., "Of Muscles and Manliness: Some Reflections on Thomas Hughes" in *Victorian Literature and Society: Essays Presented to Richard D. Altick*. Athens, OH: Ohio State University Press, 1983, pp. 300–14.

CHAPTER 2

On the making and unmaking of monsters: Christian Socialism, muscular Christianity, and the metaphorization of class conflict

Donald E. Hall

A selfish man upsets the boat in the endeavor to make his own place in it more comfortable.

In legislation, and indeed in our private conduct, there should be constant reference to great principles, if only from the exceeding difficulty of foreseeing the results in detail of any measure.

Aphorisms from *Politics for the People*, p. 112

The commonest metaphors are mostly the truest ones, if we could only feel their truth.

John Ludlow, *Politics for the People*, p. 124

As a commercial endeavor, *Politics for the People* failed spectacularly. Running for just seventeen issues between May and July of 1848, the Christian Socialist weekly never generated enough income to meet its own production costs. But even though the paper's failure was a disappointment to its founder, F. D. Maurice, it was a disappointment tempered with optimism. In his final contribution, "More Last Words," Maurice admits that the paper's writers had executed their work "very imperfectly" but asserts that "Whatever is true, must at last be mighty. The battle with principalities and powers is fought, for the most part by weak arms; which nevertheless, shall prevail" (284). The imagery in this passage tells us much about Maurice, the theologian and social philosopher who inspired both Charles Kingsley and Thomas Hughes. Indeed, the friendship alone of these three men has meant that Maurice's name is often linked with the muscular Christian movement even though he wrote only one unsuccessful religious novel and rarely mentioned fist fights or sporting events in his sermons and essays. Nevertheless, the physicality of some of Maurice's metaphors does give his work a "sinewy" quality, to

45

appropriate Norman Vance's term from his respected overview of
muscular Christianity, *The Sinews of the Spirit*. While Maurice may
have had difficulty carrying the financial burden of *Politics for the
People*, the body of that paper's text evinces its own muscularity, its
aggressive figur(e-)ative language allowing us a point of access into
the mindset and social debate that provided a foundation for Christian Socialism and its offspring muscular Christianity. For even
though *Politics for the People* was a commercial failure, Maurice's
optimism was well founded; the essays appearing in the weekly
reflected and reinforced a representational and discursive matrix
that proved both popular and resilient. Its subversive yet urgent
attempts to provide politics *for* the people reveal not only some of the
roots of muscular Christianity, but also the subtle mechanisms
whereby pedagogical programs reproduce social hierarchies, and
metaphors encode and enforce cultural ideologies.

As David Rosen explores in his essay in this volume, muscular
Christianity was born of insecurity and turmoil, as evinced clearly in
the tumultuous life of one of its progenitors, Charles Kingsley. But
Kingsley was no anomaly and muscular Christianity's aggressive,
even obdurate, response to various perceived and imagined threats
can be traced back a decade before the term was actually coined in
1857, for *Politics for the People* itself came into being at a moment of
profound social crisis. By 1848, revolution had spread across
Europe, and angry and influential Chartist leaders in England were
threatening physical violence if their petition to Parliament was
rejected, as it had been in 1839 and 1842. Feargus O'Connor and his
followers gathered almost two million signatures supporting
expanded voting rights, secret ballots, and other election reforms.
The middle and upper classes in England were nervous and, in a
very real sense, on the defensive. As historian Walter Arnstein notes,
"Almost every London gentleman was created a special constable in
order to handle the crowd which was expected to march upon the
houses of Parliament" (36). On April 10, a massive demonstration
shook the city. Charles Kingsley, the Rector of Eversley in Hamp-
shire and the newly published author of the play *The Saint's Tragedy*,
rushed to London that day and stayed up until 4 AM writing
placards addressed to the "Workmen of England." In his statement,
Kingsley first assures the Chartists of his sympathy, but finally urges
calm, respect for property, and faith in God: "Workers of England,
be wise, and then you must be free, for you will be fit to be free"

(quoted in Kendall, 45–8). In this brief yet insistent dictum one finds encapsulated not only the fervor, but also the central agenda of the Christian Socialist movement, one that (as we shall see later in this essay) remains a telling component of muscular Christianity – calming and educating the lower classes with the promise of rendering them "fit" for freedom, an aggressive pedagogical program that one month later led to the establishment of *Politics for the People*.

In his "Prospectus" that opens the paper's first issue, Maurice attempts to convey to its Chartist readers the paper's overarching purpose:

It is proposed in this Paper to consider the questions which are most occupying our countrymen at the present moment, such as the Extension of the Suffrage; the relation of the Capitalist to the Labourer; what a Government can or cannot do, to find work or pay for the Poor. By *considering* these questions, we mean that it is not our purpose to put forth readymade theories upon them, or vehement opinions upon one side or the other. We think that whatever a great number of our countrymen wish for, deserves earnest reflection. (p. 1)

Maurice thus starts by claiming a position of neutrality, of "earnest" goodwill towards all. In denying the existence of "readymade" theories among the paper's writers, Maurice denies not only ideological bias but also pedagogical intent and even seems to disavow any claim to greater knowledge or wisdom. But Maurice ends the same piece on a vaguely instructional note that revises the earlier suggestion of a hierarchy-less forum for discussion:

Many people try to convince you that it is your interest not to injure the richer classes, and to convince them that it is their interest to redress your wrongs. We, who do not, properly speaking, belong to your body or theirs, shall not try to make out that our interests are in common with either. But we believe that we have a DUTY to both, and that you have a DUTY to your own class, to every other, to God ...
We hope not to forget your different occupations; but we wish to remember that you are MEN ... Whatever knowledge is fit for men, as men, is fit for you. You have hearts and heads which can take it in. (p. 2)

"DUTY" reveals an implicit stratification. It is a term used variously to valorize the Christian Socialists' duty to educate the Chartists and the Chartists' duty to be educated. In the discourse of the contributors to *Politics for the People*, it masks ideology through an insistence that *conveying* and *absorbing* knowledge are parallel functions in an economy where a commonly shared duty to God indicates the only hierarchy not explicitly offset by others' reciprocal duties. But as we know, these are not parallel functions and Maurice here clearly attempts to cultivate passivity and receptivity in his Chartist readers. *Politics for the People* purported to be an "open forum," but was primarily a tool for education against radical social reform. (See Adrienne Munich's *Andromeda's Chains* for a complementary discussion of Kingsley's desire to educate against feminism.) While the English national "body" appears hopelessly fragmented in the passage above into warring bod*ies*, these protomuscular Christians worked to reunify the hierarchized national social body (that true body "proper" to which all of the parties above belonged), a project of (re)metaphorization whereby lower-class identity was effectively rewritten and subsumed.

The frequent references to the body in *Politics for the People*, and elsewhere in Christian Socialist and muscular Christian works, provide compelling evidence concerning the ability of figurative discourse to encode ideology; the metaphors and pedagogical goals of the Christian Socialists and muscular Christians are inextricably linked. To be sure, instructional programs are always already biased. Pierre Bourdieu quotes one academician who asserts that "the task of the teaching profession is . . . to maintain and promote . . . order in people's thinking, which is just as necessary as order in the streets and in the provinces" (70). In fact, those "orders" often reflect and reinforce each other; as Raymond Williams notes, "It is characteristic of educational systems to claim that they are transmitting 'knowledge' or 'culture' in an absolute, universally derived sense, though it is obvious that different systems . . . transmit radically different selective versions of both . . . [T]here are fundamental and necessary relations between this selective version and the existing dominant social relations" (186). Bourdieu calls this selection and transmission of "cultural arbitraries" a form of "symbolic violence"; "under the guise of neutrality" the educational system serves the interests of dominant groups and classes (67) by "imposing and inculcating certain meanings," a "symbolic system" that is power-determined, exclusionary, and inevitably oppressive (8). A key component of this "symbolic system," one that seems to fall outside Williams's and Bourdieu's particular interests, is metaphor. Metaphors, themselves, perform pedagogical work.

Eric Cheyfitz notes in *The Poetics of Imperialism* that "metaphor plays a crucial part in maintaining [a] class system" (91), for metaphor is always "instructive" – it orders, classifies, and hierarchizes (108). Such "ordering" is nowhere more apparent than in mutually reinforcing perceptions of hierarchized physical and social bodies; in fact, a recognition of this linkage is fundamental to Peter Stallybrass and Allon White's influential study *The Politics and Poetics of Transgression*: "Traversed by regulative forces quite beyond its conscious control, the body is territorialized in accordance with hierarchies and topographical rules ... which make it a point of intersection and flow within the elaborate symbolic systems of the socius" (90). "Body and social formation are inseparable," they argue (145), a transcoding that is immediately apparent in Maurice's use of the word "body" above. "We ... do not, properly speaking, belong to your body or theirs" (2) – this statement is telling not only for the way that it provides a guise of neutrality, but also for the specifically proprietary interests and worries that are inscribed in it. A few pages later, Dr. William Guy writes in an article on sanitary reform that, "whether the soldier fall by the sword or by the fever, whether his limbs be disabled by wounds, or his constitution undermined by disease, matters little; in either case, property is destroyed or injured; and that property is as well worth protecting, and has as good a claim to be protected, as if it were a gross, tangible, material thing" (7). Guy's assertions here are extraordinarily revealing. Not only does he summarily brand the soldier's body "property," but he continues to manipulate its very nature through figurative language. Of course the soldier's physical body *is* a "tangible, material thing," despite Guy's use of the subjunctive, but his phrasing implies that while the soldier's body may be rightly considered *less than* property, it is still worth treating *as* property because it does have some use value. Guy manipulates language to simultaneously erase and insist upon the materiality of the soldier's body, a process whereby the worker is thoroughly objectified and commodified. While it may help comprise the national social body, the worker's body clearly belongs to the nation, for the body of the nation is itself rigidly hierarchized, consisting of individual bodies arranged by class and function into an entity at once corporeal and corporate.

Such a metaphor implies, indeed insists, that the upper body of the nation naturally rules the lower body, just as the brain commands the physical body. John Ludlow, one of the founders of *Politics for the People*, writes that in every human body, a paralyzed nerve, a weakened sense, an open sore, impairs ... the health of the whole frame. It follows thence, that what holds good of the whole People, and that only, must hold good of every man in it; that what is good for the whole People, and that only, must be good for every man. The People cannot be honest, wise, free, intelligent, brave, worthy, unless it be composed of honest, wise, free, intelligent, brave, worthy men ... Class legislation, whether it come from the monied classes, as with us, or from the working classes, as in France now, is not legislation for the People; for this simple reason, that one man's selfishness cannot make another man happy. Class legislation is selfish legislation. Party politics are selfish politics. (p. 17)

Certainly some of the sentiments expressed here are laudable, for, as always, the Christian Socialist emphasis on cooperation between classes and individuals hinges on reciprocal responsibilities. But mitigating, perhaps even wholly offsetting, this affirmation of connectivity, is the insistently vertical axis of the body. While ameliorative in some of its implications, Ludlow's metaphor remains profoundly hierarchical, for he always assumes that the upper classes will both transmit and judge the honesty, wisdom, freedom, intelligence, bravery, and worthiness of the less privileged. Carlyle, an inspiration for much Christian Socialist thought, speaks often in "Chartism" of the "body" of the English nation and the chain of authority running from top to bottom: "Obedience ... is the primary duty of man ... Recognised or not recognised, a man *has* his superiors, a regular hierarchy above him; extending up, degree above degree" (218). Maurice agreed. In *The Kingdom of Christ* (1842) he describes his ideal of a society bound together in harmony by "sacramental bonds" which "preserve[s] all existing ranks and relations" and in which "each portion of the community" learns how to "preserve its proper position to the rest" (II 323). Those "bonds" are practically fetters, for they generally lock groups and individuals into rigidly defined social positions and functions.

In *Politics for the People* "selfishness" denotes actions and beliefs in the explicit service of the class-based self rather than the national self, but here, as elsewhere, the general principle has divergent implications for the particular parties involved. Even seemingly non-hierarchical metaphors replicate the biases of more obviously vertical constructs, for only the signifier changes, not the basic economic structure signified. "Let us not look for differences, but for agreement", writes Ludlow (274) in an article on society as a "Great Partnership." He avers, "Let us all try to love the society in which we live" and eschew "the spirit of individual selfishness jarring still against the higher spirit of fellowship" (273–4). However, that "fellowship," that social (in)corporation, remains internally stratified: "all the partners may not fill such places as they ought to fill, enjoy such share of the common profit as they ought to enjoy" (274). In fact, such class divisions appear immutable, for Ludlow writes that men must learn to "manage [the partnership] better, – nay, to work each man the more wisely and zealously" (274). The fundamental division between management and labor is thus never reconciled. That the "selfishness" of the lower classes is seen as antithetical to the interests of the national self is hardly surprising, for the latter interests are themselves the "selfish" interests of the propertied classes.

Of course identity is itself grounded in metaphor; for the lower classes to subordinate their own interests to those of the nation, to obey the wishes of the national body, would mean effectively losing the basis for their sense of oppression: their sense of selfhood. Such a process of subsumption would depend upon a fundamental and improbable (though, as we shall see, not wholly impossible) deconstruction and reconstruction of lower-class subjectivity, an upper-class ideal that remained elusive during the 1840s, for lower-class "selfishness" was resilient, rampant, and vociferously expressed. But metaphor fluidly accommodates such resistence to its ordering power. Within the broad range of body-based (con)figurations for social constitution and interaction, the schizophrenic, self-divided body became a common and useful point of reference. Always hierarchically ordered, the antagonistic components of the fragmented, binarized body appear poised for self-destruction. In Kingsley's Christian Socialist novel *Alton Locke* (1850), his poet-hero Alton encounters one such group of social antagonists: "Three-fourths, I saw at once, were slop-working tailors. There was a bloused and bearded Frenchman or two; but the majority were, as was to have been expected, the oppressed, the starved, the untaught, the despairing, the insane; 'the dangerous classes', which society creates, and then shrinks in horror, like Frankenstein, from the monster her own clumsy ambition has created" (308). The monster body of the lower classes seems to mirror even as it opposes the body comprised by the wealthy. But the members of the latter group, even if greedy and remiss above, are, by implication, both educated and sane; after all, they are not the monsters here. A. Susan Williams argues in *The Rich Man and the Diseased Poor* that the "monster" metaphor was a tool used by the upper classes to inflame public opinion and reassert dominance even as it encoded fear and perceptions of fragmentation: "The description of the poor as a monster of the Frankenstein type ... acknowledged the people's strength. On the one hand, of course, it portrayed them as an aberration, amoral and savage, unworthy of treatment as humans. But, at the same time, it invested them with the power and determination of Shelley's monster – which destroyed its creator" (124). The popularity of the image of the lower-class monster, which Williams traces throughout mid-Victorian fiction and nonfiction, captures metaphor's power when it operates in the service of entrenched cultural interests – it orders perceptions and marshalls defenses, here in response to the awakening of lower-class subjectivity, portrayed as diabolic rebellion.

Such thinking is apparent in *Politics for the People*'s frequent declarations opposing "Monster Meetings," those enormous gatherings of Chartists that Ludlow says inspire a "terror of brute force" (27). Speaking of "His" absence at these meetings, Ludlow argues that they are Godless assemblies, reinforcing their association with the unnatural, the satanically rebellious. "There is practical atheism in the cry for Monster Meetings," says Ludlow (28). In the face of such clear threat, he demands a return to "natural" law and order: "Because Parliament does not make one law, that is no reason for breaking another. Parson and minister may forget God, but that will not help a cursing beggar. Now, more than ever, perhaps, 'ENGLAND EXPECTS EVERY MAN TO DO HIS DUTY'" (18). Of course Ludlow does not address "Parliament," "Parson," or "minister" here; his demand is that the poor "do their duty" to a social body that is simultaneously paralleled to physical and religious bodies, a potent, expanding metaphoric economy. And here reciprocity reaches its limits, for finally the internally stratified social body must submit to the perceived wishes of a class-determined construction of the Godhead. Thus duty to the nation, duty to nature, and finally duty to God demanded a return to quiescence and obedience by the lower classes.

Kingsley actively teaches such social and religious dutifulness in his contributions to *Politics for the People* signed "Parson Lot." As a pedagogue and bearer of culture, Kingsley professes his desire to calm and educate his seemingly bestial audience. In his first

"Letter" to the Chartists, he chastises them for reading "French dirt" and writing with language that consists of "ferocity, railing, mad one-eyed excitement" (29). But it is as a "parson" that Kingsley constructs his most powerful argument. In one of his essays on "The National Gallery," Kingsley looks to a painting by Bellini for a behavior model, finding in the body of the painting's subject a proper alternative to the bellicose bodies of the Chartists. Kingsley fixates on the poor, aged man appearing in the portrait, noting that even though he looks as if he has had "many sorrows," he is "thoughtful," "gentle," and "kindly" – "a noble, simple, commanding old man, who has conquered many hard things, and, hardest of all, has conquered himself, and now is waiting calm for his everlasting rest" (39). Kingsley extolls patience, "self"-mastery, and "sobriety" in this essay for readers whom he hopes will long to "die the death of the righteous" (41) after reading his piece. Here, as elsewhere, the internal divisions of the social body are projected onto the lower-class body itself, which must conquer its "self," a "lowness" equated with its own subjectivity. Even death here is metaphorical, as righteousness, that state of acting in accord with divine law and deferring one's reward, clearly depends upon the death of class-based self-interest and a process of reintegration whereby one learns and accepts one's place in a social hierarchy. In his third "Letter" to the Chartists, Kingsley asks them to remember their Psalms, to be content with *"the patient abiding of the meek"* (his emphasis), not to resort to "the frantic boasts of the bloodthirsty" (136). Recalling the Sermon on the Mount, Kingsley invokes the powerful image of Christ's own body to drive home his political point – that selfishness violates the integrity of the socio-religious body, that self-mastery turns on self-renunciation and an assumption of the position of supplicant and disciple. But the tensions and fragmentations within Christ's body are also captured here, for Kingsley himself assumes the role of Christ the prophet, while demanding that his readers follow the example of Christ the self-effacing and long-suffering man.

Here we find theology at its most insistently pedagogical, a function that is clear throughout the imagined "dialogues" in *Politics for the People*, "dialogues" that follow the gradual conversion of a Chartist as they attempt to coerce a similar transformation in the reader. The term "dialogue" again masks hierarchy, for these are in fact scenes of instruction. In those written by James Spedding, the

reader is encouraged to identify with the "Chartist" participant
who at first hotly condemns social injustice, but is taught a more
moderate position. "Man was manifestly made for submission,"
asserts the "Whig" who participates in one supposed conversation
(249). He argues that before any disenfranchised individual can
realistically expect "self-government," he must first practice the
"government of himself" (254). While future political changes are
not dismissed out of hand, they are wholly contingent upon obedience and moral submission. Argues the "Whig," no change should
be made until the poor forego gin and violence. The "Chartist"
answers, "I hardly know what to think of all this – it sounds more
like divinity than politics; but there may be some sense in it, and I
will consider" (254). This observation is apt, for divinity and politics
here converge in a strong-armed attempt to counter lower-class
subjectivity. The possibility of political reform is tabled until the
lower classes prove themselves worthy by adequately submissive,
that is tractable, behavior.

And Kingsley conveniently provides yet another role model, for
Alton Locke achieves such "self"-mastery. His body is in fact a key
to understanding the novel's agenda, for it is literally inscribed by
Kingsley's politics. Many critics find Alton unusual in the Kingsley
canon, but as his only adult "working-class" hero, Alton's essential
moribundity reflects Kingsley's Christian Socialist vision. Alton is a
weak, tubercular tailor, whose potential for meekness and patience
is ever present, but whose need for self-mastery bespeaks his lack of
fitness for privileges reserved for the upper classes. Under-educated,
lacking in intellectual and religious rigor and training, he unwittingly incites a riot: "Then I first found out how large a portion of
rascality shelters itself under the wing of every crowd; and at the
moment, I almost excused the rich for overlooking the real sufferers,
in indignation at the rascals. But even the really starving majority,
whose faces proclaimed the grim fact of their misery, seemed gone
mad for the moment. The old crust of sullen, dogged patience had
broken up, and their whole souls had exploded into reckless fury and
brutal revenge" (271). This image is of the lower body unbound, the
Frankensteinian monster unleashed and venting its fury upon its
master. The problem for the Christian Socialists was finding a way
to rebind the monster and elicit the dogged patience that Kingsley
holds up as an ideal.

This transformation is effected in Alton, for through a long illness he is taught the error of his ways. In effect, the monster conveniently agrees to rebind itself. Eleanor, the novel's spokesperson for the concerned upper classes, tells Alton that "it is only by the co-operation of all the members of a body, that any one member can fulfill its calling in health and freedom" (379). And what constitutes "co-operation"? She finally reveals the answer: "Freedom, Equality, and Brotherhood ... Realise them in thine own self, and so alone thou helpest to make them realities for all. Not from without, from Charters and Republics, but from within, from the Spirit working in each; not by wrath and haste, but by patience made perfect through suffering" (386). Alton is carefully schooled in both duty and humility, finally learns his lesson thoroughly, and then quickly dies the death of the righteous. The hasty killing off of Alton may seem strange to some, but like the imagined deaths mentioned above, it demonstrates the ever-present line demarcating the boundary of the Christian Socialists' vision – while their program for inculcating docility and resolving social fragmentation (the process of "rendering them *fit* for freedom") was explicit and well developed, the moment of "freedom" itself was unimaginable. It is figured here as a point of death, for the life of the social body depends upon its proper internal constitution. No "body" can live with multiple heads and nothing below the neck; that would be monstrous.

Eighteen years later, in his substantial retrospective, *The Workman and the Franchise*, Maurice was still convinced that education could impart a "sense of unity and universality" (237) that would combat any dangerous sense of fragmentation such as that which existed in the days of the Chartist movement. His work renders vivid some of the links between Christian Socialism and muscular Christianity, for he explicitly defines "manhood" in a way that demonstrates the ease with which Christian Socialist rhetoric concerning the internal constitution of the social body can evolve into the muscular Christian focus on the external surfaces of both national and individual bodies. A man "who has earned a competence, who is able to live without depending on the bounty of others, has given a test of his manhood; that he has shown himself capable of self-restraint, and of patient toil" (208). Manhood here is equated with restraining the self, putting the "self" in the service of a larger social body that may not materially provide for one, but that expects one's labor. Suffrage, says Maurice plainly, is not one of the rights of manhood: "It will not express their serious or intelligent purpose as a body. It will not denote the serious or intelligent conviction of the distinct men who compose the body" (211). Suffrage is not out of the question for the lower-class "body," but first that body must pass "through a stage of discipline" (213) that may include submitting itself to the guidance of the upper class (221) but certainly means subordinating its will to that of the larger social body whose interests substantially mirror those of the upper class. Discipline is key here – securing the perimeters of the body in order to meet the challenges of a threatening, hostile world. According to Maurice, this unified, hierarchized, and armored social body, bound together by a common law (235), must turn its attention abroad, to investigate "the fact of our being bound to other countries as well as our own" and study England's interest "in the well-being of foreign lands" (236).

A movement abroad, through which the potentially unstable national body is disciplined and revitalized, evokes a familiar pattern. As Cheyfitz notes, "the foreign is never simply that which is outside the national, but is also that by which the national constitutes, or defines, its own identity through acts of startled recognition that entail projection and introjection" (90). Klaus Theweleit observes similar patterns in fascist literature from Nazi Germany: "Nation invariably arises out of a process of fusion, or to put it another way, out of the suppression of fragmentations and separations .... 'unity' is a state in which oppressor and oppressed are violently combined to form a structure of domination ... The concept of nation can be seen, then, as the most explicit available foundation of male demands for domination" (86–7). Theweleit argues that "the external (armed) mass becomes a particularly intense embodiment of the invisible internal mass of the soldier male" (37). For the individual warrior, battle becomes a fight against personifications of his own weakness and potential for bestiality; for society, I would add, external campaigns solidify the internal constitution.

Throughout *Politics for the People*, references to foreign threats and continental chaos operate as mechanisms for an attempted solidification of that internal body structure. And here telling metaphors abound, as society is alternately seen as an edifice, a chain, and a potential target of disease – all suggesting a bodily connectedness that demands vigilance, discipline, and the maintenance of order. In one of Ludlow's many exhortations to Chartists concerning the "Law" he warns,

The law is the great bond of human society – a chain of which no link can be snapped without danger ... [I]t is the law, and the obedience paid unto it, which prevent the crops from being ravaged by plundering savages ... Time was, when from this England of ours slaves went forth to be sold upon Roman markets. What has made the change? Law, and obedience to law. It is a great crime to break the law. (11)

Security from external threat (as well as domestic savagery) is dependent upon a rigid chain of command, a pressing concern for the Christian Socialists for they saw potential threats as numerous and varied. Ludlow repeatedly invokes the image of French social putrescence and its threat to British internal security; in his "Chapters in Recent History" he speaks of the "rotting away" of the French people under Louis-Philippe, who worked "to pervert and pollute" his nation and whose evil influences are "still everywhere rank and rampant" (15). The threat indeed has the potential for moving beyond French boundaries, for "the seeds of evil have wings, and easily take flight ... This, indeed, we see already, in the lawlessness of threatened Chartist or Irish insurrections, avowedly aping the successful barricades of Paris" (62). In his "Warnings of the Late Paris Insurrection," Ludlow paints a grisly picture of the French social body in agony: "Paris has been deluged with blood" (197). He demands that the English take heed: "[H]owever provoked, the first successful blow to established power is, in fact, the ruin of the whole edifice of society" (197). "[L]et us not lose the warning," (197) he cries. England may be next.

Victorian fiction and nonfiction repeatedly bear out Julia Kristeva's contention in *Strangers to Ourselves* that xenophobia is actually a product of discovering otherness "at the heart of what we persist in maintaining as a proper, solid 'us'" (191–2). As Patrick Brantlinger notes in *Rule of Darkness*, constructions of "foreignness" helped alleviate the worries attending the rise of "Chartism, trade unionism, and socialism" (173–4). Ludlow participates above in a widespread and well-known tendency among the Victorians to use France and the French (as well as other convenient foreign bodies) to unnerve the English reader and citizen, and, in David Lodge's words, "to dissuade the working class from organized political protest" (129). From Carlyle to Tennyson to Kingsley, Franco-phobia (and slightly later Russophobia) is manipulated in order to calm domestic discord and reassert class hierarchy.

Ludlow's article, "The Colonial System," foregrounds the potentially reconstitutive dynamic between the external and internal: "I believe the time is come for a complete and searching reform of the Colonial system of this country; but it is a reform which cannot be thoroughly carried out without corresponding changes in the Home system." Of course what follows is no call for the dissolution of the empire; instead, he wishes to find "means of firmly attaching the Colonies to the Mother-country, ... of making them constituent parts of it" (239). Are these "constituent parts" in fact new "body parts"? Such appears to be the case, for Ludlow wishes to take the outside into the national body, expanding the conception of "nation" to include all of the colonial holdings: "And what a glorious empire would this be, when an Englishman could travel from London to Labrador, to Hong Kong, to New Zealand, and find everywhere parishes and boroughs, juries and English judges, churches and schools" (240). In order to tap freely the new "boroughs'" potential for wealth-making, he would do away with import duties and excise taxes; the newly enlarged "domestic" economy would then thrive beyond imagining. He ends by asking "Is there an empire in the world that could then compare with this our England?" (240). In subsuming the colonies, the new "inside" would be economically revitalized and its predominance over the newly diminished "outside" assured. The enlarged and strengthened national body would have a secure identity through internal stability (assured by the juries and judges mentioned above) and external superiority.

As C. J. W.-L. Wee explores later in this volume, Charles Kingsley helped reinscribe British national identity during the 1850s and 1860s through his fictional search for potential sources of "vigor" from within and without the empire. But before such a process of reinvigoration – what Wee finally pinpoints as "re-racination" – could take place, substantial fractures in the internal constitution of the British social body had to be healed, even if only superficially and temporarily. Physical force Chartism did, in fact, disappear. "Why?" has been addressed in differing ways by historians. Certainly the failure of the Charter in 1848 diminished morale considerably, and Walter Arnstein makes a valid point in connecting Chartism's decline to the "renewed prosperity" of the early 1850s (37). But the Crimean War of 1853–6 also played a key, if often neglected, role. Preston Slosson in his 1916 study, *The Decline of the Chartist Movement*, notes that Chartist papers themselves helped fuel anti-Russian sentiment; by 1854 Chartist leaders and publications were actively calling for British participation in the war (203). This was in spite of the fact that at least one Chartist leader, Bronterre O'Brien, opposed the war "on the grounds that it was a ruling class device to distract the working class from its grievances" (quoted in Jones, 162).

In fact, the "bestiality" that only a few years before had been so feared and decried in the Chartists was celebrated in the 1850s as a potential source of strength for a nation preparing for war. In one 1854 *Punch* cartoon, a very aristocratically portrayed Lord Aberdeen (sporting a crown and ornate clothing) is shown barely restraining the ferocious lion of popular British anger; he states "I must let him go!" (see Warner, illustration facing p. 32). But by helping turn that bestial anger outward, the British upper classes were serving their own interests in substantial ways. David Wetzel, for one, has traced the effect of English manufacturers' grievances in stoking anti-Russian public opinion. He goes on to argue that xenophobia was the logical consequence of class tensions, but also helped assuage those tensions (15–17). In fact, J. B. Conacher, in his fine study *The Aberdeen Coalition*, argues that Lord Palmerston, who sneered at the demands of the working class and greatly feared extending the franchise "downwards," "hoped to kill reform by raising a war cry" in 1853 (221). Palmerston helped inflame public opinion against the Russians at the same time as he successfully fought to defeat Lord Russell's far-reaching 1854 Reform Bill. Kingsley himself was caught up in this war fervor, writing of the Crimean conflict, "How it makes one's blood boil!" and later adding, "The Reform Bill is shelved: excellent as it is, it does not much matter at this minute" (*Life and Works* II 167–8). Most members of Parliament finally agreed that internal fragmentation of the British social body was wholly undesirable when facing war with Russia (Conacher 296–311); said *The Times*, "At the very time when he and his colleagues were sending two immense fleets to the Mediterranean and the Baltic," Russell introduced a bill "not much less sweeping than that which some twenty years since brought us to the eve of a revolution and anarchy itself" (quoted in Conacher,

294). The bill was hastily withdrawn, for Russophobia did what Francophobia could not – solidify a sense of British "self" that effectively, if only temporarily, smoothed over the class tensions and fractures that had resulted in the Chartist movement. *Punch* illustrations from 1854 and 1855 show a personified Britain battling Russian bears and soldiers. One particularly telling cartoon shows the body of a Russian soldier literally being blown into fragments; its caption reads "Bursting of the Russian Bubble" (see Warner, illustration facing p. 32). An ordered and solid British body is repeatedly shown to triumph against a fractured foreign opponent.

But such a construction of identity is precarious to say the least, for internal political strife is never seamlessly smoothed over, only mitigated occasionally by international crises. As Regenia Gagnier traces in *Subjectivities*, British lower-class self-consciousness and drive towards self-representation continued to build through the nineteenth century. It is hardly surprising, then, that *Politics for the People* folded with its seventeenth issue and that its successors proved equally unpopular and unprofitable, for as Maurice's son noted almost forty years later, "the workingmen had felt some suspicion of its being a capitalist's trick" (*Life of Maurice* I 482). And in succeeding years, the muscular Christians still struggled with many of the same social issues that had motivated earlier works. In *Two Years Ago*, Kingsley's first novel published after the Crimean War, he again demonstrates the potentially disastrous consequences, both personal and social, of a break or inversion in the chain of class hierarchy. In the novel's first chapters, we meet the villainous Elsley Vavasour as a young man yearning to better himself and move beyond the apothecary's life for which he is destined. Another character, a relatively well-to-do physician, warns Elsley that it is the devil who is tempting him to "Throw away the safe station in which God has certainly put you, to see, by some desperate venture, a new, and, as you fancy, a grander one for yourself" (I 35–6). The narrator condemns Elsley as "Too proud to learn his business . . . , he neglected alike work and amusement for lazy mooning over books, and the dreams which books called up. He made perpetual mistakes in the shop" (I 37). His dreams of moving out of "his station" almost cost another man his health as Elsley mistakes one medicine for another and misfills a prescription; the physical body of Mark Armsworth is threatened by the individual who refuses to accept his proper role and position in the social body. But in predictably retributive fashion, it is Elsley himself who, after moving out of his station by becoming a writer, dies a miserable and drug-addicted man. Armsworth finally comments on the failed and now deceased poet: "Poor fool! ... Why didn't he mind his bottles, and just do what Heaven sent him to do?" (II 298). Again, social, cultural, and religious hierarchies are "embodied" in an insistently didactic and manipulative manner, though now removed temporally from immediate concern. One character happily remarks "two years later," "a spirit of self-reform has been awakened round here ... I find, in every circle of every class, men and women asking to be taught their duty, that they may go and do it ... .the laborers confess themselves better off than they have been for fifty years" (I 7–8).

But despite the smugness and finality of this post-Crimean statement, class tensions were never wholly erased from the novels and essays of Kingsley, Hughes, and Maurice, even if they were suppressed below more immediate crises in gender, religious, and imperialist identities. While later essays in this collection will explore these issues in depth, it is important to remember that a secure sense of a national "self" was inevitably and inextricably tied to a well-regulated class system, and policing that system remained a primary function of the muscular Christian novel. A particularly telling example of this, and one on which I will conclude here, is provided by Kingsley's final novel, *Hereward the Wake*, published in 1866. Set at the time of the Norman Conquest, the novel explores the familiar themes of Catholic effeminacy and treachery, and, of course, French perfidiousness. Its hero, the Anglo-Viking Hereward (identified often as simply the "Englishman"), is a lowlander whose brawny build and manly courage, coupled with a deep hatred of the Normans, lead to a heroism that is often jeopardized by his "low" habits. In the physical and textual body of Hereward, class tensions are vividly depicted. He is descended from royalty, but as we are reminded, such things "mattered little ... in those uncertain topsy-turvey times" (134), for "civilisation" was precarious and men able quickly to assume and lose positions of power and the trappings of refinement. Hereward, as a dweller of the fens, "has little or nothing around him to refine or lift up his soul; and unless he meet with a religion, and with a civilisation, which can deliver him, he may sink into that dull brutality which is too common among the lowest classes" (20). Hereward is full of energy and anger but, in Kingsley's depiction, has only a wavering notion of "duty" to a higher service.

His own warring instincts are best kept in check during battles with the French; likewise the army he leads epitomizes the tensions mentioned earlier in this essay: "The reckless spirit of personal independence ... prevented anything like discipline, or organised movement of masses ... His men, mostly outlaws and homeless, [were] kept together by the pressure from without" (235). We are told, "One fixed law the outlaw had – hatred of the invader" (335). But as the Normans inevitably solidify their control over the land, despair sets in; the "English" army falls apart and Hereward retreats to the fens as he and his retinue slowly degenerate: "Away from law, from self-restraint, from refinement, from elegance, from the very sound of a church-going bell, they were sinking gradually down to the level of the coarse men and women whom they saw" (353). Soon, "All the lower nature in him, so long crushed under, leapt up chuckling and grinning and tumbling head over heels" (366). This metaphor is telling, for his mutinous lower nature is itself embodied in a way that echoes the characterizations of the monstrous Chartists examined above. Even though we are told that Hereward is "the last of the old English" (412), his tale actually serves as an admonishment and lesson to the contemporary audience, especially those members of the lower classes who are urged to resist continuously their own most bestial, rebellious inclinations so as not to degenerate into their earlier, lawless selves. Hereward meets a tragic end as he finally comes under the sway of a duplicitous woman, bows to the wishes of the Normans, and is murdered. Gender, class, and nationalistic ideologies intersect in a novel that serves as a multifaceted warning to any overly-complacent or imperfectly disciplined English citizen.

In the quote above, we find that it is only during battle that the multi-conscious body works in harmony as a single unit. This psychological and social metaphor helps us understand not only the numerous references to external threats to the British nation in other muscular Christian novels, such as *Westward Ho!* and *Tom Brown's Schooldays*, but also the fact that during the same years in which the Chartist movement saw its dying gasps, the Christian Socialist brotherhood also waned and finally disbanded. As Brantlinger notes in *The Spirit of Reform*, "By 1854 Maurice had concluded that the time was not ripe for cooperation, largely because the working class was unprepared for it ... In 1857, Kingsley wrote that their co-operative ventures had failed 'because the men are not fit for them'"

(147). The interests of the men who made up this small group were drawn elsewhere. Maurice was embroiled in religious controversy during the mid-1850s; the others were fascinated by the war and the Indian mutiny that followed. With the threat of Chartism gone, the body of the Christian Socialist movement could not maintain its own perimeters.

But even though it was short-lived and some of its members are better remembered for their subsequent manifestations as muscular Christians, we are right to ask if Christian Socialism itself was an abject failure. Historian Charles Raven says resoundingly "No." The Christian Socialists "saw – how could they help seeing – the disease of the body politic" (340); "they believed themselves to possess knowledge of a principle which ... would effect a cure" (341). Raven asserts that this cure was not "association," as the Christian Socialists first believed, but education, and in their roles as pedagogues and influential writers, these few men helped change British history (340–70). Raven isolates the creation of the Working Men's College as a successful "attempt to embody what they had called Christian Socialism in a concrete form" (353), even as Brantlinger perceives it as an upper-class mechanism for "impos[ing] intelligent order on those who seem disorderly, unintelligent, 'primitive' or 'savage,' creatures of darkness" (*The Spirit of Reform* 254). Whichever perspective one wishes to take, it is worth noting that Raven's adulatory words clearly echo (or, to use an alternative metaphor, are infected by) the figurative language of the very men he praises.

So whether or not we agree with Raven in attributing such history-altering power to these remarkably "muscular" Christian Socialists, we must admit that these men made and unmade metaphors not only with a facility, but also with an effectiveness that captured the flux and flow of history itself, in particular the history of the privileged classes. Elaine Scarry recognizes twentieth-century extensions of this power in her respected work, *The Body in Pain: The Making and Unmaking of the World*, a study that demonstrates well how references to the body work to naturalize cultural constructions that all too often promote the interests of traditionally privileged bodies within the larger conceptual frame. Scarry's careful attention to the dynamics of physical and psychological torture demands that we appreciate the extent to which threats to the body politic have been and continue to be countered by deconstructions and reconstructions of the smaller bodies comprising it. The Christian Socialists and muscular Christians manipulated language as a pedagogical tool, one that they used to repudiate demands that they found uncomfortable and irreconcilable with their own class-bound view of the proper constitution of the body of the nation. Their words and representations help us understand the extent to which conceptions of identity, loyalty, and even life itself, are grounded in metaphor, which can support, reject, or work in some complexly divergent way around and through the status quo and perceptions of duty to self, class, and nation. It bears repeating (as well as remembering) that those who make meaning, both yesterday and today, do so with inevitable biases, even as their metaphors insist repeatedly on their own apolitical, ahistorical nature. As both literary and social history has shown and later essays in this volume will bear out, when words are made flesh, they often form the bodies of soldiers.

WORKS CITED

Arnstein, Walter L., *Britain Yesterday & Today: 1830 to the Present.* Boston: Heath, 1966.
Bourdieu, Pierre and Jean-Claude Passeron, *Reproduction in Education, Society and Culture,* tr. Richard Nice. London: Sage, 1977.
Brantlinger, Patrick, *Rule of Darkness: British Literature and Imperialism, 1830–1914.* Ithaca, NY: Cornell University Press, 1988.
  The Spirit of Reform: British Literature and Politics, 1832–1867. Cambridge, MA: Harvard University Press, 1977.
Carlyle, Thomas, "Chartism" in *Selected Writings,* ed. Alan Shelston. London: Penguin, 1971, pp. 151–232.
Cheyfitz, Eric, *The Poetics of Imperialism.* New York: Oxford University Press, 1991.
Conacher, J. B., *The Aberdeen Coalition 1852–1855.* Cambridge University Press, 1968.
Gagnier, Regenia, *Subjectivities: A History of Self-Representation in Britain, 1832–1920.* New York: Oxford University Press, 1991.
Jones, David, *Chartism and the Chartists.* London: Allen Lane, 1975.
Kendall, Guy, *Charles Kingsley and his Ideas.* London: Hutchinson & Co., 1947.
Kingsley, Charles, *Alton Locke, Tailor and Poet* (1850). New York: Oxford University Press, 1983.
  Hereward the Wake (1866). London: Collins, 1954.
  The Life and Works of Charles Kingsley, 19 vols. London: Macmillan, 1901.
  Two Years Ago (1857). 2 vols. New York: Taylor, 1899.
Kristeva, Julia, *Strangers to Ourselves,* tr. Leon S. Roudiez. New York: Columbia University Press, 1991.

Lodge, David, "The French Revolution and the Condition of England: Crowds and Power in the Early Victorian Novel" in *The French Revolution and British Culture*, eds. Ceri Crossley and Ian Small. New York: Oxford University Press, 1989.

Maurice, Frederick Denison, *The Kingdom of Christ* (1842). 2 vols. London: Dent & Co., n.d.

The Life of Frederick Denison Maurice, ed. Frederick Maurice. 2 vols. New York: Scribner's, 1884.

The Workman and the Franchise (1866). New York: Augustus Kelley, 1970.

Munich, Adrienne Auslander, *Andromeda's Chains*. New York: Columbia University Press, 1989.

Politics for the People, nos. 1–17. London, 1848.

Raven, Charles E., *Christian Socialism 1848–1854*. London: Frank Cass & Co., 1968.

Scarry, Elaine, *The Body in Pain: The Making and Unmaking of the World*. New York: Oxford University Press, 1985.

Slosson, Preston William, *The Decline of the Chartist Movement* (1916). London: Frank Cass & Co., 1967.

Stallybrass, Peter and Allon White, *The Politics and Poetics of Transgression*. Ithaca, NY: Cornell University Press, 1986.

Theweleit, Klaus, *Male Fantasies*, vol. 2, trs. Erica Carter and Chris Turner. Minneapolis: University of Minnesota Press, 1989.

Vance, Norman, *The Sinews of the Spirit: The Ideal of Christian Manliness in Victorian Literature and Religious Thought*. Cambridge University Press, 1985.

Warner, Philip, *The Crimean War: A Reappraisal*. London: Arthur Barker, 1972.

Wetzel, David, *The Crimean War: A Diplomatic History*. Boulder, CO: East European Monographs, 1985.

Williams, A. Susan, *The Rich Man and the Diseased Poor in Early Victorian Fiction*. London: Macmillan, 1987.

Williams, Raymond, *The Sociology of Culture*. New York: Schocken, 1982.

CHAPTER 3

Christian manliness and national identity: the problematic construction of a racially "pure" nation

C. J. W.-L. Wee

Recent work in cultural and literary studies has come to question the common assumption that each nation-state embodies its own particular culture. As anthropologists Akhil Gupta and James Ferguson observe, "[The] assumed isomorphism of space, place, and culture results in some significant problems" (7); what happens, they ask, to "Indian culture" in England? What of (post)colonial cultures and the effect they have upon their (former) masters: "To which places do the hybrid cultures of postcoloniality belong? Does the colonial encounter create a 'new culture' in both colonized and colonizing country, or does it destabilize the notion that nations and cultures are isomorphic?" (7–8). Gupta and Ferguson's questions follow naturally from Edward Said's contention that "the experience of imperialism [be taken] as a matter of interdependent histories, overlapping domains" (49–50).

My concern is with Gupta and Ferguson's second question as it applies to the origins of muscular Christianity. In the 1850s, Charles Kingsley helped create a masculinist image of an imperial English nation concerned with formal territorial expansion, one that was in reaction to an older mercantilist imperialism of free trade committed to the imperatives of progressive society.[1] Kingsley's literary and historical investigations of the "primitive" in both European and non-European cultures – which provide an important representative instance of Said's "overlapping domains" – helped give impetus to the rise of late-Victorian New Imperialism. While the analysis of one figure's work cannot answer the question of what new cultures may have emerged as the result of the various moments of colonial encounter, it certainly suggests that nations and cultures are never isomorphic. Cultural "difference" – seeing "ourselves-as-others, others-as-ourselves" (Bhabha 72) – obviously existed even in the nineteenth century, before the development of the technologies and

66

massive population movements which gave rise to such notions as postmodern hyperspace and borderlands.

In Kingsley's case, such difference makes itself felt in the rejection of an attained English modernity for the pleasures and vigors of a vital primitivism. "Modernity" is generally the concept we associate with European nationalism and imperialism, phenomena which share, as Partha Chatterjee reminds us, "the same material and intellectual premises with the European Enlightenment, with industry and the idea of progress, and with modern democracy" (3). When compared to Locke, Bentham, and Mill, Kingsley seems a retrograde figure because of his celebration of the primitive in his invocation of an organic national culture, and his desire to re-create England as a land of rugged warriors far removed from metropolitan life with its unhealthy, politically restless men (see Donald E. Hall's essay in this volume). The muscle-less modernity which surrounded Kingsley seemed insufficient for a true nationhood.

Though remembered by many now as a children's author and as the clergyman bested by J. H. Newman in his *Apologia pro Vita Sua* (1864), Kingsley in his lifetime was politically influential and highly respected. He was chaplain to the Queen, an outspoken social and sanitary reformer, a popularizer of current scientific thought, and in 1860 was named Regius Professor of Modern History at Cambridge: "His thought, spread thinly over a dozen fields ... , is frequently a better mirror of his age than that of more brilliant or more intellectual men who were atypical by their very mastery of one area of knowledge" (Martin 15). Certainly his novels sold exceedingly well: Chapman and Hall brought out three editions of *Alton Locke, Tailor and Poet* (1850) in two years, and by 1897 *Westward Ho!* (1855) had been reprinted thirty-eight times (see Colloms 126, 195). These two novels, Kingsley's best known books and the focus of my essay, participated in a process of national self-definition, through what might be called "cultural nationalism," for they embody a substantial re-imaging of race and cultural history, and their relationship to Christianity. But here Kingsley also reveals the problems surrounding the construction of a pure national-imperial identity based on racial and religious heritage, as he attempted to propagate the potent but unstable image of a masculine, charismatic, and authoritative Englishman who stands as a representative of a resolutely Anglo-Saxon and Protestant nation-empire.

Through his novels, Kingsley tries to work out the conflicts among

an unworldly Tractarianism influenced by a subversive Roman
Catholicism, an Evangelicalism he believed overly caught up with
personal piety, and his own Liberal Anglicanism, with its activist
agenda for social justice. He firmly rejected cosmopolitan standards
and economic progressivism, for they were perceived to be among
the causes of England's lackluster political and military performance
on the Continent. The Christian man, he felt, belonged to the world
of action. Kingsley's muscular Christianity (he would have preferred the phrase "manly Christianity"[2]) offered a number of ways
out of England's effete and fragmented condition. A primitive vigor
and character could be recovered either from non-European lands –
from someone else's culture – where manly energy was uncon-
strained by modern life, or from English historical precedents, where
a united nation existed. The "noble savage" (a figure analogous to
Kingsley's manly Christian) might provide the vitality missing from
modern England. However, *Westward Ho!* sees the displacement of
the image of the native as noble prelapsarian man and elects in its
place the image of the childish and degenerate savage. Kingsley
proceeds to relocate the source of primitive vigor within pre-
industrial Elizabethan England, during which a dynamic Anglo-
Saxon spirit coalesced with a nationalistic Protestantism to form a
triumphant national identity. But even though manly Christianity
thus claims pure English origins, the "other" remains needed – and
as more than a simple reflection of a presumed unitary English self.

Thus Kingsley's texts are a place of incommensurable contradictions: the difference from the modern he proposes requires a
recuperation of primitive energy now vanished from England; at the
same time, racial purity, even at a strictly literary-cultural level,
must be maintained, even though barbarous energy can only be
found in imperial frontier territories.

I

In Kingsley's work, non-European primitive vigor is closely allied to
the best historical English examples of dynamism. Certainly his own
personal history was intimately connected with the English presence
abroad: Kingsley's paternal grandfather's fortune probably came
from trading in East and West Indian produce, and his mother was
born in Barbados of a plantation-owning family. Thus, his vision of
nation and empire is itself related to an earlier expansive phase of

English history and contains contradictory and even chaotic attitudes towards both Europeans and "natives."

Kingsley's importance within the literary-cultural tradition that related "culture" to "society," as assembled by Raymond Williams in *Culture and Society*, merits re-evaluation in light of his conscious incorporation of imperial elements into his model for an organic society in which there is interrelation and traditional continuity in human activities and history. One finds a "hybridity," as Homi Bhabha would put it, involved in the Victorian conceptualization of a supposedly insular nation-state. Certainly, Kingsley made an impact on Victorian intellectual and cultural life: from the 1850s onwards, his notions of manly Christianity and Christian responsibility spread throughout the privileged educational worlds of public schools and ancient universities. David Newsome argues that while the Anglican Church may not have fully come to grips with the Christian Socialists until after their deaths,

the widespread popularity which the writings of Kingsley and [Thomas] Hughes immediately enjoyed suggests that they were the spokesmen of that large section of their countrymen who, in the middle years of the century, were beginning to feel that England's glory lay in her potentiality to develop under-developed countries and to civilise less civilised peoples, and who were quick to grasp that successful Empire builders needed a touch of Spartan discipline and Spartan qualities to equip them for their task. The belligerence and the militant patriotism which the Crimean War had called forth were indications of what was to come. (227–8)

The term "spokesmen" is misleading: it would be more accurate to say that successful novels like *Tom Brown's Schooldays* (1857) and *Westward Ho!* not merely reflected but also encouraged the imperialist mood among sections of the English population. (This, after all, is what Newsome shows in his last chapter, "Godliness and Manliness.") The bringing together of the elements of English high culture that Kingsley thought important – Edmund Spenser and the tradition of an *English* literature and religion – and the image of the romantic adventurer tramping his way through exotic lands makes for an imaginatively powerful and (dangerously) attractive idea of national community. The national and the imperial are presented as complex and even perversely interlinked parts of what it means to be English.

Philip Corrigan and Derek Sayer, among other revisionary Marxists influenced by the work of Raymond Williams and Stuart Hall, contend that culture and "cultural images," reflecting the falsely perceived static nature of national character,

> provided the moral energy for … the successive imposition of English civilization on the "dark corners" of England itself, Wales, Scotland, Ireland and eventually that British empire which covered a quarter of the globe. To say this is far from denying the brutality of conquest (or the rapacity of commerce) … Our point is that it took a national culture of extraordinary self-confidence and moral rectitude to construe such imperialism as a "civilizing mission" … *and* for long periods, with a fair degree of success, to bedazzle the domestically subordinated with the spectacle of empire. (193–4)

While Kingsley is a good instance of how the imaginatively concrete presentation of a national and racial culture could contribute to an expansionist mission, it is too much to suggest that a culturally cohesive England simply expanded and domesticated first the outer reaches of the British Isles and then the non-European world. That would be to accept Kingsley's ideology without observing the conditions of its making. It is not even that a unified English "self" finds itself "reflected" and thus "affirmed" in its clash with less developed peoples: this, for instance, is what Abdul JanMohamed suggests:

> While the surface of each colonialist text purports to represent specific encounters with specific varieties of the racial Other, the subtext valorizes the superiority of European cultures, of the collective process that has mediated that representation. Such literature is essentially specular: instead of seeing the native as a bridge toward syncretic possibility, it uses him as a mirror that reflects the colonialist's self image. (84)

JanMohamed's argument serves "as a necessary reminder that imperialism was a protean phenomenon and its epistemic violence inseparable from material and institutional force" (Parry 45). But while discussions of literature, religion, culture, and resistance should not suggest that the subjugated ever wield the sort of power the imperialist has, "domination" is a double-edged sword: the imperialist's socio-political and economic choices made in relation to the "Other" redefine and constrain his *own* self. There is a dialectic involved between the colonizer's initial image of himself and that of the potential colonized person before him, both of which become, as it were, "re-written" even while the natives are being subjugated to imperial authority. Syncretism always occurs, though denied by the wielder of imperial power, and even if, as in Kingsley's case, it is used to assert English superiority.

But what is particularly interesting in Kingsley's work is the fact that "primitive" culture is not that which is merely Other to superior English national-imperialism, but that the "primitive" is appropriated as a category to disrupt modernist conceptions of nation and empire. Kingsley rejected a pragmatic and progressive "self-help" image which had been represented in the eighteenth century by Daniel Defoe's *Robinson Crusoe* and, in Kingsley's own time, by the various civilizing missionary and engineer heroes of Samuel Smiles's books. Incipient within this rejection of Victorian industry, in both senses of that term, seems to be a fear of the cultural homogeneity modernity was supposed to bring. As Eric Hobsbawm notes, "it was accepted in theory that social evolution expanded the scale of human units from family and tribe to country and canton, from the local to the regional and eventually the global" (3). What Kingsley, the historian J. A. Froude, and other imperialist writers of the mid-nineteenth century manage to do is to wrench or perhaps capture the narrative of progress for their own purpose: "progress" now means strengthening the nation-state as an end in itself, so that England's distinctive history – a proven primitiveness, as it were – would not be abolished. The late-Victorian national imperialism which develops with help from Kingsley's work is an attempt to confront England's urban-industrial circumstances as well as the anxieties raised by the increasing competition and might of the United States and Germany. However, it must be added that national-imperial discourse, even in Kingsley's writings, never attains a stable perspective on English identity. In the end, whether the English as a race possess either the qualities of modernity or primitiveness, and whether each quality is truly "good" or "bad" remains unclear.

II

Alton Locke and *Westward Ho!* seem at first glance to be unconnected: while the earlier work is a "condition of England" novel written from a Liberal Christian perspective as the pseudo-autobiography of a Chartist tailor, the later work is an Elizabethan romance extolling English Protestant virtues in an age of vile Spanish imperial dominance. And yet, they are related: Victorian England could be a great, united nation, as Elizabethan England had been, if only the false religious alternative of Mammon could be overcome. Mammon

engenders the selfish individualism that proponents of liberal
economics thought would improve society, but which actually
caused the decline of a once vital Anglo-Saxon race. Old England
offers an alternative model of common commitment sustained by a
humane and pious cultural life. Kingsley rejects what Herbert
Butterfield called the "Whig interpretation of history" – the analysis
of the past with too strong a commitment to the ratification and
glorification of the present – for a more romantic view of history.
While empire did not have a potent part in Whig history (see
Burrow 233), it had a place in the slowly ascending romantic
nationalism which provided a common idiom in discussing national
identity during Kingsley's time.

It is significant that *Alton Locke* and *Westward Ho!* were written
within a period traditionally held by a number of historians to be
anti-imperialist – when statesmen and officials alike distrusted
expansion and were even indifferent to the maintenance of the
empire which did exist.[3] Kingsley represents a period of reformation
for national culture, marking a shift from informal to formal empire,
and in his works, empire makes a center-stage appearance in the
world of primitives. But while it is romantically admired in *Alton
Locke* as a primeval center of potentially rejuvenating energy, this
world becomes, finally, the scene of racial decline. In *Westward Ho!*,
Kingsley displaces the regenerative energy he had hoped to find in
the noble savage, and instead relocates it within the pre-industrial
scene of England's Teutonic origins. His reformed national-imperial
culture was a highly problematic synthesizing effort at trying to hold
together the civilized and the atavistic. Considerations of primitive
vigor are thus fundamental to Kingsley's discourse on organic
national culture: it is this dynamic manliness that can unify and save
an industrial and commercialized England.

Certainly Kingsley had a Christian Liberal[4] distaste for a society
of exploiters and exploited with no connection with each other. In
an early issue of the Christian Socialist journal *Politics for the People*,
he makes explicit the spiritual source of English brotherhood: "All
that is wanted is the Spirit of self-sacrifice, patriotism and brother
love – which God alone can give – while I believe He is giving more
and more in these very days" (quoted in Colloms, 99). Kingsley's
specific Christian model for a national community potentially
enabled through contact with the primitive is most emphatically
stated in *Alton Locke* by Eleanor, the widow of Lord Lynedale, who,

by the end of the novel, has taken on the role of a prophetess. As the incarnation of "feminine" moral virtues and "culture," she is obliged to instruct Alton that moral regeneration must first occur if a true spiritual nationhood is to be achieved. Alton's fruitless participation in frenetic Chartist violence, while understandable, shows that "disorder cannot cast out disorder" (369). A state must be more than abstract ideas of rights, external acts of parliament, and social contracts: the working class must claim their "share in national life, only because the nation is a spiritual body" (364). Eleanor encourages Alton to become a "poet of the people" (384) and distill his acquired spiritual knowledge into an educational poetry for the underprivileged.

While what Kingsley conveys seems universal enough, a specific "Englishness" emerges in his text connected not only with English history, but, strangely enough for a modern nation, with the tropics as well. Eleanor sees Alton's new-found educational commitment as a resurgence of "the old English spirit ... as it spoke in Naseby fights and Smithfield fires" (383). Given a need for proletarian education, the novel ends oddly with Eleanor sending Alton off to Texas (which she somehow thinks of as "the Tropics" [383]). Apparently, Alton can escape an enervating European life in Texas and find new energy as "Drake, ... Hawkins, and the conquerors of Hindostan" (383) had before him in order to revitalize a weakened English identity. Modernity alienates the English from their history:

I have long hoped for a Tropic poet; one who should leave the routine imagery of European civilisation, its meagre scenery, and physically decrepit races, for the grandeur, ... the paradisiac beauty and simplicity of Tropic humanity ... See if you cannot help to infuse some new blood into the aged veins of English literature; ... bring home fresh conceptions of beauty, fresh spiritual and physical laws ... that you may realise them here at home. (384)

Kingsley, at several points in the novel, identifies the original English vigor that needed resuscitation as being Teutonic. At Cambridge, the "true English stuff," potentially the property of all Englishmen, is revealed to Alton when he looks at some undergraduates manfully rowing: they manifest a "grim, earnest, stubborn energy, which, since the days of the old Romans, the English possess alone of all the nations of the earth" (132). Alton later tells us that it was only because the Reformation in Germany had been transferred to sixteenth-century England that the chains of medieval, Romish superstition had been broken. Primeval Teutonic energy was then allowed to link with the true religion in "the new light of the Elizabethan age" (138). Modern England – with its scientific and commercial successes and a strong artistic tradition – then became possible as a nation-state.[5] It is this unifying and, after the sixteenth century, nationalistic Protestant energy which has dissipated. At the juncture in history that Alton occupies, exposure to pre-industrial lands may help rejuvenate a weakened national culture and "blood." Atavism can be an oddly restorative tonic for selfish English values.

While the novel is driven by an attraction to and sympathy with the Chartist cause and the working class in general, Kingsley in the end refuses the latter's primitive and unrestrained fervor as a potential source for national renewal (at least until they are spiritually remade). While Alton is supposedly the representative of working-class consciousness, he is made to throw over his given role for a middle-class self apprehensive of working-class violence: the narrating Alton ultimately repudiates the narrated Alton. Kingsley then looks instead at another "Other" for inspiration – Eleanor's "Tropic humanity." Kingsley's search for reinvigoration causes him to explore a variety of possibly vital others – only to deny his first attraction when the connection appears unsuitable. In fact, the primitive other will suffer the working class's fate at the end of *Westward Ho!*.

Alton's fever-induced dream in Chapter 36 gains clarity and centrality in the novel in the light of the above discussion. The reader receives key details of the history of the ancient Indo-European, or, more specifically, Indo-Germanic identity which Kingsley feels has been lost. The exact relationship between tropical lands suited for imperial domination and the English homeland also surfaces.

The seemingly random elements in the dream have to be read against the backdrop of Eleanor's exaltation of "paradisiac beauty." The dream is neatly divided into two sections: in the first, Alton pays for his Chartist misdeeds by being made to fall off "the golden ladder" (336) of humanity and by being transformed into a madrepore – a coral-producing organism. He has to re-evolve and thereby gain genuine progress following a Lamarckian scheme of development; this is important, for Lamarck's faith in acquired characteristics here gives a scientific basis for Kingsley's commitment to the possibility of an English racial regeneration. In the second section, having been rehumanized, Alton finds himself as a baby who is part of an "Arian" tribe moving out from the Pamir area north-west of Kashmir going "westward, westward ever": he is only one of a number of "Titan babies" who providentially bear inside them "the law, the freedom, the science, the poetry, the Christianity, of Europe and the world" (343). Kingsley unfolds a schematic overview of English racial development.

The world in which Alton is redeveloping into humanity has non-European settings within which elements of fantasy occur – India, an *Arabian Nights* setting, Borneo, the Andes; this suggests that primitive regions are prehistorical and are, in that sense, out of time. They are Eleanor's paradisiac places, and they contain the same boundless possibilities as *Westward Ho!*'s South America. How English Anglo-Saxon energy can be revivified and tested is the concern of the later novel. Alton himself is too much a denatured Londoner to become an outstanding representative of English life. His quick death en route to Texas is the strongest indictment of Victorian life in *Alton Locke*.

However, despite Alton's ultimate failure to reach Texas and the earlier lapse into working-class violence, his fall from humanity in his dream is not altogether a bad thing: it puts him back in touch with his animal and hence primal origins, and with a time, as Barnakill says in Kingsley's *Yeast* (1848), when the earth still heaved "with the creative energy of youth ... [and from which] the highest spiritual cultivation [emerged] in triumphant contact with the fiercest energies of matter; ... where the body and the spirit ... [were not] separate" (319). The "old English spirit" of Drake and Hawkins resulted only because man's spirit was developed in conjunction with his body, that seat of primal energy. Elizabethan progress came about, paradoxically enough, because ancient racial memory was not neglected – an oddly "atavistic" progress, to be sure. (See David Rosen's essay in this volume for a discussion of the "saving sacred primitivism" which pervaded Victorian intellectual life.)

The question which arises, then, is: how exactly did the Elizabethans attain this balance between the spirit – the civilized – and the primitive? How did they manage to find (and exploit) an authentic masculine vigor in the non-European territories of their time, a vigor which enabled England to stride forth as a modern European power?

III

Westward Ho!, published after *Hypatia* (1853), functions effectively as a sequel to *Alton Locke*. Kingsley's general literary method is to highlight contemporary deficiencies through presenting Elizabethan England as a model of alterity: England then was led by a virtuous Protestant queen who encouraged the development of a national culture for a nation united in warfare against papist tyranny and Spanish oppression of South American Indians.[6] The novel was tellingly dedicated to the "White Rajah" James Brooke of Sarawak and to Bishop George Selwyn of New Zealand, two aggressive and manly colonists of the day. And in this, Kingsley's foundational epic, the English emerge as the race fit to take over the Spaniards' decaying American empire. We would expect, given Eleanor's hopes for Alton to become a "Tropic poet," that England's representative, Amyas Leigh, might find a way to link up with New World energy. This desire for miscegenation and identification with the primitive, however, is precisely what is denied: the "native" woman Amyas eventually marries turns out to be European. The American primitives are found to be not prelapsarian in nature, but postlapsarian, without even the redeeming grace of civilized rationality. The English must hence look within their own selves for the dynamism necessary to divert the dangers of modern competitive life. England thus "discovers" its essential self through an interdependent relationship with the Other which Kingsley is unwilling to acknowledge even as he imaginatively presents it.

Kingsley's didactic intentions in *Westward Ho!* are as apparent as in *Alton Locke*. The narrator tells his reader "that by careful legislation for the comfort and employment of 'the masses' (term then, thank God, unknown), she [Elizabeth] had both won their hearts, and kept their bodies in fighting order" (485). Like Eleanor, Elizabeth possesses a restraining moral spirit which thankfully pervades her political concerns. The aristocratic leaders and heroes in her realm follow her lead. Commercial leaders and men in business are not excluded from the land's highest positions: selfish behavior in the economic sphere is not inevitable if the role of justice is acknowledged. This is the nation to be tested in the realm of the primitive.

A united English nation also meant an internationally strong England: "(now that our late boasting [regarding military might] is a little silenced by Crimean disasters) [we might] inquire whether we have not something to learn from those old Tudor times, as to how to defend a country" (485). First, in the mid-1800s, there had been the French invasion scare, with the drumming up of old Protestant-Catholic enmities; and then in 1853, there had been the Crimean campaign. The Light Brigade's decimation had shocked Kingsley tremendously, and *Westward Ho!* is a concrete instance of how an English intellectual can use a serious attempt at art to try to spur a nation on to greater national effort and unity in the face of grave difficulties: the novel was officially distributed to English troops during the Crimean War.

Amyas's aspirations to a vigorous English masculinity are obvious from the novel's beginning. As our boy hero walks home and surveys the rich historical landscape of North Devon, Kingsley causes him to reinvest the landscape with the grandeur of racial memories of a coarser era against which Victorian torpor can be measured:

Beneath him, on his right, the Torridge, like a land-locked lake, sleeps broad and bright between the old park of Tapeley and the charmed rock of the Hubbastone, where, seven hundred years ago, the Norse rovers landed to lay siege to Kenwith Castle, a mile away on his left hand; and not three fields away, are the stones of "The Bloody Corner," where the retreating Danes, cut off from their ships, made their last fruitless stand against the Saxon sheriff and the valiant men of Devon. (15)

Kingsley's description is combined with a concrete historical sense to give the past an immediacy that is almost graspable. While Amyas longs for the chance to defend England as "the men of Devon did then," the narrator reveals that much more is in store for Amyas: he "is a symbol, though he knows it not, of brave young England longing to wing its way out of its island prison, to discover and to traffic, to colonise and to civilise" (15). Though Amyas does not see the full plan of Providence, his vision is clearer than Alton's at Cambridge. Amyas's mandate will serve as a path-breaking example to all like-minded Englishmen.

Jacqueline Rose has stressed the role of "geography and history" in her analysis of the adventure motif in children's fiction: "at its simplest, the [geography and history] idea is one of going somewhere else in order to get back to our own past. But already we can note that seeing these distant communities as one stage of our own historical development is a way of subordinating them to us" (54). But while there may be a domination of one society over another in the imaginative process of "recovering" the past, there is also a negotiation which is undertaken between "them" and "us"; this suggests that "we" may actually need something from "them" even if the final goal is the subordination of "them" to "us." This form of adventure tale goes back, in Rose's reckoning, to the late eighteenth century – a period when Kingsley's family had been overseas making their fortune – and the adventure tale is a form which Kingsley exploits with considerable skill. In using the adventure motif, though, Kingsley finds himself in a genuine bind at times when he wonders how to regard the primitive *vis-à-vis* the European. The blatant didacticism and propaganda value of the novel in the wake of the French scare and then the vicissitudes of the Crimean War should not obscure the point that the desire for domination crucially affects the home culture's self-definition.

The fascination with primitives in relation to national regeneration begins closer to home than the New World, though – in Ireland. Ireland's ambiguous status in the novel – it is a European land suitable for English colonization – serves as a warning of what can occur if vigor is stripped of civilized standards. For instance, Walter Raleigh speaks to Amyas of "Noble Normans sunk into savages – *Hibernis ipsis hiberniores!*" (207). The Irish, like the working class, are part of Kingsley's hesitant internal differentiation of the nation. He approves of the Irish presence in the Crimean campaign and, through Raleigh, indicates that Amyas's easy condemnation of Celtic "savages" denies the possibility of a united kingdom. Though racially connected with Normans rather than Saxons, Raleigh says the traitorous Irish lords "are better English blood than Saxons who hunt them down" (206). But in spite of Kingsley's desire to have an inclusive nation, Irish "savagery" is never considered a possible source of reinvigorating primitivity: "some uncivilising venom in the air" (207), Raleigh says, plays them out. Catholicism is named as one ingredient in this "venom." Kingsley makes the Irish serve as a warning to Amyas of the consequences of undirected vigor; they are an unacceptable model of alterity.

Ireland, first major site of imperialism in *Westward Ho!*, prefigures what will occur in the outer reaches of English expansion. The

Irish/Celts/Normans are uneasy foils for English-Saxon identity, since they indicate what the English themselves could turn into. Kingsley, however, at least allows the Irish to be human, while around him "Paddy" was being simianized in comic caricatures due to "the coincidence of Fenianism with the [eventual] debate over *The Origin of Species* and the increase in social and political tensions arising out of the economic expansion of the mid-Victorian era" (Curtis 101). The fear of potential English barbarism recurs in Kingsley's last novel, *Hereward the Wake, the Last of the English* (1865), where a surprising connection with the Norman is allowed at the novel's end. Kingsley clearly finds the road to identity affirmation a rocky one.

The "defending" of this early colonized territory from the Spanish allows the formulation in *Westward Ho!* of a national-imperial high cultural identity. In the midst of war, Sir Walter Raleigh and Edmund Spenser are incongruously found arguing over what verse forms English poetry ought to take. Raleigh is against classical literature, while Spenser remains of two minds between English "barbarous taste" (170) and ancient beauty; he is yet to be convinced that Englishness in verse can be anything but provincial. Like the boy Amyas, Spenser is unconscious of God's plan for him – that he, Spenser (the narrator tells us), "was laying the foundation" for the "great dramatists ... not yet arisen, to [later] form completely that truly English school" (170).

The discussion between Raleigh and Spenser is interrupted when Amyas starts singing a homely Christmas carol taught to him by his mother. The carol Amyas sings gives Raleigh the opportunity to point out the greater emotional capacity of the English ballad to inspire "love and loyalty" (172) than that of stilted hexameters, sapphics, and trimeters. Through Amyas, Spenser sees that fairy-land will be present wherever any true Englishman stands. As for the religion that emerged from imperial Rome, it would destroy English homeliness. The Spanish fail to see that the moment belongs no longer to an older imperial culture but to the *novus ordo*, a younger if coarser provincial culture. Spenser realizes that he is duty-bound to reject the implicit Catholic assertion that they are the civil and religious voice of the metropolitan whole. The classical tradition as represented by Homer, Ovid, Virgil, and Petrarch is not civil (it leads to the oppression of American natives) and is characterized only by an unacceptable universality – paganism. Raleigh berates

Spenser: "Did you find your Red Cross Knight in Virgil, or such a dame as Una in old Ovid? No more than you did your Pater and Credo, you renegado baptized heathen, you!" (171). As the older empire is translated into a newer empire, so must there be a *translatio studii* to accompany the realization of English racial genius: cultural and intellectual work must now be carried out not on the basis of the old European humanist tradition, but on an English tradition – the provincial is transformed into the national. A new global order is developing which is ostensibly grounded in benign exchange between independent states – except when uncivil and undeveloped peoples require stewardship and guidance, as *Westward Ho!* will indicate.

The search for a source of regenerative vigor proceeds to the New World. However, only one true encounter with the unfallen primitive occurs in the Americas, and this takes place early in the journey, when the heroes are off Cape Codera. A local boards Amyas's ship to trade, thinking they are Spaniards. The description of this native suggests some equality with the Europeans: "[The Guayqueria Indian] was full six feet high, and bold and graceful of bearing as Frank or Amyas' self" (311). In fact, the Indian seems *better* than Amyas or his delicate brother Frank, for, unlike either of them, he manages to combine physical prowess with some innate sense of cultured grace. It takes "some trouble to master him, so strong was he" (311) when he tries to escape from the sailors; and when he is allowed to leave the ship, he leaves "the whole crew wondering at the stateliness and courtesy of this bold sea-cavalier" (312). This idealized native, whom Amyas commends for his bravery, ought to be indicative of the type of person who might be living in the New World.

The spectacular native never reappears. Except for his meeting with Ayacanora, who turns out to be a focal point in Kingsley's convoluted national-imperialist ideology, Amyas finds no other evidence of a native "higher race." After the breathtaking first encounter with Ayacanora, he meets with some members of the tribe that has raised her: "Amyas, who expected to find there some remnant of a higher race, was disappointed enough at seeing on board [the canoe] only the usual half-dozen of low-browed, dirty Orsons, painted red with arnotto" (381). The dehumanization of the natives proceeds at a rapid pace after this contact. What seem habits and practices similar to those of European life turn out to be lurid lower-order counterfeits.

Despite his disappointment, Amyas in fact does not easily give up the idea of finding the vigorous primitive. The hunt for the city, Manao, for instance, is partially connected with the romantic and nostalgic search for the noble "remnant of the Inca race" (388). The first meeting between the hero and Ayacanora, clearly the heroine, conveys Amyas's desire for biblical and primitive origins and, also, allows a cautious connection between European and native to emerge:

It was an Indian girl; and yet, when he looked again, – was it an Indian girl? Amyas had seen hundreds of those delicate daughters of the forest, but never such a one as this. Her stature was taller, her limbs were fuller and more rounded; ... her whole face of the highest and richest type of Spanish beauty ... All the strange and dim legends of a higher race than Carib, or Arrowak, or Solimo, which Amyas had ever heard, rose up in his memory. She must be the daughter of some great cacique, perhaps of the lost Incas themselves ... [S]he, unabashed in her free innocence, gazed fearlessly [at Amyas] in return, as Eve might have done in Paradise, upon the mighty stature, and the strange garments, and above all, on the bushy beard and flowing yellow locks of the Englishman. (378–9)

The distant, mythic past and the present collide for both Amyas, as he beholds Ayacanora, and the narrator, as he wonders if Ayacanora and Amyas are later types of Adam and Eve. In Ayacanora, we get an image of mankind in a state of primitive perfection, as "a higher race." She is mighty in "stature," as Amyas is, and we learn that a youthful, creative energy from a distant past – from "strange and dim legends" – can be found in the present.

But Kingsley's characteristic ambivalence surfaces in the uncertainty as to whether any native could truly possess as statuesque a figure as Ayacanora possesses. Is this the desired connection with the primitive? While at this point in the novel, the trip to discover the origins of man seems successful, Kingsley is finally unable to affirm common origins for all men. Though his text represents a clear restaging of the late-eighteenth-century admiration of the noble savage, we see a more cautious appropriation of the primitive.

The reader has been prepared for this momentous occasion, in which the past and present, the primitive and civilized, coalesce, only a few pages earlier, when Kingsley conflates two unrelated landscapes – that of the primeval forest and that of England: "there reigned a stillness which might be heard – such a stillness (to compare small things with great) as broods beneath the rich shadows of Amyas's own Devon woods, or among the lovely sweeps of Exmoor, when the heather is in flower" (376). Thus, in spite of England's less impressive landscape, it, too, is connected to the vibrant force that generates the tropical forest. The scene is of some moment in the narrative. Perhaps the Englishman doesn't *need* non-European primitivism; perhaps he need only look inside his own culture for renewal; perhaps it is internal "re-racination" rather than reinvigoration that is at issue here. With these thoughts in mind, we can proceed to look at the unfolding tale of Ayacanora, who turns out to be the major figure who undergoes such re-racination.

Her transformation takes place in two stages. First, Ayacanora decides that it would be better for her if she identified herself with the Europeans; and, second, she discovers that she is indeed white. The first stage occurs when she saves Amyas and his men from the tribe's capricious behavior. The tribe's "Piache," or witch doctor, has threatened to go to another village and take along with him a "magic" trumpet which could supposedly blight palm trees as an indication of his displeasure with the tribe for their positive response to the foreigners. Ayacanora bursts upon the scene: "Choose between me and your trumpet! I am a daughter of the Sun; I am white; I am a companion for the Englishmen! ... I shall go to the white men, and never sing you to sleep any more; and when the little evil spirit misses my voice, he will come and ... make you dream of ghosts" (391–2). She has instinctively recognized the superior prowess of the white men, and how only they are fit companions for someone who may be an unfallen Inca: Ayacanora desires an honorary "white" status. This recognition was implicit in her first meeting with Amyas: a mutual (and sexual) dynamism draws her to Amyas, as it does Amyas to Ayacanora, deny it as he might. Instinct (or "blood") can be a deeper form of truth than rational thought.

It is the Europeans' arrival that enables Ayacanora to establish her superior credentials within the tribe: she has seen the Europeans laugh at the idea of a "holy trumpet." Taking heart from that, Ayacanora is "determined to show [the tribe] ... that a [superior] woman was as good as a [native] man" (409) and steals the trumpet from under the nose of the Piache. In the process, she acquires a "white" authority over the natives, and simultaneously, by becoming this honorary white woman, comes under Amyas's dominion.

She tells him, "I did beat [the Piache] . . . a little; but I thought you would not let me kill him." Amyas is "merely half amused with her confession of his authority over her" (410). If Ayacanora gains the high ground over the locals, Amyas gains a higher ground over her, with the result that he comes to dominate the entire native landscape.

The next stage of her transformation occurs on the return to England. Salvation Yeo recognizes Ayacanora as the "little maid" he had lost years ago, the daughter of John Oxenham and his Spanish mistress. It takes a while, but Ayacanora finally grasps that she is literally and not only figuratively white; when this happens, a change occurs:

The thought that she was an Englishwoman; that she, the wild Indian, was really one of the great white people whom she had learned to worship, carried with it some regenerating change: she regained all her former stateliness [as opposed to her generally childish comportment on board ship], and with it a self-restraint, a temperance, a softness which she had never shown before. (460)

In other words, she finds within herself the cultural strengths of morality and self-restraint that Kingsley believes to be the essential complement to male prowess. Ayacanora's primitive strength now turns out to have been apparently nothing more than a degenerate wildness: the self-sufficiency and possible competitiveness of the primitive woman are now gone, with the result that Ayacanora can be Amyas's true complement. He becomes the sole possessor of physical vigor and master of the native landscape. Through his marriage to Ayacanora, Amyas, as Martin Green says, "incorporates – without any miscegenation – primitive powers" (217). Vigor must be male and imperial, and the possibly non-European source of that force must be suppressed.

While Ayacanora seems to have an innate sense of feminine virtue, she is only incorporated into the domestic sphere when she becomes suitably trained through the efforts of Frank and Amyas's mother who, like the unseen Queen, is the visible standard-bearer for womanly behavior. For Ayacanora, to be tutored by Mrs. Leigh is to be surrounded by "a perpetual genial calm of soft grey weather, which tempered down to its own peacefulness all who entered its charmed influence" (475). From Mrs. Leigh, Ayacanora learns to add on to the "boundless hospitality of the savage" the ability "to give to those who can give nothing in return" (474). Ayacanora thus also learns to be part of the mission to foster a sense of national community which seems to have a place for all Englishmen, whether rich or poor.

But Kingsley continues to reveal important gaps in English life to us. Amyas relentlessly hunts down his arch-enemy Don Guzman without any consideration for his own men's welfare, and, since he has forsaken his Christian family responsibility, becomes no better than the economic exploiters in *Alton Locke*. As a result, he is melodramatically struck blind, and only thereafter can he forgive Ayacanora for being half-Spanish and accept her in marriage. The realization that he has violated his own Teutonic code of honor and has also failed to see (the irony is obviously intended) how an English Ayacanora complements his value system dawns on him only in his literal darkness. With tropical humanity tested, we are supposed to realize that non-European primitivism cannot rejuvenate industrial England; the spirit for renewal must come from the wells deep inside the Teutonic psyche (see David Rosen's discussion in this volume of a Victorian "deep structure" of masculinity). The connection with the primitive is papered over.

And what of Ayacanora? For all of Kingsley's insistence on the priority of racial identity, her dual role as noble wildwoman and virtuous Englishwoman is the outstanding example of how "innate" racial identities are culturally assimilated: her primitivism is the result of being reared in the American Eden; her nurturing and increasingly domestic self is largely learned at Mrs. Leigh's feet. Kingsley wants to make Ayacanora inherently native and English, while yet revealing that either identity can be instilled by circumstance. Kingsley's confused, double representation of Ayacanora's essential selves indicates his wish to keep her a *tabula rasa* who obviates the threat of racial miscegenation while still imparting *both* primitive powers and civilized English restraint to Amyas. And even here he does not succeed, for the event that enables the marriage to take place compounds an already complicated narrative with an unintended but severe irony that undermines the renewal project. Ayacanora does indeed become Amyas's helpmate, but can only do so *after* he is symbolically emasculated through his blindness and literally stripped of his manly capacities. At the end of this renewal procedure, she comes in to *take charge* of Amyas, rather than complement him. In bringing in the weight of Victorian gender narratives, Kingsley hopes to create an identity-confirming woman for Amyas. This step patently fails. Perhaps the move to make Ayacanora an Englishwoman is designed to make her more controllable by dissipating her threatening racial otherness. That is to say, the otherness of gender identity seems preferable to and is less exotic than racial otherness. But either way, given Amyas's effective emasculation, the relationship with the primitive (or the gendered Other) is never fully erased, as Kingsley hopes that it might be.

Having said this, the larger narrative of the romance is sustained and moves inexorably on to the triumph of England. The defeat of the Spanish Armada reaffirms Teutonic vigor and sets the stage for the apotheosis of a national-imperial culture. The Spanish descendants of the supranational European empire, the *imperium Romanum*, make way for an emergent provincial culture and empire; as in Milton's *Paradise Lost*, there has been a *translatio* from the false to the true, and "the people of Rome yield to the people of England the title of *populus Christianus*" (Kermode 55).[7] Indeed, Milton is invoked by Kingsley: "those poor Vaudois sheppard-saints [of Piedmont], whose bones for generations 'lie scattered in the Alpine mountains cold'" (524) join the world in celebrating the vanquishing of the Spanish. All repressive empires – Russian, Byzantine, and papist – have given way to the nation which brings freedom and equality to all. A shout of joy emerges from Europe and "all mankind," "a shout that was the prophetic birth-paean of North America, Australia, New Zealand, the Pacific Islands, of free commerce and the colonization over the whole earth" (524). While trying to reject any connection with Roman origins, Kingsley proceeds to domesticate the Roman *sacrum imperium*, and the historical fact of England's triumph attains mythic proportions. Spenser becomes the national poet of this emergent nation and national culture. However, given Kingsley's religious antipathy toward anything Roman Catholic, he deliberately purges Spenser of his actual pro-Latin inclinations: Spenser's Elizabeth in *The Faerie Queene* had been seen as Astraea, who, Frank Kermode argues, was for Dante "a figure for sacred empire" (58). No such classical identification is allowed for Kingsley's picture of Elizabeth I: English thought and action must possess purity. And with such purity, the action of re-racination seems complete, and a former outlying territory of the Roman Empire becomes a nation-empire.

To the end of *Westward Ho!*, the complex interplay of home and overseas concerns in Kingsley's writings does not abate. If, through his rejection of a more cosmopolitan idea of imperialism, Kingsley helped England move towards the New Imperialism, which Joseph Chamberlain, Colonial Secretary under Lord Salisbury, for instance, espoused, he managed this because he peeked imaginatively over the fences that marked cultural boundaries in order to see who "they" were; as a result, Kingsley attained a refined vision of a national "English" heritage of vigor and how the English people of an effete, modern society must stand in relation to this heritage. Kingsley tries to fire a cultural nationalism in which the distinction between "race" and "nation" is blurred, and in which the nation is represented as a homogeneous and cohesive formation. While his national-imperial discourse attempts to establish a dominating identity through writing out native peoples, the result is a more ambivalently negotiatory discourse in which the imperialist's identity itself has been reinscribed. An attraction to miscegenation has not entirely been erased by a simultaneous loathing of it, and the racial and cultural composition of the nation-empire that surfaces from both *Alton Locke* and *Westward Ho!* remains profoundly unstable.

NOTES

I wish to thank Elizabeth Helsinger, Jean Comaroff, Norman Vance, Ronald Inden, Walter Reed, Paul Gilroy, David Bunn, and Catherine Hall for reading various early versions of this essay.

1 Despite the adjective "British" in the phrase "British Empire," talk of the "British" during the nineteenth century usually meant talk of the English and "Englishness." I hence use the term "English" rather than "British."

2 Kingsley ties in the spiritual and intellectual aspects of man to the passional through the Platonic idea of *thumos*, or "spirit," which he interpreted as referring to the righteous indignation that could drive the social reformer or imperial civilizer. Kingsley, however, did not enjoy having the phrase "muscular Christian" applied to him. He complains about it in a sermon on King David: this "clever expression" misleads for there must be both masculine and feminine virtues: "[David] has personal beauty, daring, prowess and skill in war. He has the generosity, nobleness, faithfulness, chivalry of a mediæval and Christian knight. He is a musician, poet, seemingly an architect likewise. He is, moreover, a born king" (*David* 5, 14). Thus, in David, masculine "vigor" and feminine "virtue," with its related "soft" skills in spiritual and intellectual arts, are both present: he is a positive pre-industrial example of a responsible leader with superlative vigor animated and restrained by other matters of substance: "The first and last business of every human being ... is morality" (13).

3 The "Robinson-Gallagher thesis" of "informal imperialism" in 1953 challenged this view.
4 As opposed to the political liberalism of, say, Macaulay or Mill.
5 Kingsley was not against political economy *per se*; what he disliked was its not being subject to human and humane control. English overseas commercial activities are seen as good in *Westward Ho!*.
6 The choice of Elizabethan rather than medieval England as the model for national community is in sharp contrast to the preferred medievalism of the period, from the Romantics to Tennyson. It indicates Kingsley's attempts to conjoin a nostalgic sense of history within a larger notion of providential progress not utilitarian in its scope.
7 I found Kermode's notion of the "imperial classic" and its relation to "provincial" texts helpful in thinking through what Kingsley is attempting.

WORKS CITED

Bhabha, Homi K., "Location, Intervention, Incommensurability: A Conversation with Homi Bhabha," *Emergences* 1 (1989): 63–88.
Burrow, J. W., *A Liberal Descent: Victorian Historians and the English Past.* Cambridge University Press, 1981.
Butterfield, Herbert, *The Whig Interpretation of History* (1931). New York: AMS Press, 1978.
Chatterjee, Partha, *Nationalist Thought and the Colonial World: A Derivative Discourse?* London: Zed Books, 1986.
Colloms, Brenda, *Charles Kingsley: The Lion of Eversley.* London: Constable, 1975.
Corrigan, Philip and Derek Sayer, *The Great Arch: English State Formation as Cultural Revolution.* Oxford: Basil Blackwell, 1985.
Curtis, L. Perry, *Apes and Angels: The Irishman in Victorian Caricature.* Washington, DC: Smithsonian Press, 1971.
Eldridge, C. C., *Victorian Imperialism.* London: Hodder and Stoughton, 1978.
Green, Martin, *Dreams of Adventure, Deeds of Empire.* London: Routledge and Kegan Paul, 1980.
Gupta, Akhil and James Ferguson, "Beyond 'Culture': Space, Identity, and the Politics of Difference," *Cultural Anthropology* 7.1 (February 1992): 6–23.
Hobsbawm, E. J., *Nations and Nationalism since 1780: Programme, Myth, Reality.* Cambridge University Press, 1990.
JanMohamed, Abdul R., "The Economy of Manichean Allegory: The Function of Racial Difference in Colonialist Literature" in *"Race," Writing and Difference*, ed. Henry Louis Gates, Jr. University of Chicago Press, 1986, pp. 78–106.
Kermode, Frank, *The Classic.* London: Faber and Faber, 1975.

Kingsley, Charles, *Alton Locke, Tailor and Poet: An Autobiography* (1850). Oxford University Press, 1983.

　David: Four Sermons Preached Before the University of Cambridge. Cambridge: Macmillan, 1865.

　Westward Ho! or The Voyages and Adventures of Sir Amyas Leigh, Knight of Burrough, in the County of Devon, in the Reign of Her Most Glorious Majesty, Queen Elizabeth (1855). New York: Airmont, 1969.

　Yeast (1848) in *The Works of Charles Kingsley*, vol. iv. Philadelphia: John Morris & Co., 1899.

Martin, Robert Bernard, *The Dust of Combat: A Life of Charles Kingsley.* New York: Norton, 1960.

Newsome, David, *Godliness and Good Learning: Four Studies on a Victorian Ideal.* London: John Murray, 1961.

Parry, Benita, "Problems in Current Theories of Colonial Discourse," *Oxford Literary Review* 9.1–2 (1987): 27–58.

Rose, Jacqueline, *The Case of Peter Pan, or the Impossibility of Children's Fiction.* London: Macmillan, 1984.

Said, Edward W., "Third World Intellectuals and Metropolitan Culture," *Raritan* 9.3 (Winter 1990): 27–50.

Williams, Raymond, *Culture and Society 1780–1950.* London: Chatto and Windus, 1958.

PART II

Varieties of muscular Christianity

CHAPTER 4

Charles Kingsley's scientific treatment of gender

Laura Fasick

Nineteenth-century popular fascination with scientific knowledge and discoveries (Russett 5) amply bears out Thomas Laqueur's contention in *Making Sex* that empirical discoveries in science often are interpreted only as further support for accepted ideas. Regardless of the factual accuracy of Victorian theories of disease transmission or of heredity, for instance, the theories themselves could influence larger concepts of human society and personality.[1] The "sudden acquisition of much physical knowledge" that Walter Bagehot claimed as one of Victorian England's chief distinctions (quoted in Gay, *Education*, 52) provided a way to naturalize a wide range of prescriptive notions. As scholars grow increasingly interested in the ways in which ideology subtly structures both "practical" knowledge and the literary texts that draw upon that knowledge, the works of formerly neglected writers such as Charles Kingsley become increasingly accepted as subjects for serious consideration. In his combination of moral earnestness and scientific enthusiasm, his eagerness to find moral significance in natural patterns, Kingsley represents some of the major tendencies in Victorian culture.

The "factual" basis on which Kingsley founded his concern for the maintenance of distinct gender roles was not only scientific, but specifically hygienic. Relying on a model of scientific impartiality and certainty, Kingsley praises the "valuable light" of objective knowledge, and declares that "enough, and more than enough, is known already" to preserve personal health ("Science of Health" 30). As writers from Mary Douglas to Peter Stallybrass and Allon White have pointed out, however, issues of cleanliness have often encoded social priorities, values, and hierarchies. Kingsley is as obsessed with sexuality, for him sanctified by monogamous marriage, as with hygiene,[2] and these interests effectively merge into one.

Kingsley attempted "to identify spiritual or moral law with physical law" (Hanawalt 603) and, to him, hygienic principles were among God's "simplest laws of physical health, decency, life" ("Mad World" 300).[3] His advocacy of the "laws of nature, which are nothing but the good will of God expressed in facts" ("Science of Health" 31) bears on gender roles in two ways: the acceptance of a two-sex model for human personhood (for Kingsley, part of the "scientific" truth about God's creation); and the belief that reverence for the physical realities God created includes a healthy sexuality. For Kingsley, urges towards sexual and familial life are among the natural energies and impulses implanted by God,[4] and no one should "abandon trust in his own instincts and natural desires" (Hanawalt 601).[5] (See David Rosen's essay in this volume for a discussion of the ambiguities in Kingsley's conception of energy.) Conversely, repressed sexuality, based on an impious disdain for the world God has given us, creates the conditions for unhygienic waste and thus for physical and moral degeneration.

One statute of the "natural law" to which Kingsley subscribed was the two-sex model of the world that Thomas Laqueur has described as emerging during the eighteenth and nineteenth centuries. Kingsley's differentiation between male and female is one instance of the nineteenth-century shift from viewing men and women as "hierarchically, that is vertically ordered" "according to their degree of metaphysical perfection ... along an axis whose telos is male" to a view of the sexes as "horizontally ordered, as opposites, as incommensurable" (Laqueur, "Orgasm" 3). "Henceforth, women were not to be viewed as inferior to men but as fundamentally different from, and thus incomparable to, men" (Schiebinger 217). The doctrine of complementarity, which Kingsley enthusiastically accepted,[6] fits well with the pattern of Victorian science to think in terms of "division and classification" (Russett 6–7). It also meshes with Darwinian evolutionary theories, in which the success of evolving forms depended partially on their triumph over their competing fellows and partially on their adaptation to an environment that included other, differing organisms (Beer 45). That competitive struggle went on between males, often for the possession of females (Beer 125). Men and women, on the other hand, did not compete with each other; they adapted, entering into a symbiotic relationship that allowed each sex to benefit from contact with the other. In individual cases, this symbiosis could intensify into romantic love; for all individuals, the contrast between the opposing yet complementary qualities of the two sexes helped to establish and define gender identity itself (Russett 11–12).

For Kingsley, this version of natural law, in which men and women defined their gender identities through and against each other, decreed the proper forms for individual and familial life. Kingsley can accept "practical" celibacy when marriage was "inexpedient," as it often was in missionary work or in the explorations that contributed to the British Empire (Vance, *Sinews* 37), provided that the celibate still demonstrated emotions Kingsley considered normal.[7] But the conscious choice of sexual abstention as "withdrawn spirituality" (Vance, *Sinews* 37) is abhorrent to him because man (and presumably woman) is "unsexed by celibacy" (*Letters* I 211). The "binary law of man's being" is "the want of a complementum" in monogamous marriage; in strikingly evolutionary language, Kingsley declares that in marriage, husband and wife "became one being of a higher organisation than either had been alone" (*Letters* I 151).

They could only achieve this mutually beneficial union, however, by retaining the distinctive features of their respective sexes. A man without a masculine spirit cannot even hope for any of the virtues of femininity; as Vance points out, "manliness" is "counter not so much to womanliness as to effeminacy" (*Sinews* 8), an inherently unnatural state. At its worst, a turn away from gender identity is a turn away from human identity as well. A Jesuit, for instance, is "a man no longer," a loss that makes him (or "it") neuter rather than feminine. However, since all humans are either male or female, a creature that belongs to neither sex is not even human. "[W]ithout a will, a conscience, a responsibility ... to God or man," even a "soul" – all that defined the human for nineteenth-century religion – the Jesuit is a "thing" (*Westward Ho!* II 152). The horror of mystical talk, "both Romish and Puritan" (*Letters* I 210), about Christ as the bridegroom of the soul is that it characterizes the soul "as feminine by nature, whatever be the sex of its possessor" (*Letters* I 210). Such talk is a dehumanization of the soul, for the image "is indeed only another form of the desire to be an angel" (*Letters* I 210). The "common conception of an angel" is that of "a woman, unsexed" (*Letters* I 210), and because unsexed, no longer human. And while the mystics may imagine that such a transformation is an exaltation, Kingsley leaves no doubt that it is a turn away from "the eternal idea of pure humanity, which is the image of the Lord God" (*Letters* I 207).

For Kingsley, a more appropriate model of human exaltation is to imagine human sexual divisions perpetuated in divine form. In heaven, he assured his future wife, they would "be able to enjoy uninterrupted sexual intercourse" (quoted in Chitty, 81), their then eternal masculinity and femininity joining in what Kingsley termed "a union which shall be perfect" (quoted in Chitty, 81). This is indeed seeing in "rich animal life" a sanctity that God brings to "ideal fulfill[ment]" (*Letters* I 210). Kingsley's perception of "the sanctity of the family, hereditary and national ties, and the dependence of those on the very essence of the Lord" (*Letters* I 210) makes the Godhead the source of his own highly specific ideals of gender relations. In a daring move, he even makes fixed gender identity and sexual feeling itself a necessary precursor to true religion:

"Go to the blessed Virgin," said a Romish priest, to a lady whom I love well. "She, you know, is a woman, and can understand all a woman's feelings." Ah! thought I, if your head had once rested on a lover's bosom, and your heart known the mighty stay of a man's affection, you would have learnt to go now in your sore need, not to the mother but to the Son – not to the indulgent virgin, but to the strong *man*, Christ Jesus – stern because loving – who does not shrink from punishing, and yet does it as a man would do it, "*mighty* to save." (*Letters* I 211)

Here Kingsley offers sharply demarcated and strongly sexualized gender roles, rather than the ambiguous sexlessness of angels, to facilitate contact with the highest human nature, that of the God/Man Christ. (One notes, incidentally, that such facilitation reserves for men the closest identification with the Godhead.) Despite (or because of?) this disparity between the sexes, this passage is the optimistic counterpoint to Kingsley's connection of celibacy with blurred gender roles and therefore the loss of human identity.

The two-sex model was not Kingsley's only scientific support for his ideas about gender, however. His novels, the repositories for his preaching on both sanitation and sexuality, draw the two issues together by an emphasis on health and its basis in nature. As Mary Douglas points out, however, "pathogenicity" is one of the most "recent" of "idea[s] about dirt" (35). By contrast, the "old definition of dirt as matter out of place" implies not the fear of contagion present in theories of pathogenicity, but rather "a set of ordered relations and a contravention of that order" (35) that is also relevant when considering Kingsley's combined acceptance and abhorrence of refuse. The physical matter that endangers bodily health is a source of horror only because people have gone against nature in their treatment of that matter, as when feces foul drinking water rather than serve as manure. "God has forbidden that anything should be merely harmful or merely waste in this so wise and well-made world," Kingsley declares ("Two Breaths" 72).[8] Human perversity, however, too often opposes God's plan and brings down upon itself Nature's terrible punishment. It is perverse to deny the physicality of human existence, but such perversity is common. One form it takes is the prudery that would deny the existence of sewage. Such a denial defeats sanitary reform and invites the plagues of cholera, typhoid, and dysentery. Then indeed waste is not "merely" waste: it is the home of "Baalzebub, god of flies, and of what flies are bred from," who comes in the form of disease "to visit his self-blinded worshippers, and bestow on them his own Cross of the Legion of Dishonor" (*Two Years Ago* II 85). Kingsley's rhetorical shift from praise for divine providence to warnings of satanic predation illustrates Donald E. Hall's argument (in his essay in this volume) that metaphoric language prescribes as well as describes.

In *Yeast*, Kingsley illustrates the interconnectedness he finds among sexual repression, dirt, and disease. Here, Argemone Lavington's dream of living "like the angels single and self-sustained," rather than having "to give up [her] will to any man" (134) is part of a false fastidiousness that also makes her unwilling to investigate the conditions of the poor, including her own tenants. Her cottagers live in misery while Argemone fantasizes about joining a convent for the sake of its "romantic asceticisms and mystic contemplation" (132). Only after Argemone is forced into confessing sexual love by the "almost coarse simplicity" and "delicious violence" of Lancelot Smith's "manly will" (142–4) does she take the first step towards cleansing the filth. Argemone's "purity" had actually been the precondition for dangerous and disgusting squalor among the poor and for her own spiritually dangerous sexual ambiguity. Comparing his heroine to Sappho, Kingsley warns that attempting to deny sexual feeling only leaves the "self-deceiver" more vulnerable to "mere passion ... and so down into self-contempt and suicide" (32–3). Whether or not Kingsley intended an allusion to lesbianism in his reference to Sappho,[9] he certainly meant to emphasize that

Argemone's rejection of conventional sexual life is unnatural and
that it is unhealthy in its consequences, both for her and her tenants.

The same complex of associations among sexuality, sanitation,
and true religion appears in *Two Years Ago*. Grace Harvey, "to woo
[whom] was more than any dared" (I 72), is saintly despite believing
in the "Manichaeism" (I 73) that Kingsley despises. But her detachment from the physical world could easily be the prelude to "spiritual intoxication, followed by spiritual knavery" (II 54). She is saved
when her love for Tom Thurnall awakens her sexuality: "her heart
throbbed, her cheek flushed, when his name was mentioned; . . . she
watched, almost unawares to herself, for his passing" (I 155). Tom
introduces her to another aspect of physical life when he convinces
her that their town's faulty sewage system threatens the place with
cholera. Grace responds by "offering to perform with her own hands
the most sickening offices; to become, if no one else would, the
common scavenger of the town" (II 53). But while Grace had
enjoyed a "fancied queenship" as a puritan (II 54), now her "noble
enthusiasm" for "a great practical work" (II 53) wins her only
"peevishness, ridicule, even anger and insult" from a people willing
to hear "talk . . . about their souls" but not to "have their laziness,
pride, covetousness, touched" (II 53).

The villagers' new denigration of Grace is more than defensiveness, however. They genuinely perceive her as degraded by her
new crusade. They are thus operating in accord with the "high/low
opposition . . . [that] is a fundamental basis to mechanisms of ordering and sense-making in European cultures" (Stallybrass and White
3). Among the symbolic domains where this opposition has traditionally received most attention are "psychic forms, the human
body, . . . and the social order" (3). One can see this opposition at
work both in Grace's initial influence and in her later fall into public
disfavor. Prior to Grace's involvement in sanitary reform, her
psychic affiliation with the "heights" of heaven had gained her an
influence disproportionate to her low worldly position, in which she
lacks both money and rank. Detachment from the body functions
like class elevation; it gives Grace the authority to intervene in the
villagers' lives and lifts her too high for the marital aspirations of the
male villagers. However, by aligning herself with what Stallybrass
and White term "the grotesque body" (defined by orifice and
elimination), Grace lowers her place in the village hierarchy.[10] The
villagers are disgusted not only by her new excremental interests,

but by the sexual urges they assume those interests imply. "[C]oarse viragos" attempt to shame Grace by claiming that her crusade is prompted by amorous pursuit of "the curate or the doctor" (II 53). Eager to cover up their literal dirtiness, they show their inner foul-mindedness by equating sexual love with disgrace. Of course, the values by which the villagers are judging Grace at this point are directly opposed to those that Kingsley himself is using and expecting his readers to use. Grace is indeed in love with the doctor, but just as her ability to contemplate sewage with equanimity is proof of her purity, so is it a sign of her health that she is "not ashamed at the discovery" of her own passion (I 155).

Sexuality as part of the "wise and well-made world" is natural and healthy; religious doctrines that would repress sexuality, on the other hand, go against nature and health and ultimately produce the spiritual equivalent of "Baalzebub's" filth and disease. The problem, as Kingsley sees it, is that sexuality is as inescapable as sewage and as prone to fester when ignored. Unable to accept the Roman Catholic ideal of virginal purity, he attacks the "prudish and prurient foulmindedness" ("Poetry of Sacred" 287) he finds in tales of the Virgin Mary. He defines prurience itself as contingent on celibacy, for prurience is "lust, which, unable to satisfy itself in act, satisfies itself by contemplation, usually of a negative and seemingly virtuous and Pharisaic character, vilifying, like St. Jerome in his cell at Bethlehem, that which he dare not do, and which is, after all, only another form of hysteria" (*Letters* II 249).

Kingsley's definition is particularly interesting because at that time hysteria was considered both a disease of sexual frustration, and a "morally repulsive" one at that (Showalter 133). Associated particularly with women's rebellion against "the female domestic role," it seemed not only a disease but a "moral perversion" (133). As a label, it implies a weak gender identity in either men or women: in men, because hysteria was "the classic female malady" (18); in women, because a hysterical female was clearly not fulfilling her natural role as "self-sacrificing daughter or wife" (133). As a disease, hysteria could be seen as the inevitable result of going against nature and nature's division of the sexes. The one truly virile character in Kingsley's *The Saint's Tragedy* refers scornfully to monks as "these male hysterics, by starvation bred / And huge conceit" and urges his lord not to "cast off God's gift of manhood" (lines 17–18). Grace Harvey, whose mysticism takes her dangerously close to denying the flesh, is lucky to live in a Protestant country. Otherwise, misdirected spirituality might have led her to equal "the ecstasies of St. Theresa, or of St. Hildegardis, or any other sweet dreamer of sweet dreams," in which case, she would "have died in seven years, maddened by alternate paroxysms of self-conceit and revulsions of self-abasement" (*Two Years Ago* 287). Here, treating sexual denial as a disease further naturalizes the gender roles that conduce to "healthy" sexuality. Kingsley's equation of the natural with the divine blocks the last escape from this circular trap: it removes the possibility of an identity "above" the natural and the gender-identified. Movement away from fixed gender roles means not exaltation but degeneration.

Kingsley's writings provide ample illustrations of nineteenth-century theories of degeneration,[11] a concept particularly frightening if one accepts, as Kingsley does, the inseparability of spirit and flesh.[12] When discussing degeneration, Kingsley explicitly links physiological decline with the failure to live up to gender ideals. In "Nausicaa in London," he sees the physical deterioration of English females as indicative not only of sickly bodies, but of sickly personalities, marred by unfeminine prudery. Homer's heroine is the superior of modern women both because of her greater physical grace and because of her willingness to admire and wish for a strong man as a husband. More dramatically, the poet Elsley Vavasour, in Kingsley's novel *Two Years Ago*, descends into sickliness, neurosis, opium addiction, madness, and death (thus encapsulating in one life the hereditary pattern for the nineteenth-century degenerate[13]) because he abandons his male role, which for Kingsley must necessarily function through interaction with a female (Elsley's wife). Elsley's dereliction is both the result of "effeminate habits" and intensified by those habits, which deepen his "internal malaise" (1 313). Since Elsley's wife is womanly enough to yearn for male guidance, Nature fills the vacuum with Major Campbell, one of those men to whom "women will bow" (1 64). But Elsley mistakes the inevitable outcome of his own shaky gender identity as an act of betrayal by his wife. His subsequent flight leads not only to his own death but to his wife's miscarriage of Elsley's unborn son, the symbol of his now irretrievably lost masculinity.

To accept one's masculinity (or femininity), on the other hand, presumably is to accept both spiritual and physical life. Certainly Kingsley's typical hero, whether incarnated as Lancelot Smith in

Yeast, Amyas Leigh in *Westward Ho!*, Tom Thurnall in *Two Years Ago*, or Hereward in *Hereward the Wake*, is consistently a broad-shouldered specimen of "healthful manhood," whose "sinewy limbs" and "daring, fancy, passion" require a wide "sphere of action" (*Hypatia* I 2).[14] Kingsley's emphasis on his heroes' muscularity provoked exasperated comment even among contemporaries,[15] but for the historical novels at least, he could cite science in his defense. As Norman Vance comments about *Hereward the Wake*, "the modish Darwinian theory of the survival of the fittest is invoked in defence of Hereward and the lawless men of his time: in such a primitive age only the savage and the strong could expect to survive at all" (*Sinews* 99). Kingsley's heroines also tend to conform to his ideal of robust beauty. They rarely suffer from the "literal and figurative sickness" that Gilbert and Gubar find endemic among nineteenth-century heroines (*Madwoman* 55) unless, like Argemone and Honoria Lavington, they are being punished for their own turn away from healthy sexuality.[16] Yet health and vitality do not exempt Kingsley's women from physical suffering, any more than robustness preserves Kingsley's men from pain. Both men and women in Kingsley's fiction are subject to extreme bodily trials, but the differing patterns of their vicissitudes indicate more general differences between the sexes. Kingsley shows a world in which the male body is distinguished by its capacity for aggression, while the female body is marked by its capacity to endure assault.

Kingsley's belief in righteous "rage" and a virtue based on "combative defence against cruelty, injustice, and wickedness" (Vance, "Kingsley's Christian Manliness" 31)[17] explains why he can find nature at once the expression of a divine love and also a destroyer that "kills, and kills, and kills" in a massacre worse than human war (*Letters* II 97). God created a world that abounds in natural dangers, but he also created men to fight against those dangers. Certainly man must obey natural law, but "Nature is to be obeyed only in order to conquer her" ("Mad World" 278). Such conquest is not impiety against God's decrees; it is instead the fulfillment of God's expectations. He placed men in the world in order to *be* fighters.

Thus, even though disease results from going against nature, it is appropriate to battle disease fiercely when it occurs, no matter if human folly itself invited its appearance. Tom Thurnall in *Two Years Ago* is a doctor, but as such he is primarily a wager of war against disease rather than a bestower of comfort. When a cholera epidemic occurs, "brave Tom ... wrestle[s]" with this personified monster who "fleshes his teeth on every kind of prey" (II 87). Tom's motivation is aggression rather than compassion: "I have got – and what greater pleasure – a good stand-up fight with an old enemy ... I have written off for help to the Board of Health, and I shall not be shoved against the ropes till the government man comes down" (II 92).

Here even the preservation of life is defined as combat. We find the same desire to magnify aggressive motives at the expense of compassionate ones in Kingsley's discussion of mythic heroism, one of the few instances where Kingsley does *not* detect a hidden sanitary motif.[18] He rejects "the theory that the tales of Hercules and the Hydra, Apollo and the mud-Python, St. George and the Dragon, were sanitary-reform allegories, and the monster whose poisonous breath destroys cattle and young maidens only typhus and consumption" ("Poetry of Sacred" 298). Instead, he cites recent discoveries by geologists and naturalists to support his belief in the existence of supposedly "fabulous" monsters (297). Science lends credence to a version of heroism that valorizes the combative male body.

In comparing this account with the description quoted above of the cholera epidemic in *Two Years Ago*, one notes that rather than allegorizing dragons into disease, Kingsley prefers to picture disease as a dragon, the better to make soldiers out of the men who battle it. Much nineteenth-century fiction used disease to soften and feminize male characters (Mitchell 40–41), but for Kingsley, the weakness induced by actually suffering disease, as opposed to combatting it, is a terror rather than a benefit. When one of Tom's recruits finally succumbs to the "sword" of infection, Kingsley's single, grim detail of the horror is that he "scream[s] like a woman, though he has bitten his tongue half through to stop his screams" (II 111).

Vulnerability, in Kingsley's world, is feminine, but since Kingsley treats disease as an emblem of spiritual ills, he must find some other way to mark his heroines' bodies as vulnerable and therefore female. Women's subjection, or at least threatened subjection, to masculine violence becomes a way to fix gender identity in both heroine and hero: in a heroine because her susceptibility establishes her femininity, in a hero because her weakness becomes the justification for his forcefulness. Kingsley's sketch of the evolutionary system in reverse in *The Water Babies* reveals his own ideal of female sexual selection:

the female will inevitably choose the male who can best protect her in a hostile world (223–4). This pattern, inflated and idealized by romantic rhetoric, provides a model for love in many of his novels. The would-be self-sufficient Argemone first experiences "the delight of dependence – the holy charm of weakness" when she realizes that a man's "personal prowess," no matter how seemingly "coarse and brutal," will make her "quite safe in his strength" (*Yeast* 93–4). This scene transforms even an English pastoral landscape (the scene of Argemone's epiphany) into a lawless Darwinian jungle where female requires male for survival as well as for pleasure.[19] At the same time that Kingsley spiritualizes female susceptibility as "holy" and invests male "prowess" with the stature of chivalry, he naturalizes the inevitability of female dependence and even of female suffering. The fact of female vulnerability both distinguishes women as a sex and invokes masculinity as a necessary and protective complement. Thus not only maleness, but the virtue of maleness, can exist only in distinction from femaleness and its "holy charm."

Kingsley's fiction therefore displays an extraordinary emphasis on sexual violence, at times so vividly portrayed as to shock contemporaries (Vance, *Sinews* 112). And Kingsley consistently associates such violence – and the protective retribution it provokes – with a healthy turn away from female celibacy into sexual (and sexually dependent) life. In novels from *Yeast* to *Hypatia* to *Two Years Ago* to *Hereward the Wake*, the possible threat of another man's assault upon the woman is a precipitating factor in bringing lovers together. Yet the interplay between power and desire is at times disturbingly ambiguous. Tom Thurnall, after rescuing Grace from a drunken attacker, proceeds to force his own embraces on her. Angered by her rebuff, Tom recognizes that he is in love only because he feels "a flush of rage, and a strong desire ... to slay ... any one else who dared even to look sweet on Grace" (1 395). Here involvement with a woman is both provoked by other men's (often violent) interest in her and expressed through proprietary retaliation against those men. Such a formula confirms masculinity as much through combativeness as through sexual desire. In *Hypatia*, violence can be turned even against the beloved object: "the human heart" of Raphael Aben-Ezra, "asleep for many a year, leap[s] into mad life" when he witnesses what he believes to be an attempted rape (1 258). Raphael's defense of the woman he only now realizes he loves is to "[draw] his dagger" and proclaim to the suspected assailants that "I

will balk you! She shall die first!" (I 258). Kingsley treats this display
as Raphael's emergence into moral and emotional reality after long
pseudo-philosophical hermeticism. In this version of reality,
however, female peril is merely a means to awaken the male to a full
experience of life.

The ultimate fate of Raphael's beloved Victoria goes further to
suggest that such peril is an acceptable, even necessary, price for
women to pay for feminine fulfillment. Raphael saves Victoria from
the sterile convent life to which her father had wished to consign her,
but their marriage, signifying Victoria's healthy acceptance of "the
primary laws of ... being" (II 12), is an acceptance as well of
"trouble in the flesh" (II 296). Her father's desire that Victoria take
the veil had been practical as well as devout: the "safe shelter of a
nunnery" is the best "lot for a defenseless girl" in "such times as
these" (II II). Yet this protection from physical danger is characterized as a form of punishment: Raphael, in a speech filled with
Kingsleyan terminology about religious celibacy, calls it "perpetual
imprisonment" (II II). Victoria is better off married to Raphael
himself, but Kingsley goes to great lengths to emphasize that the
union comes at a (justifiable) cost of far more fleshly "trouble" than
the normal travails of childbirth and sickness. He hints darkly that
after Raphael's death leaves Victoria without a protector, "persecu-
tors" subject her to "strange misery and disgrace," to "shame and
agony," and that "the scars of fearful torture" mark "her delicate
limbs" (II 297). Victoria's "joyful" acceptance of this pain and her
continued work as an "angel of mercy" reveal her heroism (II 297),
but it is a heroism sharply differentiated from that of her menfolk,
who die "the deaths of heroes" in combat against "the invading
swarms" (II 297).

The contrast is an oddly revealing comment on the implications of
Kingsley's enthusiasm for a specifically feminine heroism in a world
that Kingsley sees as constantly torn by masculine strife.[20] "The
brute male force of the wicked world which marries and is given in
marriage" ("Review of *Froude's History*" 217) is brutal as well in its
treatment of the vulnerable, but such dangers are an acceptable
price for sexual life. The problem is that while Kingsley not only
allows but expects his men actively to oppose those dangers, he
cannot formulate a proper female response aside from long-suffering. Men may die, but they are not barred from fighting for their
lives or for those of others.[21] Women are, and their acceptance of

womanhood is acceptance of passivity within a tumultuously violent world. Both Victoria and Raphael solidify their gender identities through marriage, but while Victoria's turn away from a nun's sexlessness entails the passive suffering of physical torture and humiliation, the formerly dandyish Raphael's parallel assumption of masculinity makes his body an instrument of combat (albeit unsuccessful) rather than of endurance.

In *Two Years Ago*, as well, a woman's tortured body connotes both her immersion in sexual life and a heroic feminine endurance carefully distinguished from the heroism of masculine activity. Kingsley's fascination with gender is particularly noticeable here because his story touches upon, and yet avoids, one of the most sensitive of nineteenth-century "scientific" debates: the controversy over the status of the African races. Kingsley's own attitudes towards race are confused and contradictory beyond even the usual chaos of his opinions,[22] and constitute a baffling, sometimes painful mixture of humanitarianism, distaste, and outright cruelty. (C. J. W.-L. Wee's essay in this volume offers a fuller examination of this rich topic.) In *Two Years Ago*, however, Kingsley introduces race only to elide it under the more compelling (for him) category of gender. One of the book's many plots is the love story between the beautiful former slave Marie, light-skinned enough to pass as an Italian, and her devoted white suitor, Stangrave. Marie will not marry Stangrave until he proves himself as a man through his vigor against some evil; the evil against which Marie hopes he will devote his energies is slavery. So far this sounds like exemplary abolitionist propaganda. Sexuality, however, complicates the issue.

In dramatizing the evils of slavery, Kingsley focuses on the sexual exploitation of slave women as the most trenchant of reasons why it is "dreadful ... to be a slave" (I 50–51). By pursuing this (resolutely heterosexual) emphasis, Kingsley chooses to ignore the plight of male slaves, for whom, interestingly enough, he reserves the bulk of his racial distaste (I 159). Perhaps Kingsley found the expression of empathy with black men difficult because of their race, or perhaps their slavery-enforced abjection was too threatening to his ideals of masculinity to confront, much less to explore. By focusing on slaves as exclusively female and as beautiful enough to tempt the men at "the New Orleans market, or some devilry" (I 50), Kingsley allows himself the vigor of humanitarian indignation and the pleasure of erotic contemplation, without risking self-identification with the helplessly vulnerable. However, since beauty for Kingsley entails light skin and Caucasian features, the slave herself must be all but white: Marie is the novel's representative slave, yet Kingsley takes pains to emphasize that she possesses only "some drops" of African blood (I 227).

Disconcertingly, as well, the historical fact of African-American slavery glides into the willing "slavery" of woman's self-abnegating love (as Kingsley perceives it). The impetus for Marie's deliverance comes from her southern white lover, whose dying wish that Marie be spirited to Canada the novel's hero feels impelled to carry out (I 50). But Marie herself separates the "sacred fight" against black slavery (I 161) from women's yearnings for subjection, for "what are women meant for but to be slaves?" (I 159). Speaking for a sex rather than for a race, Marie declares that "[w]oman must worship, or be wretched" and that "to hear [her white lover] call me slave would have been rapture; to [him] I would have answered on my knees, Master, I have no will but yours" (I 159). Admittedly, Kingsley ascribes to Marie some of that "instability, inconsistency, hasty passion" that he declares typical of "quadroons" (I 241), yet her protestations are typical of the rhetoric indulged in by other Kingsley heroines who equate feminine love with abjectness before the beloved.[23] In this context, Marie's story becomes the story not of her emancipation but of her eventually successful search for a "true" (because worthy) "master" (I 161). Kingsley's story, likewise, becomes not a tract against slavery, but an account of individuals' assumption of proper gender roles. Marie's "theatric passionateness," too self-aggrandizing to be feminine, must give way to "pure womanly" humility (II 386); even more urgently, the insufficiently masculine Stangrave must rise from modern dilettantism to the type of heroism found in "Mort [*sic*] d'Arthur" and Homer (I 220–21).

The models are literary classics of warfare. The militaristic motif continues as Kingsley motivates Stangrave's commitment to a humanitarian cause through growing and bloody-minded assertiveness rather than through empathy with the oppressed. Stangrave's first revulsion against slavery is founded in his disgust at the self-abasement of northerners who fail to protest slavery's evil, northerners among whom he includes himself: "white slaves," "we have steadily, deliberately cringed at the feel of the wrong-doer [the southern slave-holder] ... and received as our only reward fresh insults" (II 252–3). This contempt for Yankee unmanliness recalls Marie's earlier comparison of the "cold Northerner" to the castrated "ox" and her description of his fear lest "the Southern aristocrat ... should transfer ... the cowhide from the negro's loins to his" (I 100), another castration image. Stangrave's embrace of the abolitionist cause, a cause that Kingsley implies is almost as little supported above as below the Mason-Dixon line, is therefore figured primarily as a move from emasculation to masculinity. His new model of human life is one in which all must take their place as "the slayers and the slain" (II 255). Perceiving himself as a warrior, Stangrave speculates that "the art of war" may be, after agriculture, "the most necessary of the human arts" (II 255). "Armed industry" with its attendant bloodshed is not only "the history of the human race," it is the biblical prescription for "the normal type of human life" (II 255). Suitably, Stangrave's initiation into this heroism is signaled by his willingness to enter into personal combat: only after engaging to duel with Tom can Stangrave both consummate his love for Marie and announce his new willingness to fight a national, rather than an individual, battle.

Even more clearly here than in *Hypatia*, however, the only role for the female body within this militaristic model of heroism is that of an inspirational icon of suffering. Earlier in her history, speaking of her endurance of the "scourge" and her resulting scars, Marie hopes that her "torments" might "madden a people into manhood" (I 161). Kingsley gives no hint of black men who do more than "crouch before the white like brutes" (I 159), but Marie's hope comes true in the effect of her marked body upon Stangrave. The scars upon her "fair, pure, noble flesh" (II 386) will be "God's commandment to [him]" to fight slavery, cause for Marie not only to "rejoice" but to "glory in them" (II 386).

The enraptured tone is striking because it contrasts so sharply with Kingsley's refusal to romanticize the diseased female body. Popular didactic fiction throughout much of the nineteenth century idealized the patient long-suffering of the invalid as a model of religious resignation, with a concomitant avoidance of distasteful sickroom details (Nelson 21–4, 73, *passim*). This was an attitude with which Kingsley had no patience. He himself credits his lack of emotionality towards disease to his approaching the matter from a scientific, rather than religiously Manichaean, angle. But the swooning sentiment that Kingsley withholds from the idea of the

body racked by sickness he pours forth in full measure upon images
of the female body agonized and marked by torture.[24] It is fitting
that this should be so, for thus the gender distinction that Kingsley
constantly strives to preserve can best be maintained. For Kingsley
as much as for other Victorians, disease, as noted above, dissolves
the differences between the sexes, reducing men as well as women to
dependent endurance. The infliction and endurance of torture,
however, is for Kingsley a gendered affair. Certainly men suffer and
die in Kingsley's novels, but they do so primarily as active agents,
falling in combat rather than enduring in passivity. Women, on the
other hand, can only endure. The virtue of their suffering is that the
pains to which evilly directed male aggression subjects them are a
spur to countervailing male heroism. Thus Kingsley iconizes the
female martyr whose martyrdom marks her difference from men,
rather than the female invalid who diffuses ideals of patience and
tenderness to both sexes. The distinction retains female suffering as a
morally positive influence while dramatically altering the effects of
that influence into an intensified, rather than weakened, sense of
gender difference.

This use of female pain stands in uneasy conjunction with Kingsley's advocacy of bodily health and sanitary reform on the basis of
concern not only for physical suffering but for souls that cannot
thrive while trapped within sickly bodies. In Kingsley's idiosyncratic blending of spirituality and materialism, acceptance of disease is
a moral degradation and the consciousness of physical debility
destroys self-respect. Disease is caused by dirt and the presence of
dirt is facilitated by the denial of the body, on which sexual and
therefore individual identity depends. Disease, dirt, and the unsexed
individual alike provoke disgust. Yet the female body that has been
ravaged by male aggression rather than illness is neither contami-
nated nor repulsive: Victoria's tortured limbs are an emblem of her
"purity" (II 297); Stangrave will "prize" Marie's scars "more than
all [her] loveliness" (II 386).

The apparent contradiction in Kingsley's valuation of physical
integrity seems to turn on the gender significance of vulnerability.
Feminine awareness of physical dependence upon male strength is a
psychological necessity for true womanhood and hence a moral
benefit. That such dependence can entail suffering only increases its
uplifting qualities. Kingsley's willingness to romanticize feminine
martyrdom to male aggression as he will not romanticize human

martyrdom to disease, however, indicates that his horror at disease is not simply revulsion at pain as such. Illness is terrifying because it dissolves gender and thus (for Kingsley) human identity. It *is* waste because it "wastes" human beings, depriving even their suffering of any nobility. The experience of pain caused by human aggression, however, can reinforce and even ennoble identity when the sufferers divide along gender lines of male resistance and female endurance. That experience then becomes an occasion for the triumphant enactment of gendered identity. Perhaps this willingness to accept gender-enhancing pain, repugnant to us yet for Kingsley consistent with deeply felt humanitarianism, sheds some light on the apparently fatalistic acceptance in the works of other Victorian writers of suffering that appears to modern readers both socially created and remediable. Members of a culture that prided itself on ever-expanding knowledge, Victorians struggled with how to interpret that knowledge. Often they chose the interpretations most consistent with prior social constructions, including constructions of gender difference.

NOTES

I would like to thank Donald J. Gray and Donald E. Hall for their comments on earlier versions of this essay.

1 See Williams, *The Rich Man and the Diseased Poor*; Haley, *The Healthy Body and Victorian Culture*; Drinka, *The Birth of Neurosis*; and Morton, *The Vital Science: Biology and the Literary Imagination, 1860–1900* for a fuller study of literary and social manifestations of Victorian ideas about the roles of heredity and environment on physical and psychological disease. For more general background in the interchange between Darwinism and literature, Gillian Beer's *Darwin's Plots: Evolutionary Narrative in Darwin, George Eliot, and Nineteenth-Century Fiction* provides an extensive and thoughtful discussion of Darwin's own "literary" formulation of his ideas, with a consideration of how fiction absorbed and used them. George Levine's *Darwin and the Novelists: Patterns of Science in Victorian Fiction* examines the movement from natural theology to various interpretations of Darwinism in selected novels from *Mansfield Park* to *Under Western Eyes*.

2 "Of sanitary reform I shall never grow tired," Kingsley wrote in 1859 (*Letters* II 88), and the labors revealed both in his letters and in Lady Susan Chitty's biography bear this out. Chitty's book also documents the personal history of Kingsley's feelings towards the sexual and gender issues on which he wrote so copiously.

3 For specifics on Kingsley's scientific knowledge and activities, see

Hanawalt, "Charles Kingsley and Science"; and Meadows, "Kingsley's Attitude Toward Science."

4 See *Letters* I 205–6 for a discussion of "human relations" as "antitypes" of divine union.

5 For Walter Houghton, this trust in the natural renders Kingsley's whole theology suspect. See his "The Issue Between Kingsley and Newman."

6 References to complementarity run throughout Kingsley's writings. In addition to instances cited in the text, see *Letters* I 182; and *Lectures to Ladies on Practical Subjects*.

7 Thus Kingsley is happy to absorb the barren woman or spinster into Victorian pieties about motherhood. Women, he writes, are more immersed than men in "the stern mysteries of pain, and sorrow, and self-sacrifice; – they who bring forth children, weep over children, slave for children, and, if they have none of their own, then slave, with the holy instinct of the sexless bee, for the children of others" ("Science of Health" 32). Note that feminine self-sacrifice here becomes an instinctual and unconscious process, rather than a moral choice.

8 He makes this point again in *Letters* II 243, and in the essay "Thrift." Christopher Hamlin's "Providence and Putrefaction: Victorian Sanitarians and the Natural Theology of Health and Disease" establishes that the moral significance of sewage was a widely accepted concept among the Victorians.

9 Peter Gay claims that the nature of Sappho's relationships was a debatable issue "through the first half of the nineteenth century" (*The Tender Passion* 238), with most classicists rejecting the lesbian hypothesis.

10 Kingsley himself saw women as the ideal dispensers of hygienic knowledge. For him, that role in itself justified "the training of women for the medical profession" ("Science of Health" 35).

11 Even before the publication of Darwin's *Origin of Species* (1859), Kingsley had prefigured evolutionary theories in the "Dreamland" chapter of *Alton Locke* (1849). (See Lionel Stevenson's "Darwin and the Novel" for mention of some other literary foreshadowings of Darwin.) Alton's dream vision shows him progressing upwards on the evolutionary ladder, but it also hints at the possibility of degeneration when Alton, in the form of an ape, loses intellectual capacity as he matures. Kingsley's tracing of "the fearful degradation which goes on from youth to age in all the monkey race, especially in those which approach nearest to the human form" (*Alton Locke* II 270) is one of several passages in this chapter that explicitly reflect contemporary physical anthropological thought. At puberty, closure of the cranial sutures was supposed to end intellectual growth among "the anthropoid apes" and blacks (Russett 53); Kingsley's Alton describes his ape face as one that "might have been a negro child's" (*Alton Locke* II 270).

The Water Babies provides Kingsley's most explicit treatment of degeneration in the story of the Doasyoulikes. They live up (or down) to their name and consequently degenerate from human beings into apes. Kingsley is explicit that their physical degeneration is a result of their moral inadequacy: their laziness is an abdication of human responsibility and therefore humanity itself (*The Water Babies* 219–25). Arthur Johnston's "*The Water Babies*: Kingsley's Debt to Darwin" examines the Darwinian implications of this novel in detail. Gillian Beer also contributes a sensitive discussion in *Darwin's Plots* (133–9).

12 In one of his most striking statements, Kingsley claimed that "the soul of each living being ... secretes the body thereof, as a snail secretes its shell, and ... the body is nothing more than the expression in terms of matter of that stage of development to which the being has arrived" (*Letters* II 133).

13 See Russett, *Sexual Science*, 67–74, and Drinka, *The Birth of Neurosis*, 167–8 and 251–7, for a fuller discussion of ideas about the fate of the degenerate.

14 Alton Locke, Kingsley's only sickly male protagonist, is also his only working-class one, and Kingsley's uneasy class-consciousness is nowhere more apparent than in this fact. Not only is Alton's frail physique itself a marker of his low social standing, but it also justifies his eventual submission to the most enlightened representatives of a men-tally as well as physically stronger aristocracy. For Victorian per-ceptions of the poor as physically deficient and sickly, see Porter 159. Susan Williams's *The Rich Man and the Diseased Poor* examines this phenomenon in detail.

Raymond Williams's discussion of *Alton Locke* in *Culture and Society 1780–1950* remains a rewarding examination of Alton's eventual class submission. It may be worth noting that Alton's physical weakness is not his only difference from Kingsley's other heroes, a generally homo-geneous group. In his hysterical tendencies, defensiveness, and self-absorption, he greatly resembles Elsley Vavasour, Kingsley's other upwardly aspiring lower-class poet, who is emphatically the anti-hero of the book in which he appears.

15 See Vance, *Sinews* 104 and Haley 108–9.

16 Argemone, who has already been discussed as a would-be celibate, dies after catching fever at one of the slum dwellings she had allowed to fester on her land. On her deathbed, her beauty gone, she explicitly acknowledges that her death is an expiation for previous sins of pride and indolence (204), sins that Kingsley had linked to her idealization of female autonomy.

Unlike her sister, who accepts a man's love before dying, Honoria Lavington definitely rejects the man who could have fulfilled her passionate nature. The result is her deterioration. By the novel's end, she is the victim of "some mysterious and agonizing disease, about which the physicians agree on one point only – that it is hopeless" (275). Linking Honoria's ill health to her female singleness, Kingsley declares that "there she lies – and will lie until she dies – the type of thousands more ... who find not mates in this life" (275–6).

17 But see Henry Harrington's "Charles Kingsley's Fallen Athlete" for another view. Also of interest is William Baker's look at *Westward Ho!* as an example of bloodthirstiness in didactic disguise.

18 Norman Vance's "Heroic Myth and Women in Victorian Literature" discusses Kingsley's idea of mythic women as one instance of a larger Victorian literary fashion.

19 Kingsley leaves no doubt of Argemone's sexual arousal as she realizes her dependence upon Lancelot's protection. See *Yeast* 93–4.

20 Norman Vance perceptively comments that "Kingsley's imagination relishes the almost brutal ruggedness of the worlds" he conjures up in his historical novels "not least" because "it highlights the role of ... [his] ideal of womanhood" ("Heroic Myth" 182). I would only add that this role may seem ideal to Kingsley partly because it facilitates, rather than bars, the free play of "ruggedness."

21 Torfrida in *Hereward the Wake* does provide battle strategies for her husband, but this is behind-the-scenes wifely assistance. Only in *Westward Ho!* does Kingsley show a woman who fights like a man; Ayacanora slays the man about to kill her beloved Amyas Leigh. Amyas, however, recoils from his savior as a "bloodthirsty" woman (II 362) until the "sacred fire of sorrow" at his distaste burns all "fallen savageness" out of Ayacanora and leaves her "all-enduring" (II 368).

22 Michael Banton's "Kingsley's Racial Philosophy" provides a thoughtful overview though downplaying some of Kingsley's less palatable comments.

23 See, for instance, *Westward Ho!* II 453–4 and *Hypatia* II 255.

24 Susan Chitty has documented Kingsley's ambivalent attraction to chastisement as a religious discipline both for himself and for his wife (80), despite his vehement denunciations of its practice among Catholic communities. His drawings, a selection of which are included in Chitty's biography (following p. 160), include some depictions of sexualized pain, for example a naked St. Elizabeth's mother carrying a cross while being jeered at by grotesques, and Elizabeth's mother being stripped and murdered by her subjects, a process that, as Peter Gay notes, includes "being burned in her genitals by a long, wicked, phallic torch" (*Tender Passion* 310). In his review of "The Poetry of Sacred and Legendary Art," Kingsley confesses to finding many "an exquisite story" (292) in tales of the martyrs. Although rejecting their use as Catholic propaganda, he is stirred by accounts of "tender girls" suffering "tortures ... too horrible for pen to tell" (291): illustrations of "God's strength made perfect in woman's weakness" (292).

WORKS CITED

Baker, William J., "Charles Kingsley and the Crimean War: A Study of Chauvinism," *Southern Humanities Review* 4 (1970): 247–56.

Banton, Michael, "Kingsley's Racial Philosophy," *Theology* 78 (1975): 22–30.

Beer, Gillian, *Darwin's Plots: Evolutionary Narrative in Darwin, George Eliot, and Nineteenth-Century Fiction*. London: Ark, 1983.

Chitty, Lady Susan, *The Beast and the Monk: A Life of Charles Kingsley*. New York: Mason/Charter, 1975.

Dale, Peter Allen, *In Pursuit of a Scientific Culture: Science, Art, and Society in the Victorian Age*. Madison: University of Wisconsin Press, 1989.

Douglas, Mary, *Purity and Danger: An Analysis of Concepts of Pollution and Taboo*. New York: Praeger, 1966.

Drinka, George, *The Birth of Neurosis: Myth, Malady, and the Victorians*. New York: Simon & Schuster, 1984.

Gay, Peter, *Education of the Senses*, vol. I, *The Bourgeois Experience: Victoria to Freud*. Oxford University Press, 1984. *The Tender Passion*, vol. II, *The Bourgeois Experience: Victoria to Freud*. Oxford University Press, 1986.

Gilbert, Sandra and Susan Gubar, *The Madwoman in the Attic: The Woman Writer and the Nineteenth-Century Literary Imagination*. New Haven: Yale University Press, 1979.

Haley, Bruce, *The Healthy Body and Victorian Culture*. Cambridge, MA: Harvard University Press, 1978.

Hamlin, Christopher, "Providence and Putrefaction: Victorian Sanitarians and the Natural Theology of Health and Disease" in *Energy and Entropy: Science and Culture in Victorian Britain. Essays from Victorian Studies*, ed. Patrick Brantlinger. Bloomington and Indianapolis: Indiana University Press, 1989, pp. 93–123.

Hanawalt, Mary Wheat, "Charles Kingsley and Science," *Studies in Philology* 34 (1937): 589–611.

Harrington, Henry R., "Charles Kingsley's Fallen Athlete," *Victorian Studies* 21 (1977): 73–86.

Houghton, Walter, "The Issue Between Kingsley and Newman," *Theology Today* 4 (1947): 80–101.

Johnston, Arthur, "*The Water Babies*: Kingsley's Debt to Darwin," *English* 12 (1959): 215–19.

Kingsley, Charles, *Alton Locke, Tailor and Poet: An Autobiography* (1848), introd. Maurice Kingsley, 2 vols. New York: Fred De Fau, 1899.

"Great Cities and their Influence for Good and Evil" in *Sanitary and Social Lectures and Essays*, pp. 187–222.

Health and Education. New York; Appleton, 1874.

His Letters and Memories of his Life, ed. F. E. Kingsley, 2 vols. London: Macmillan, 1894.

Hypatia; or, New Foes with an Old Face (1853), introd. Maurice Kingsley, 2 vols. New York: Fred De Fau, 1899.

Lectures to Ladies on Practical Subjects. Cambridge: Macmillan, 1855.

"A Mad World, My Masters" in *Sanitary and Social Lectures and Essays*, pp. 271–300.

"Nausicaa in London, or the Lower Education of Woman," in *Health and Education*, pp. 69–88.

"The Poetry of Sacred and Legendary Art," *Fraser's* 39 (1849): 283–98.

"Review of *Froude's History of England, vols. VII and VIII*," *Macmillan's* 9 (1864): 211–24.

The Saint's Tragedy (1848) in *Poems*, introd. Maurice Kingsley. New York: Fred De Fau, 1899.

Sanitary and Social Lectures and Essays. London: Macmillan, 1889.

"The Science of Health" (1872) in *Sanitary and Social Lectures and Essays*, pp. 21–45.

"Thrift," in *Health and Education*, pp. 122–149.

"The Two Breaths" in *Sanitary and Social Lectures and Essays*, pp. 49–74.

Two Years Ago (1857), introd. Maurice Kingsley, 2 vols. New York: Fred De Fau, 1899.

The Water Babies (1862). Philadelphia and London: Lippincott, 1917.

Westward Ho! (1855), introd. Maurice Kingsley, 2 vols. New York: Fred De Fau, 1899.

Yeast: A Problem (1849) in *The Life and Works of Charles Kingsley*, 19 vols. London: Macmillan, 1901.

Laqueur, Thomas, *Making Sex: Body and Gender from the Greeks to Freud*. Cambridge, MA: Harvard University Press, 1990.

"Orgasm, Generation, and the Politics of Reproductive Biology," *Representations* 14 (1986): 1–41.

Levine, George, *Darwin and the Novelists: Patterns of Science in Victorian Fiction*. Cambridge, MA: Harvard University Press, 1988.

Meadows, A. J., "Kingsley's Attitude Toward Science," *Theology* 78 (1975): 15–22.

Mitchell, Sally, "Sentiment and Suffering: Women's Recreational Reading in the 1860s," *Victorian Studies* 21 (1977): 29–45.

Morton, Peter, *The Vital Science: Biology and the Literary Imagination, 1860–1900*. London: George Allen and Unwin, 1984.

Nelson, Claudia, *Boys will be Girls: The Feminine Ethic and British Children's Fiction, 1857–1917*. New Brunswick: Rutgers University Press, 1990.

Porter, Dorothy, "'Enemies of the Race': Biologism, Environmentalism, and Public Health in Edwardian England," *Victorian Studies* 34 (1991): 159–78.

Russett, Cynthia Eagle, *Sexual Science: The Victorian Construction of Womanhood*. Cambridge, MA: Harvard University Press, 1989.

Schiebinger, Londa, *The Mind has no Sex? Women in the Origins of Modern Science*. Cambridge, MA: Harvard University Press, 1989.

Showalter, Elaine, *The Female Malady: Women, Madness, and English Culture, 1830–1980*. New York: Pantheon, 1985.

Stallybrass, Peter and Allon White, *The Politics and Poetics of Transgression*. Ithaca, NY: Cornell University Press, 1986.

Stevenson, Lionel, "Darwin and the Novel," *Nineteenth-Century Fiction* 15 (1960): 29–38.

Vance, Norman, "Heroic Myth and Women in Victorian Literature," *Yearbook of English Studies* 12 (1982): 169–85.

"Kingsley's Christian Manliness," *Theology* 78: 30–38.

The Sinews of the Spirit: The Ideal of Christian Manliness in Victorian Literature and Religious Thought. Cambridge University Press, 1985.

Williams, A. Susan, *The Rich Man and the Diseased Poor in Early Victorian Literature.* Atlantic Highlands, NJ: Humanities Press International, 1987.

Williams, Raymond, *Culture and Society 1780–1950.* New York: Harper, 1958.

CHAPTER 5

Young England: muscular Christianity and the politics of the body in "Tom Brown's Schooldays"

Dennis W. Allen

Perhaps the most significant body in *Tom Brown's Schooldays* is one that does not appear in the text itself: the body of Christ. As the word made flesh, the embodiment of the logos, Christ's materiality provides the doctrinal basis for Hughes's novel. Following F. D. Maurice, Hughes reads the incarnation as evidence of the value and sanctity of the human body and as the basis of human solidarity, the unity of all men as "brothers in Christ" (Vance 54–6). Thus Hughes's ideals of muscular Christianity, the interrelated development of the individual's physical and spiritual strength, and of Christian Socialism, the equality of all men, are grounded on the oxymoronic conjunctions of the material and the spiritual, and the individual and all mankind, in the incarnate Christ. Yet, even as it articulates Hughes's principles, *Tom Brown's Schooldays* reveals the ideological tensions inherent in his ideals. This essay will examine Hughes's attempts to resolve two of these tensions: the latent incompatibility of the values of physical prowess and spiritual aspiration that combine to form muscular Christianity and the conflict between the ideal of democratic equality that underlies Hughes's Christian Socialism and his implicit assumption of a middle-class perspective in the novel.

These ideological frictions are interrelated in Hughes's novel, the solution to one conflict providing the basis for another conceptual dilemma. Like Hughes's doctrine itself, the difficulties begin with a body or, rather, bodies: the ideologically charged bodies of Tom Brown and the boys of Rugby. The incommensurability of muscular Christianity's stress on both athleticism and spirituality first becomes apparent in Hughes's problems in depicting a body that adequately represents both values. Hughes resolves the difficulty through his appropriation of the Disraelian term "Young England," which is rewritten as the ideal of a corporate, bourgeois body, that, metonymically linked to the English land, is both material and transcendental. Yet this equation between the middle-class body and the national landscape raises its own difficulty, implying a belief in bourgeois hegemony that clashes with Hughes's Christian Socialist ideal of human equality. Finally, although Hughes resolves the latter dilemma by positing the bourgeoisie as capable of symbolically representing the working classes, it is this idea of representation itself that finally unbalances the text, uncovering the class biases of Hughes's muscular Christianity. As we shall see, if Hughes's text begins in the mysteries of Christ's body, it rests, in the end, on the representational politics of the body of the bourgeoisie.

I

Given Hughes's emphasis on the values of sport and physical fitness, and the continual descriptions of cricket matches, rugby scrummages, and foot races that fill *Tom Brown's Schooldays*, it is curious that the novel contains surprisingly little physical description of the characters. East, for example, is introduced as "a boy of just about [Tom's] own height and age" (66), while Flashman is presented as "about seventeen years old, and big and strong of his age" (131). Even Arthur, whose lack of physical stamina is a matter for concern throughout much of the narrative, is described only as "a slight pale boy, with large blue eyes and light fair hair" (158). With their tendency to substitute vague comparisons ("big ... [for] his age") for specific details, such descriptions subtly encode Hughes's concern with athletic competition, yet their overall effect is less to delineate the body than to erase it from Hughes's narrative, and it is difficult to reconcile this erasure with Hughes's overall glorification of athleticism. Why does Hughes choose to present a muscular Christianity without any muscles?

The answer is suggested by one of the exceptions to the principle, the scene in which Tom visits Arthur's sickbed. Finally allowed to enter Arthur's room, Tom is shocked by the effects of illness on his friend: "Arthur was lying on the sofa by the open window, through which the rays of the western sun stole gently, lighting up his white face and golden hair. Tom remembered a German picture of an angel which he knew; often had he thought how transparent and golden and spirit-like it was; and he shuddered to think how like it Arthur looked, and felt a shock as if his blood had stopped short, as he realised how near the other world his friend must have been to look like that" (223). Kneeling at Arthur's bedside, Tom's reflections move from his perceptions of Arthur's body to a vivid sense of his own, so that he feels "ashamed and half angry at his own red and brown face, and the bounding sense of health and power which filled every fibre of his body, and made every moment of mere living a joy to him" (223).

Tom's comparison here of himself and Arthur summarizes Hughes's use of the relation between the two boys to articulate his notion of muscular Christianity. Associated with physical prowess and high animal spirits, Tom has been given the responsibility of taking care of Arthur. This task is designed to imbue Tom with moral principles, to make him Christian as well as muscular, both through the responsibility of his role and through his association with the high-minded and sensitive Arthur. By the same token, the relationship is supposed to make Arthur more sturdy, to supplement his spiritual strength with physical vigor. The central scene in this interaction, the final blending of the muscular and the Christian, is the encounter at Arthur's sickbed. If Tom has previously succeeded in making Arthur physically fit enough that he will eventually survive this illness, Arthur uses the present opportunity to improve Tom morally, making him swear to stop cribbing his lessons.

Yet the incompatibility of these principles, the physical and the spiritual, is suggested by the fact that they must be materialized in *two* bodies. And the corporeal description employed in the passage continually stresses the differences between these bodies so that, as Arthur lays his "thin white hand" on Tom's "great brown fist," an ideological conflict at the heart of Hughes's philosophy becomes clear. Although muscular Christianity is explicitly predicated on an analogy between physical and spiritual vigor and invokes Victorian belief in the doctrine of *mens sana in corpore sano*, the interaction of a healthy mind and a healthy body (Haley 4), Hughes's novel is subtly animated by an alternate, ascetic doctrine of the incommensurability of the corporeal and the spiritual. Thus Arthur, who is "more spirit than body" (22) to begin with, is further etherealized by illness, becoming ever more "transparent and golden and spiritlike" as his body wastes away. As such, the novel implies that the muscular and the Christian are inherently opposed, and this opposition is materialized in different corporeal images: the sturdy athletic body versus the evanescent "house of the soul." Although, by the novel's end, Hughes presents characters who are psychologically capable of joining the physical and the spiritual (Pickering 42–3), the tension between the muscular and the Christian becomes evident in the inability of any individual to embody simultaneously the radically different somatotypes allied to these ideals. The incarnation of physicality, Tom can thus only evince his spirituality here as a psychologized process of dematerialization: through a sense of shock that feels "as if" his blood has stopped and through shame and anger about his body.

If, as Norman Vance has noted, the synthesis of the manly and the Christian in the writings of Hughes and Kingsley is inherently unstable, always threatening to revert to two separate concepts (6), it is precisely in images of the body that the tensions in Hughes's philosophy become evident in *Tom Brown's Schooldays*. As such, Hughes's erasure of the body seems, finally, designed to mystify these tensions, to elide the incompatibility of the ethereal and athletic bodies, of spirituality and athleticism themselves, by reducing the individual body to an abstract outline. Yet, as the existence of the passage itself suggests, the ideological difficulties inherent in Hughes's conception of muscular Christianity cannot be so easily dismissed, and the chapter concludes with a metaphoric displacement of the conflict. At the end of the episode, Arthur turns the talk to his home in Devonshire, with its "red bright earth, and the deep green combes, and the peat streams like cairn-gorm pebbles, and the wild moor with its high cloudy Tors for a giant background to the picture – till Tom got jealous, and stood up for the clear chalk streams, and the emerald water meadows and great elms and willows of the dear old Royal county" (235).

If the competing demands of the physical and the spiritual, embodied in the contrasting somatotypes of Arthur and Tom, are finally irreconcilable as corporeal ideals, Hughes's solution is to re-present the conflict as a debate about the merits of Tom's and Arthur's respective counties, to displace the conflicting terms onto the land. Thus Arthur is associated with mountains and moors, the landscape of the sublime, with its suggestions of the transcendental, while Tom is identified with a vaguely pastoral scene that implies the transformation of nature by human effort, that "subduing of the earth" (1) that Hughes continually insisted was one of the physical tasks of the muscular Christian. Taken by itself, this restatement serves merely to conceal the larger conflict since it duplicates the problems we have already noted: here nature is divided into two opposed landscapes, the spiritualized scene of sublimity and the land domesticated by physical labor, and neither Arthur nor Tom is identified with both. Yet the larger principle at work here, the identification of the boys and the land, displaces the conflict into terms that allow the opposition to be resolved. Hughes's equation of the corporeal and the geographic, evident in his tendency throughout the novel to substitute lyrical descriptions of the English countryside for physical descriptions of the characters, provides a solution to the difficulty of reconciling the material and the spiritual.

Despite the specific identification of Tom and Arthur with their individual counties, the novel as a whole insists on a larger link between English boys and the English land. This is nowhere clearer than in the novel's first chapter, where Hughes presents the intimate connection between a boy and his native landscape as an ideal that has been neglected. Noting that nowadays boys spend their vacations wandering across Europe, Hughes points out that they no longer know their "own lanes and woods and fields" (5). In his time, he continues, they "went over the fields and wolds and hills, again and again, till we made friends of them all" (5). Then, Hughes continues, the boys were closely identified with their counties, but now, in this age of "larger views," they are "young cosmopolites, belonging to all counties and no countries" (5). Much of the rest of the first chapter attempts to remedy this problem. If it is no longer always possible to link individual boys with their home counties, Hughes attempts instead to reunite English boys as a group with the English land, and he presents a description of the delights of the Berkshire landscape in a conscious attempt to interest "Young England" in the splendors of their native countryside.

This insistence on the connection between "England," the English countryside as a whole, and the boys who collectively constitute "Young England" uncovers a series of metonymies at the heart of Hughes's novel. As Hughes's concern with national identity suggests, "England" here is simultaneously a physical, geographical place and a patriotic construct, both the land itself and a larger national idea. This national idea is not only materialized in the land, however. Although the phrase "Young England" was coined by Disraeli in 1842 to refer to a small group of young aristocratic Conservative MPs and originally connoted a strain of romantic Toryism (specifically the doctrine that a responsible aristocracy and a paternalistic feudalism could protect the working classes from the evils of industrialization), Hughes redefines the term here to suit his own purposes. Applied to middle-class schoolboys, "Young England" suggests that the national idea is also incarnated in the bodies of the boys, who stand as a living embodiment of the nation.[1] Thus, as signifiers of the same signified ("England"), the land and the bodies of the boys themselves are interchangeable. This equivalence not only allows Hughes to substitute natural description for corporeal description but enables him to reconcile the opposition of the physical and the spiritual. If the individual bodies of Tom and Arthur reveal the disjunction of the material and the immaterial, the impossibility of representing the two in a single body, the idea of "Young England" is predicated on an interaction of the concrete and the abstract. Thus, like the land, the bodies of the boys take on a significance only when considered as materializations of an abstraction ("England"), while, conversely, "England" is an idea whose "reality" is assured by its incarnation in the landscapes and the bodies of the boys who compose it. Moreover, just as the landscapes of individual counties are conceptually consolidated as the (English) land, so the individual bodies of English boys are consolidated as "Young England," and, because this corporeal incarnation is corporate, Hughes elides the semiotic inadequacies of the individual body. If no single boy can corporeally manifest both physical prowess and the ethereal body of the ideal Christian, the corporate body of "Young England" is always simultaneously material and immaterial, flesh and ideal.

II

If the boys at Rugby constitute the corporate body of "Young England," this body is also a class body, the body of the bourgeoisie.[2] As the novel's epigraph, a quotation from *Rugby Magazine*, suggests: "As on the one hand it should ever be remembered that we are boys, and boys at school, so on the other hand we must bear in mind that we form a complete social body."[3] This "social body" is complete in more than one sense, for it is not simply a localized metaphoric body, the "society" formed by the boys at Rugby, but the materialized embodiment of "England" itself, a synecdoche that stands for the nation as a whole. As such, if the equivalence between this corporate body and the land works to reconcile the conflict of the physical and the spiritual, the same equation raises its own ideological difficulty. As Donald E. Hall demonstrates in his essay in this volume, the classless ideals of Christian Socialism often concealed a deeper belief in the class system and in bourgeois hegemony. The resulting conceptual dilemma is revealed in *Tom Brown's Schooldays* by the identification of the middle-class boys of Rugby with the English land.

Overtly, the work is animated by pronouncements against class division, articulating Hughes's Christian Socialist beliefs. Addressing the "young swells" who aspire to Parliament, Hughes urges them not to tour the country making speeches but rather to make friends with the working classes: "Let them be men of your own ages, mind, and ask them to your homes; introduce them to your wives and sisters, and get introduced to theirs; give them good dinners, and talk to them about what is really at the bottom of your hearts, and box, and run, and row with them, when you have a chance" (32). If Hughes's suggestions conclude with an emphasis on sports, this is because the body is implicitly posited here as a universal biological substratum beneath or behind the artificial distinctions of class. As such, class divisions are erased in athletic competition, where the bourgeoisie and the upper classes are revealed to be "of the same flesh and blood as ... Bill Smith the costermonger" (32). Not surprisingly, then, before Tom is sent to Rugby, Hughes stresses that Tom and his brother play with the village boys "without the idea of equality or inequality (except in wrestling, running, and climbing) ever entering their heads, as it doesn't till it's put there by Jack Nastys or fine ladies' maids" (44).

Arguing against the separation of classes and presenting the body, or at least the male athletic body, as democratic, as the sign of the commonality of all men, Hughes advocates a social ideal that transcends class barriers.[4] Yet, having presented the utopian vision of Tom at play with the village boys, Hughes unconsciously reverts in the next paragraph to the tacit assumption of social inequality that he has just rejected. Thus Hughes's rather left-handed defense of the village boys is that they are as manly and honest as "those in a higher rank" (44) so that Tom receives more harm from his "equals" at school than from his "village friends." Within the space of a page, then, Tom is implicitly inserted into the two conflicting social conceptions that underlie Hughes's text: the classless democracy of the athletic body and the hierarchical structure of the class system. Thus the village boys are simultaneously Tom's (physical) equals and his (social) inferiors. Generally, however, the conflict between Hughes's ideal of a classless society and his assumption of the validity of the class system is less obvious than this, played out indirectly on and through the landscape.

Although Hughes posits the athletic body as democratic, it is nonetheless striking that his vision of social harmony involves pitting these bodies *against* each other so that class tensions are symbolically reinscribed in the conflictual nature of sports. If such conflict is sometimes overt, as in boxing, it is more often implicit, articulated through the function of the land in sport. Because games and sports are extended against or over a "ground," this ground is often coded as the object of contention, either directly (in territorial games such as rugby) or indirectly (as the basis for comparative measurement of the competitors, as in foot races). Athletic competition, as Hughes was fully aware, is thus a form of symbolic warfare, a battle over land. War is, of course, Hughes's favorite metaphor, one that he relentlessly invokes to describe everything from sports themselves to internal conflict, but, for our purposes, the most significant use of the metaphor is Hughes's characterization of the relations between the boys at Rugby and the "louts," the townspeople and neighboring farmers, as a state of continual "warfare." If the boys' clashes with the louts are the closest Hughes comes to depicting class tensions openly in the novel, this "war," too, is a battle over land, over occupation or use of space, for the conflict centers on schoolboy traditions that allow trespassing and poaching. Because such traditions are implicitly predicated on a sense of the boys' deeper right to the land, they uncover additional implications of the equation of the boys at Rugby with the English land: the assumption that England is, finally, the possession of the bourgeoisie. As the incident with Farmer Thompson suggests, the larger issue of the validity of the class system is thus played out in the novel as a question of who "owns" England.

Returning from an expedition to collect wild birds' eggs, Tom, East, Arthur, and Martin cross a field owned by Thompson, whose poultry is subject to frequent depredations by the boys from Rugby. Flushing one of Thompson's guinea-hens out of a hedge, the boys give chase but are apprehended by Thompson and one of his shepherds just as Holmes and Diggs, two older boys, are passing. The ensuing debate aptly illustrates Hughes's conflicting attitudes

towards class difference. On the one hand, as Holmes later notes in a
lecture to the boys, school traditions that distinguish poaching from
ordinary theft are wrongly based on a belief in class privilege:
"There's nothing so mischievous as these school distinctions, which
jumble up right and wrong, and justify things in us for which poor
boys would be sent to prison" (204). Yet, on the other hand, this
argument is offset by Holmes's earlier remark to Thompson, "you
ought to be ashamed of yourself for leaving all that poultry about
with no one to watch it so near the School. You deserve to have it all
stolen. So if you choose to come up to the Doctor with them, I shall
go with you and tell him what I think of it" (203). Aptly, this
remark leads Farmer Thompson to take Holmes for one of the
masters, for it is grounded in a sense of class mastery: not only in
Holmes's reversion under the pressure of the situation to a defense of
the boys that is based more on class solidarity than on the facts of the
situation, but also in the implicit assumption that everyone involved
is subject to the authority of Dr. Arnold. And, however sophistical
the argument, Thompson never challenges Holmes's assertion that,
in effect, the boys have an implicit right to his unguarded property.
Tom and company finally get off by paying three shillings. Holmes's
ability to argue both sides of the issue here is not idiosyncratic but
rather an apt condensation of an ambivalence at the heart of the
novel about competing doctrines of human equality and the class
system. Throughout the narrative, Hughes simultaneously insists on
a universal morality beyond social class and demonstrates a nostalgic identification with the boys that implicitly validates the sense of
class privilege animating such escapades. In this instance, Hughes's
Christian Socialist belief in democratic equality is articulated
through the universal applicability of the moral principle that theft
is wrong and through a parallel juridical principle that the law
should apply equally to everyone, as Holmes's reference to prison
suggests. These ethical and legal doctrines are juxtaposed, however,
with the boys' sense of class privilege, which must finally be understood here as a particular conception of the land and of property.
What Holmes's defense of the boys implies – and what is implicit in
Hughes's conception of the boys as England itself – is their intrinsic
right to "England," a right that transcends Thompson's appeal to
the notion of private property. Ideologically, since the boys are
symbolically equivalent to the land, they cannot really be said to
trespass, and it is apt that, at Tom's first view of Rugby, he sees the

boys standing by the gates "looking as if the town belonged to them" (65). By the same token, the boys' sense of a deeper right to Farmer Thompson's poultry, a sense that Hughes both contradicts and supports, is merely an extension of the same doctrine: the assumption that, because it is ideologically coextensive with the nation, the bourgeoisie can appropriate the fruits of the land and the products of working-class labor.

Despite Hughes's explicit presentation of the Christian Socialist ideal of a classless society, then, the novel implicitly assumes not only the validity of the class system but also the hegemony of the middle classes, a hegemony based on the symbolic equivalence of the land, of England, and the bourgeoisie. Yet the resulting ideological conflict, Hughes's simultaneous insistence on human equality and on social hierarchy, is resolved by the very symbolic equation that generates the conflict. The identification between the boys at Rugby and England itself that creates the problem also means that, because the boys incarnate England, they can actually *represent* it. As such, issues of class difference and dramas of class conflict can be played out and resolved among the boys themselves. This is nowhere clearer than in the chapter on "The War of Independence," which details the younger boys' rebellion against the practice of fagging.

Generally, Hughes approves of fagging, the tradition by which the younger boys are required to perform chores for boys in the sixth form. Several years after Tom's arrival at Rugby, however, the praepostors come to be dominated by smaller boys, promoted for cleverness, who cannot keep order, or else "big fellows of the wrong sort," whose "friendships and tastes had a downward tendency" (123). The result is a period of "chaos," during which the fifth form boys "usurp power" and fag the younger boys although their "only right over them stood in their bodily powers" (123). As a result, Hughes notes, the strong feeling of "fellowship" in the house dissolves, and the house breaks up into factions. In response to this "tyranny," Tom and East initiate a "revolution," persuading most of the younger boys not to fag for the fifth form, and, after a period of "war," the younger boys prevail. If the novel as a whole mystifies the relations of class domination on which the privilege of the boys at Rugby is implicitly based, such relations surface and are symbolically resolved here. By casting the younger boys in the roles of an oppressed working class, Hughes is able to reconcile his beliefs in human equality and in the hierarchy of the class system, adumbrating a conception of democratic equality that is, finally, compatible with a hierarchical social structure.[5]

What is at stake here is the boys' insistence on the right to control their own bodies. This control is overtly centered on the issue of labor power, on, for example, Tom's refusal to fetch Flashman's hat, but the deeper principle is the contemporary notion of the body and labor as property. As Eric Cheyfitz has demonstrated, the equation goes back to Locke, who finds the basis for property in the individual body. Thus, each man "has a property in his own person," which includes his capacity for labor, and it is labor that creates additional property (Cheyfitz 54).[6] As such, the rebellion is ultimately based on the boys' insistence on the right to the possession and disposition of their bodies and labor as (private) property in contrast to the older boys' assumption, based on their position in the school hierarchy, of an overriding "right" to fag the younger boys. Given the underlying similarity of this "war" to the boys' "warfare" with the louts, it is not surprising that the rebellion is played out in spatial terms, both literally and symbolically. The older boys' attempts to quell the rebellion involve two parallel violations of what is "proper" to the fags, two forms of "trespassing": forced entry into the private spaces where the younger boys have barricaded themselves and acts of violence imposed on the bodies (the "property") of the younger boys. Thus the rebellion begins when Tom and East refuse to answer Flashman's call for a fag and bolt the door of their study, inciting Flashman to a series of attempts to break the door down, and the war continues through a period of "constant chasings, and sieges and lickings of all sorts" (129). When the fifth form boys finally give up such attempts at domination and accede to the "revolution," they implicitly admit the equality of all the boys in certain fundamental rights of self-possession and self-determination, rights to the disposition of their bodies as property.

In a sense, then, the "War of Independence" can be seen as an elucidation of Farmer Thompson's perspective: an insistence on a right to private property based on a sense of the intrinsic democratic equality of all individuals, a perspective that is only implicit in the poaching incident itself. Yet Hughes is not really contradicting himself by arguing for a pure democracy of equal individuals here; rather, this notion of individual equality is inserted within a larger hierarchical structure. If the revolution is presented under the seemingly paradoxical aegis of "law and order" (126), this is because Hughes is not questioning hierarchy itself or fagging as a system of forced labor. Instead, he is concerned to define the acceptable limits of domination (Worth 29). As the equation of the fags' rebellion with the American War of Independence suggests, the fifth form boys' attempt to fag the younger boys is "tyrannical," not because fagging is wrong but because the fifth form has exceeded the legally determined limits of its power. The fifth form doubly violates the juridical structure of Rugby, both by usurping fagging privileges and by disrupting the school's chain of command since, unlike the praepostors, who must answer to Dr. Arnold, the fifth form boys need not justify their actions to any higher authority. As Tom "indignantly" notes, they are "responsible to nobody" (125). The juridical and hierarchical structures of the school are finally restored when the "better fellows of the fifth" admit the injustice of their behavior and give up the attempt to fag the younger boys. And the incident as a whole thus allows Hughes to insist that the fundamental legal equality between the older and younger boys is nonetheless contained within and compatible with the larger structures that constitute Rugby.

Transcoding interclass questions of equality and hierarchy into the intraclass conflicts of the boys at Rugby, Hughes is thus able to reconcile the two concepts because, within the school hierarchy, the "law" posits both the juridical sameness of the boys (and hence certain limited rights of corporeal self-determination) and their differences (in a hierarchical structure organizing the distribution of labor, power, and responsibility). Moreover, such differences are based on a mutable characteristic – age. Thus the interplay of sameness and difference, of equality and hierarchy, is reinforced by the fact that, in time, the fags will become praepostors, that each individual boy will eventually occupy all the positions in the hierarchy.[7]

Finally, this section of the novel reconciles the ideological conflict between the premises of Christian Socialism and Hughes's belief in the class system by reconceptualizing the problem. If the dilemma arises from positing the body as the basis of democratic equality in contradistinction to the hierarchical structures of society, Hughes inverts those assumptions in this section of the novel. Here, the difficulty lies in the fact that bodies are unequal. The fifth form boys' assertion of their "right" to fag is, finally, based on their greater physical size and strength rather than on the rules of the school, and it is the social system of Rugby, in the form of those rules and in its assumptions about the fundamental juridical sameness of the boys, that asserts the principle of human equality. Thus, if the battles with the "louts" in the novel usually end in an ideological stalemate for Hughes, in a simultaneous insistence on and denial of bourgeois hegemony, this stalemate is resolved by the intraclass struggles of the boys at Rugby, which allow Hughes to reconcile the doctrines of Christian Socialism with the class system.[8]

III

Hughes's conceptual dilemmas and their resolutions are aptly summarized by the concept that links contemporary ideals of the body and the land: the notion of work. The idea is introduced in Arthur's description of his sickbed vision, in which a "mighty spirit" shows him a great river that represents death. On the other bank, Arthur sees multitudes, who all "work at some great work," and he then sees the "myriads on this side" who are also laboring. Among the hundreds of people he knows, in fact, are Tom and himself "doing ever so little a piece of the great work" (231). The idea is expanded and elucidated near the novel's end when Tom, preparing to leave Rugby, discusses the future with one of the masters. Tom is impatient to be "at work in the world," which he defines as making one's living and "doing some real good" (265). As the master notes, Tom is conflating two different ideas here: "You may be getting a very good living in a profession, and yet doing no good at all in the world, but quite the contrary, at the same time. Keep the latter before you as your one object, and you will be right, whether you make a living or not; but if you dwell on the other, you'll very likely drop into mere money-making, and let the world take care of itself for good or evil" (266). The essence of work, then, is not the pursuit of Mammon but for each individual to attempt to make things "a little better."

This vision serves as a final means of reconciling the contradictions of Hughes's text. If Hughes conceives of work as an inherently spiritual task, this task must nonetheless be accomplished on the material plane. Thus the concept of work reconciles the dichotomy of the physical and the metaphysical that haunts the text. Moreover, since "every man may do some honest work in his own corner" of the world (266), the idea of work is inherently democratic, a universal, equalizing vision: working, one joins with the laboring multitude, and the essence of work is that it is unselfish. Moreover, if the notion of work is democratic because everyone should work, this ideal is reconciled to the class system through the assumption of a class division of labor. Tom's work, the master insists, is properly at Oxford and not, as Tom initially argues, out in the world. Tom can best serve God by receiving the education appropriate to his station.

Yet the scene raises a lingering difficulty, an unbalancing of Hughes's resolution of the novel's ideological conflicts. Significantly, Tom's discussion with the master takes place over tea at the master's house, where, it transpires, the servants have taken advantage of the master's absence at the cricket match to sneak off to the country dances in the close. Tom, of course, proves equal to the situation, finding a way into the locked house and, "by a sort of instinct," discovering all the materials necessary to prepare a tea better than any that "had appeared there probably during the reign of his tutor" (264). Hughes's vision of the multitudes at work, then, is presented with a peculiar twist, for the vision is solely (and doubly) represented by the bourgeoisie, who, in the absence of the "truant servants," perform both the physical and the intellectual labor necessary.

The passage is disturbing, not simply because Hughes suggests that the bourgeoisie could do a better job at the work of their servants if they chose, but also because the episode uncovers a latent insistence on bourgeois hegemony, an insistence articulated through Hughes's assumption of the superior fitness of the bourgeoisie to illustrate his beliefs. Just as the boys at Rugby can play out and resolve class tensions because, as England, they can represent all of England, both the bourgeoisie and the lower classes, so here the middle classes are identified with and represent *all* work. Positing the bourgeoisie as the signifier of the universal (England, work), Hughes thus models novelistic representation on contemporary conceptions of political representation. Just as his address to the "young swells" implicitly assumes that the bourgeoisie and the upper classes will politically represent the working class, so Hughes assumes the validity of a parallel process whereby the middle classes can *symbolically* represent the lower classes. As such, the working class is finally subsumed in a representational process in which they have no "say" and in which their potential for self-representation is delegated by

Hughes to the boys at Rugby: through the attribution of working-class activities (such as poaching) to the boys and through the fags' symbolic appropriation of the very feature that defines the working classes – work itself. The representational domination of the upper classes is also evident in Hughes's own attempts to "stand up for the underdog" by standing in for the underdog, by positioning himself as part of the masses. The clearest instance of this tendency, aptly enough, is Hughes's apostrophe to the "young swells" during his discussion of parliamentary representation. You try to "make us think, through newspaper reports, that you are even as we of the working classes," Hughes notes, concluding that "we 'ain't so green,'" (32). Even as he denies the similarity of the classes and interrogates the validity of both political and journalistic represen-tation, Hughes nonetheless enacts an identical representational process by speaking for the masses as one of the masses.

As such, Hughes's class perspective transcends the rather obvious fact that the few "louts" who enter the narrative are a bourgeois construction of working-class experience. This construction itself is submitted to an additional process of symbolic co-optation so that it is not, finally, Farmer Thompson who represents the masses but middle-class characters like East, who "was always a people's man" (265), or Hughes himself acting as the voice of the working class. Thus, if class dominance is balanced within the novel by an insist-ence on the Christian Socialist doctrine of human equality, the text itself reasserts such dominance in the very logic of its representa-tional techniques. Yet this representational privileging of the bour-geoisie cannot be seen as a simple contamination of Hughes's relig-ious doctrine by class ideology. Rather, it is finally inherent in the very logic of muscular Christianity itself. To understand this logic, we must return briefly to the status of the body in muscular Chris-tianity.

We can see that the emphasis on physical vigor in muscular Christianity is also an act of co-optation, the ideological annexation by the middle classes of the body itself, which had formerly been associated, as Regenia Gagnier notes, with the working classes (56–7). Yet, despite Hughes's stress on sports and fighting, the body in *Tom Brown's Schooldays* is less the concrete material body than the body as sign, a signifier of something beyond itself: as an emblem of the spiritual (in the case of muscular Christianity *per se*) or as evidence of the ontological and hence moral or even juridical commonality of all men (as in the case of Christian Socialism). And it is for this reason, finally, that the body is both present and absent in the novel. Because the semiotics of the body are more important than its actual physical existence, Hughes continually enacts what might be called a "semiotic presentation" of the bodies of the boys at Rugby, which are everywhere suggested and rarely actually described, so that the stress falls finally on the meanings of the body rather than on the body itself.

This distinction is significant precisely because it uncovers a fundamental fissure in class relations to the body, a fissure resulting, as Elaine Scarry has demonstrated, from nineteenth-century conceptions of the relation of the body to production. Analyzing Marx, Scarry identifies the belief that the creation of artifacts is an extension of the human body into the made world and the concomitant conclusion that, projected out onto the world, the human becomes disembodied (244). As Marx realized, however, this process of disembodiment is not universal, and Scarry goes on to note how, under capitalism, the two aspects of this process are split so that the working class is reduced, in a very real way, to the laboring body that creates the artifacts, while the capitalist, distanced from the laboring body by his association with a process of abstraction (the transformation of the object into a commodity, and of the commodity into money, and of money into capital), becomes disembodied, his sentient relation to the world mediated by his material possessions (259–63).

Unlike the working class, then, for whom bodily experience would be intensely real, the aches and pains of a hard day's work, the bourgeoisie, ideologically divorced from the body by the capitalist economic system, is free to see the body as something other than itself. As a result, the body in *Tom Brown's Schooldays*, as in muscular Christianity, is a bourgeois conception, a semiotic body that articulates the transcendental. It is because this body is, in effect, dematerialized that its semiotic function can be transferred so easily in Hughes's text to equally dematerialized conceptions of the land or of "work." Thus the land in *Tom Brown's Schooldays* is not an actual site of agricultural labor but is politically abstracted into "England" and aesthetically abstracted into Hughes's nostalgic, lyricized landscape descriptions just as the novel's ideal of work transcends the real conditions of production in a vision of work as a spiritual duty. Moreover, Hughes is able to co-opt the very concepts of the body and work associated with the working classes precisely because, identified with unmeaning materiality, the working class cannot represent itself, either in politics or in literature, while the bourgeoisie, associated with the notion of representation, becomes the universal signifier, which must of necessity stand in for the working class. Such assumptions are, finally, the basis of Victorian middle-class paternalism, the notion that the bourgeois male represents all men. And the same logic informs Hughes's conception of muscular Christianity itself. Identified with the semiotic body, Hughes's muscular Christian is, ultimately, a middle-class Christian who stands as the signifier of a universal spiritual brotherhood. As such, the novel's stress on bourgeois hegemony is evident not only in the content of the work, and in the boys' triumphant battles with the "louts," but it is also embedded in the very logic of representation that underlies the political, aesthetic, and religious philosophies that shape, and overdetermine, the politics of the text. Unlike the body of Christ, which is both material and spiritual, Tom Brown's body enters a representational process, signifying the latter through the former, and it is this process that dooms, even as it is used to articulate, Hughes's doctrine of human equality.

NOTES

1 For Disraeli's use of the term, see Bradford 118–31. While Hughes's nostalgia for England's rural past bears some affinity to the ideals of Disraeli's "Young England" movement, his use of the phrase looks ahead, anticipating turn-of-the-century readings of national geography as a projection of the male body. For a trenchant analysis of the "topography of masculinity" in America during the 1890s, see Seltzer 140–58.
2 Although Hughes is traditionally associated with the country gentry, an association that is also established for Tom Brown in the opening chapters of the novel, I agree with Ian Watson that the work as a whole reflects the contemporary consolidation of the squirearchy and the industrial bourgeoisie into a unified "middle class" (116–29). Significantly, this minor redefinition of class boundaries and the resulting construction of a generalized "bourgeois" class identity was effected in part by Rugby itself, which, under Dr. Arnold in the 1830s, positioned itself as a "middle class" school (in contrast to Eton and Harrow) by discouraging enrollment by the aristocracy and the lower classes (Honey 15). Note that the novel assumes this collective identity. Once Tom arrives at Rugby, there is virtually no mention of the (class) backgrounds of individual boys.

3 J. R. de S. Honey has identified the schoolboy author of the 1835 article from which this quotation is drawn as A. P. Stanley, who would later act as Dr. Arnold's biographer (17).

4 The gender inflection of Hughes's doctrine, his failure to include women as subjects in this vision of class harmony, is not accidental or inadvertent. As Donald E. Hall notes in "Muscular Anxiety," *Tom Brown's Schooldays* reflects the gender anxiety of many mid-Victorian men in the face of the feminist movement. Hughes's response to this anxiety, Hall argues, is not simply to create an all-male utopia at Rugby, but also to "colonize the feminine" (11), to appropriate traditionally "feminine" characteristics such as "tenderness" for his male characters so that women are finally subsumed in a vision of male "gender omnipotence" (18). As Laura Fasick suggests in an essay on Kingsley included in this volume, such appropriations do not undermine (in fact, they depend on) a rigid ideology of gender difference.

5 The equation between fags and the working classes did not escape contemporary schoolboys. See Gathorne-Hardy 120.

6 The most obvious contemporary statement of this notion can be found in *Grundrisse*, the notebooks Marx was compiling at the same time that Hughes was writing *Tom Brown's Schooldays*. For Marx, the notion of the body and labor power as property are the defining characteristics of the worker under capitalism (471–514; see especially 498–502).

7 This principle was evident to Hughes's contemporaries, who often argued that the process trained the boys for their eventual role as leaders of society (Chandos 99, Gathorne-Hardy 120–21, Honey 218, Gagnier 178, Quigley 48). Although the movement through the system was based in part on merit, whether academic or athletic, promotion to positions of higher authority within the school hierarchy was largely automatic.

8 As Watson has demonstrated, Hughes's simultaneous insistence on social hierarchy and on individual achievement is another reflection of the contemporary alignment of the residual feudal values of the country gentry with the emerging ideology of industrial capitalism (123).

WORKS CITED

Bradford, Sarah, *Disraeli*. New York: Stein and Day, 1983.

Chandos, John, *Boys Together: English Public Schools 1800–1864*. New Haven: Yale University Press, 1984.

Cheyfitz, Eric, *The Poetics of Imperialism: Translation and Colonization from The Tempest to Tarzan*. New York: Oxford University Press, 1991.

Gagnier, Regenia, *Subjectivities: A History of Self-Representation in Britain, 1832–1920*. New York: Oxford University Press, 1991.

Gathorne-Hardy, Jonathan, *The Old School Tie: The Phenomenon of the English Public School*. New York: Viking, 1978.

Haley, Bruce, *The Healthy Body and Victorian Culture*. Cambridge, MA: Harvard University Press, 1978.

Hall, Donald E., "Muscular Anxiety: Degradation and Appropriation in *Tom Brown's Schooldays*," *Victorian Literature and Culture*. Forthcoming.

Honey, J. R. de S., *Tom Brown's Universe: The Development of English Public Schools in the Nineteenth Century*. New York: Quadrangle, 1977.

Hughes, Thomas, *Tom Brown's Schooldays* (1857). New York: Dutton, 1906.

Marx, Karl, *Grundrisse: Foundations of the Critique of Political Economy*, tr. Martin Nicolaus. New York: Vintage, 1973.

Pickering, Samuel, "The 'Race of Real Children' and Beyond in *Tom Brown's Schooldays*," *Arnoldian* 11.2 (1984): 37–46.

Quigley, Isabel, *The Heirs of Tom Brown: The English School Story*. London: Chatto & Windus, 1982.

Scarry, Elaine, *The Body in Pain: The Making and Unmaking of the World*. New York: Oxford University Press, 1985.

Seltzer, Mark, "The Love-Master," in *Engendering Men: The Question of Male Feminist Criticism*, eds. Joseph A. Boone and Michael Cadden. New York: Routledge, 1990, pp. 140–58.

Vance, Norman, *The Sinews of the Spirit: The Ideal of Christian Manliness in Victorian Literature and Religious Thought*. Cambridge University Press, 1985.

Watson, Ian, "Victorian England, Colonialism and the Ideology of *Tom Brown's Schooldays*," *Zeitschrift für Anglistik und Amerikanistik* 22 (1981): 116–29.

Worth, George, *Thomas Hughes*. Boston: Twayne, 1984.

CHAPTER 6

Muscular spirituality in George MacDonald's Curdie books

John Pennington

"One thing more ... have you courage as well as faith?"
The Princess and Curdie

In *Secret Gardens*, Humphrey Carpenter writes that "the Christian Socialists, whose doctrinal liberalism was combined with some rather vague attempts at social reform, played no small part in the creation of more than one of the outstanding children's books that were about to appear" (6). Carpenter is referring primarily to Thomas Hughes's *Tom Brown's Schooldays* (1857) and Charles Kingsley's *The Water Babies* (1863). No less an authority on the Victorian age, Richard Altick claims of the Christian Socialists: "Like their inspirer, Coleridge, they were convinced that the Church had an obligation to initiate and guide social action, even so far as to defend the workers against capitalistic exploitation" (142). With Kingsley's reforming zeal and Hughes's rough-and-tumble, black-eyed spirituality, this brand of Christian Socialism was dubbed "muscular Christianity," a virile, strong-armed Christianity, a man's religion, so to speak, that melded courage and faith, spirit and body. Though Kingsley himself dismissed the term "muscular Christianity," Carpenter posits that these men "actually ... seem to have been rather flattered by it" (31).

A central figure in the Christian Socialist movement was F. D. Maurice, a friend of and influence on Kingsley, Hughes, and William Morris. Maurice felt universality was fundamental to Christianity: people should exist in cooperation, in a universal community centered on God. Maurice's "social theology" rested on the assumptions that humans "cannot be content with a spiritual society that is not universal, or with a universal society that is not spiritual" and that such "a universal spiritual society ultimately implied a redistribution of wealth" (Prickett, *Romanticism and Relig-*

ion 142). As Donald E. Hall points out in his essay in this volume,
Maurice, "theologian and social philosopher" and founder of the
Christian Socialist weekly *Politics for the People*, can be categorized as
a muscular Christian because his socialist reforming spirit is captured in "the physicality of some of ... [his] metaphors ... [which]
give[s] his work a 'sinewy' quality" (45). In 1853 Maurice was
kicked out of King's College for preaching, in part, that eternal
punishment was mere superstition. Another man of God was forced
from his pulpit that year for preaching that the heathen would be
welcomed into the Kingdom of God – and for subscribing to
German theology. That man was George MacDonald, Scottish
poet, preacher, novelist, fantasist, fairy tale writer, and friend and
disciple of Maurice. In fact, Maurice wanted to collaborate with
MacDonald on a spiritual work, he writes in a letter to MacDonald,
"that would cheer men's hearts and kindle their hopes of something
better to come" (Greville MacDonald 399).

Maurice, Kingsley, Hughes, and MacDonald all fought for the
retention of Christian values in a rapidly changing industrial world.
As Jerome Buckley suggests in *The Victorian Temper*, Kingsley, as
spokesman for muscular Christianity,

saw the tangible evils of the industrial system and the terrible consequences
to body and soul of a determined Mammon-worship; yet he saw also that
there could be no retreat from an age of railroads and steam-ploughs and
electric telegraphs. He, therefore, chose to fight materialism by accepting
matter itself and by arming its agents with moral and spiritual purpose.
(123)

Thus Kingsley armed himself for a spiritual fight, blending spirituality with the material world. "Man, endowed with strength and
natural affections and the capacity to explore and understand the
natural and moral order," writes Norman Vance of Kingsley's
Christian activism, "should put all these gifts to work in the service
of his brother man and God, as patriot or social reformer or crusad-
ing doctor" (105). But as Vance indicates, there are varieties of such
muscular activism; Kingsley reflects one kind, MacDonald another.
In his full-length fairy tales, *The Princess and the Goblin* (1872) and
The Princess and Curdie (1883), MacDonald defines his muscular
Christian activism. Though labeling MacDonald a strict muscular
Christian may misrepresent the man, we can see how he revised,
adapted, critiqued – how he "poeticized" – much of this movement
in his fairy tales directed towards children. MacDonald's brand of

muscular spirituality can best be called a version of "moral man-liness" (Vance 10), but it does indeed have the power, strength, and conviction of the movement headed by Kingsley and Hughes.

MacDonald advocates a spiritual muscularity, one that requires strength of spirit rather than strength of body. This is an important distinction, for MacDonald was also an admirer of Darwin, making him in a sense a Christian Darwinist, but of a particular sort. In *George MacDonald and His Wife* (1924), Greville MacDonald writes that his "father's sense and understanding of ethical Evolution is implied throughout his writings, and must have discovered itself in quite early days long before he knew anything of the *Descent of Man* or *The Origin of Species*" (217). In her essay in this volume, Laura Fasick argues that Kingsley's "eagerness to find moral significance in natural patterns" led him to embrace both "moral earnestness and scientific enthusiasm" (91). Like Kingsley, MacDonald was able to meld evolution with Christianity, and we see this most profoundly in the Curdie books. Though many Victorians were depressed by Darwin's exposure of the survival of the fittest and accidental evolution, MacDonald found it an apt metaphor for his Christian faith: people evolve or devolve according to faith; the strongest do survive, but they are the spiritually strong, not neces-sarily the strong in body.

Thus the Curdie books are muscularly Christian in a profoundly spiritual sense. Yet MacDonald was also a social commentator, arguing for the inherent goodness of all people, whether rich or poor, but condemning the industrial age for creating two nations, one centered on money, the other on displacement for lack of money. In *At the Back of the North Wind* (1872), for example, he takes Dickensian swipes at capitalism that crushes the weak and underpri-vileged. Jack Zipes contends that MacDonald's fairy tales "nur-tured his religious mysticism and fundamental beliefs in the dignity of men and women whose mutual needs and talents could only be developed in a community that was not based on exploitation and profit-making" (*Fairy Tales and the Art of Subversion* 103). MacDonald actively condemns Social Darwinism for its peculiar survival of the fittest theology: the strong and privileged survive and flourish; the poor do not. MacDonald Christianizes Darwinism, and in doing so, truly "socializes" it. Darwinism therefore becomes the basis for an evolved ethical system that is positive and constructive; at the same time Darwinism is condemned when it is appropriated for use in a materialistic, capitalistic system that is morally remiss and destructive. MacDonald denounces greed and self-interest, especially where capitalism invades organized religion and erodes its spiritual foundation by placing the excessive weight of materialism on it. Stephen Prickett writes in *Romanticism and Religion*, "The England of capitalism and commerce seemed to MacDonald one of the [most] hideous moral distortions that [the] world had known" (242). The Curdie books contain a complex poetics of evolution and spirituality: the strong survive only if spirit – love of Christ and neighbor – is stronger than the desire to love Mammon.

There is yet another factor: MacDonald's brand of muscular spirituality and Darwinism grew out of his personal life. Mac-Donald's family inherited a susceptibility to tuberculosis, and his father, two brothers, and four of his eleven children succumbed to the disease. MacDonald fought the disease throughout his life, continually plagued by his weak lungs. He writes in one letter to his father in 1850 about his tubercular attacks: "But I am not unhappy about it ... Perhaps such attacks might come and go, and one yet *wrastle on* for some years. But I have no *idol of chance*, as many young Christians seem to have. All will be well with me" (Greville Mac-Donald 147). Just as David Rosen argues, in his essay in this volume, that Kingsley "himself became a text for his manly ideal" (18), the same claim can be made about MacDonald. It is interesting to speculate that MacDonald revises Darwin and muscular Christianity to account for his own physical and spiritual condition. That he writes in the fairy-tale mode also has implications: children are not "strong," not the fittest in body, but they can evolve into the strongest spiritual beings and do indeed survive in a competitive world. The body-weak, spirit-strong Diamond in *At the Back of the North Wind* campaigns for both spiritual and social change; he actively becomes the embodiment of MacDonald's muscular spirituality. *The Princess and the Goblin* and *The Princess and Curdie* follow in the *North Wind* tradition, for these texts depict two children – one male, one female – who fight the good fight for Christianity. In a sense, MacDonald "feminizes" muscular Christianity to reflect his own less-than-muscular physical state; he balances his conceptions of the masculine, active body with the feminine, more spiritual body to create a composite hero in Curdie and Irene.

The Princess and the Goblin is often considered MacDonald's finest work directed at children. G. K. Chesterton, in his introduction to

Greville MacDonald's *George MacDonald and his Wife*, claims that *Goblin*, "of all the stories I have read, including even all of the novels of the same novelist ... remains the most real, the most realistic, in the exact sense of the phrase the most like life" (9). Chesterton contends that the fairy tale "made a difference to my whole existence ... a vision of things which even so real a revolution as change of religious allegiance has substantially only crowned and confirmed" (9). Certainly C. S. Lewis, "baptized" by MacDonald's *Phantastes*, would understand Chesterton's exuberant claim. But Chesterton's assessment of *Goblin* may at first glance seem contradictory: how can a Grimm-inspired original fairy tale be considered realistic? The answer resides in reading the comment figuratively, emphasizing the key words "crowned" and "confirmed." Chesterton finds a religious spirituality that is itself realistic, or perhaps a spirituality in which he finds truth and emotional realism. The religious strength of *Goblin* pervades the entire fairy tale without ever becoming didactic. Though the word "God" never appears in the tale, we can agree with Carpenter, who suggests that "MacDonald uses the stuff of folklore to construct a parable about the Christian universe ... Really, *The Princess and the Goblin* is as powerful a piece of religious teaching as ever came the way of a Sunday School child" (83).

MacDonald indeed constructs this parable powerfully, using many of the tenets of muscular Christianity to drive home his spiritual point concerning muscular faith. Hints of spiritual devolution are clear in the first chapter: the goblins, living in the hollows of the mountains, have metamorphosed into such creatures that "there was no invention ... of the most lawless imagination expressed by pen or pencil, that could surpass the extravagance of their appearance." Yet MacDonald emphasizes that these creatures have devolved from humans:

The goblins themselves were not so far removed from the human as such a description might imply. And as they grew misshapen in body they had grown in knowledge and cleverness, and now were able to do things no mortal could see the possibility of. But as they grew in cunning, they grew in mischief, and their great delight was in every way they could think of to annoy people who lived in the open-air storey above them. (10)

Goblins, we find out, are physically strong, but spiritually weak; thus, MacDonald creates a complex muscular and Christian poetics: pure "masculine strength" is negative unless complemented and

tempered by a "feminine spiritual" agent. It is appropriate that
Thomas Hughes argues in *The Manliness of Christ* (1879) that a
complete muscular Christian requires "self-sacrifice for the welfare
of another" (19) and "tenderness, and thoughtfulness for others"
(17–18), for MacDonald, strong in spirit and weak in body, stresses
just such a vision of muscularity and Christianity.

The goblins are pitted against the king; their goal is to kidnap the
young Princess Irene and force her to marry Prince Harelip. The
battle lines are then drawn: the spiritually devoid, physically strong
goblins versus the two children – Irene and the miner Curdie – who
must transform into muscularly equipped Christians in order to win
this battle by using both their strength and faith. Irene and Curdie
become figurative and literal Christian soldiers.

MacDonald develops two parallel stories which reflect the convergence of the spiritual and the physical – Irene's spiritual development and Curdie's physical and more frustrated spiritual development. The teacher of these children is the mystical Grandmother
who weaves her spiritual threads on her spinning wheel. Irene
discovers this spiritual mentor by "losing" herself in her home and
finding the Grandmother in the attic. Says the Grandmother to
Irene: "But you would have found me sooner if you hadn't come to
think I was a dream" (77). A key question the Grandmother asks the
girl "is whether you will believe I am anywhere – whether you will
believe I am anything but a dream" (82). The simplicity of Mac-
Donald's lesson here depicts the artistry of the fairy tale: the Grandmother is talking about belief and faith in God, but she uses
accommodation to make her point: she is a concrete incarnation of
belief and faith. An important symbol suggesting this function is the
Grandmother's ring, which spins an invisible thread; this ring is, in a
sense, Irene's guardian when the Grandmother is not physically
present. "The thread is too fine for you to see it. You can only feel it"
(103), teaches the Grandmother to Irene. "But, remember, it may
seem to you a very roundabout way indeed, and you must not doubt
the thread" (104). Irene's lesson revolves around the simple concept
that seeing or touching is not necessarily believing, that the spiritual
should, and must, have dominance over the material. Again we see
MacDonald's brand of muscular spirituality in action, for the
Grandmother, a spiritually powerful entity, teaches Irene, a
physically weak child, the power of faith.

Irene is easily convinced, but Curdie presents a greater challenge.

As a miner, Curdie is of the earth, close to matter, while Irene lives above in more spiritual air. Thus it is important that MacDonald have Curdie rise above his earthiness, separating himself from the spiritually void goblins. Curdie is a hard-working boy, a model son, but he has not yet developed his faith. The fairy tale, then, traces his development, which continues in *The Princess and Curdie*. While Irene converses with the ethereal Grandmother, Curdie labors in the mine and overhears the goblins' plot to steal Irene. While Irene has a spiritual thread to guide her, Curdie uses a commonplace ball of string to navigate the goblins' caverns and thwart their sinister designs. Here, thread versus string can be read as spirit versus body. When Irene follows her thread and finds Curdie imprisoned by the goblins, she tries to persuade him to follow her as she follows the invisible, spiritual thread. "What nonsense the child talks," complains Curdie. "I can't understand it" (141). And when Curdie is presented to the Grandmother by Irene, he sees only the attic, nothing more. The Grandmother tells Irene: "People must believe what they can, and those who believe more must not be hard upon those who believe less – I doubt if you would have believed it all yourself if you hadn't seen some of it" (150). She goes on: "You must give him time . . . and you must be content not to be believed for a while. It is very hard to bear; but I have had to bear it, and shall have to bear it many a time yet" (151). Implicit here is the fact that Irene must bear part of the weight of Curdie's spiritual trials.

The climax of the story rests on two processes: the physical defeat of the goblins and the spiritual victory that Curdie wins over himself. Repeatedly, MacDonald fuses the physical and the spiritual in the fairy tale. After Curdie is shot in the leg by the king's men, his spirit and faith heal as his body heals, suggesting that his physical wound is symbolic of his spiritual wound. Late in the novel, he is able to engage the goblins in physical battle as a spiritually well-equipped muscular Christian. Theologically, Curdie's defeat of the goblins symbolizes the victory of spirit over base matter. But as Prickett explains in *Victorian Fantasy*: "Materialism is forced to be reductionist with spiritual experiences; mysticism very often fails to take account of material forces. We cannot fully reconcile the two realms" (187). Thus the muscular Christian's triumph here is only temporary, as material forces continually tempt and undercut the spiritual. We see this warfare continue in MacDonald's sequel, *The Princess and Curdie*.

Goblin's simplicity is its greatest asset; MacDonald's simple sermon of spiritual strength enlists fairy-tale functions of binary opposition: good/evil, light/dark, spirit/matter. To turn from *Goblin* to *Curdie*, however, is to move from the simple to the complex, from the safety of spiritual victory to the urgency of unending battle for spiritual survival. *Curdie* is a darker, more foreboding work. Carpenter contends that in the second Curdie book MacDonald becomes "a destroyer rather than a creator. Something went wrong between the two Curdie books ... In fact the conclusion of *The Princess and Curdie* is reminiscent not of the book of Revelation but of the fall of Sodom and Gomorrah" (82–3). Carpenter's appraisal of the fairy tale captures its essence: *Curdie* finds an even more muscular Christian at the pen; the message is a direct attack on the weak spirituality that capitalism breeds.

Curdie is one of the few Victorian novels to appropriate Darwin's *The Origin of Species* naturally and profoundly into its imaginative framework. MacDonald "found Darwin an immediate ally," says Prickett, "but, as his son points out, ethical evolution was implied throughout his work long before Darwin published his research results – and, moreover, however some Victorians may have interpreted him, 'ethical' evolution is not implied by Darwin's theory" (*Romanticism and Religion* 243). Colin Manlove suggests that the primary difference between Kingsley and MacDonald is found in their attitudes towards science: "Kingsley is acutely conscious of the scientific discoveries of Darwin and Huxley and of the need to square them with his Christian faith. MacDonald's reaction to contemporary scientific discovery is ... simply to dismiss it as irrelevant to true insight into the world" (150). Such a claim, however, undercuts MacDonald as an artist, thinker, and Victorian. Though he was to write in *Creation in Christ* that "human science cannot discover God, for human science is but the backward undoing of the tapestry-web of God's science" (145), he writes in *The Miracles of the Lord* that "in my theory, the spiritual *both* explains and accounts for the material" (164).

In his essay, "The Imagination: Its Function and its Culture," MacDonald further clarifies his position on imagination and science: God is the great creator, man and woman mere arrangers of God's universal spiritual laws. God is poet, maker. Consequently, "all the processes of the ages are God's science; all the flow of history is his poetry" (4). To MacDonald, the poet and scientist are variations upon a single theme: "The influence of the poetic upon the scientific imagination is ... especially present in the construction of an invisible whole from the hints afforded by a visible part; where the needs of the part, its usefulness, its broken relations are the only guides to a multiplex harmony, completeness, and end, which is the whole." This "multiplex harmony" by necessity must be seen "through the combined lenses of science and imagination" (15). In another essay, "Wordsworth's Poetry," MacDonald reiterates this view: "The poet may be a man of science, and the man of science may be a poet; but poetry includes science, and the man who will advance science most is the man who, other qualifications equal, has most of the poetic faculty in him" (256). Darwin, it follows, is scientist *and* poet, his theory of evolution can be seen as a "hypothesis ... [coming from] the work of the imagination" (256–7).

MacDonald, then, does not reject science; he finds it an apt metaphor, for by re-imagining and further poeticizing Darwin's theory he melds scientific materialism to religious spirituality. Darwinism becomes the key metaphor; he poeticizes scientific materialism and finds a spiritual dimension that provides room for faith in the evolving industrial age. On the material level, Darwin's theory can account for the spiritually devoid, those who have devolved into beastly creatures; on the spiritual level, it can account for the spiritually strong, those who have evolved into humane spiritual beings. "Survival of the fittest" by all means, MacDonald suggests, for the spiritually strong will survive. Thus MacDonald's Darwinism complements his muscular spiritual ethic by depicting the evolutionary struggle of spirit over body.

The beginning of *Curdie* echoes *The Water Babies*; it is a cosmogony myth centered around a scientific account of the universe. Chapter One – "The Mountain" – connects the material with the spiritual, for the mountains are alive, like humans, and they have a Wordsworthian power to evoke "beautiful terrors" (9). MacDonald brings the mountain to the individual: "Well, when the heart of the earth has thus come rushing up among her children, bringing with it gifts of all that she possesses, then straightaway into it rush her children to see what they can find there" (11). And herein lies the rub: those who find the spiritual power of nature will benefit, but those who find its material allure will become spiritually void. Mining, then, becomes a key metaphor for MacDonald: on one level exist the miners – Curdie, for example – whose "business was to bring to light hidden things; they sought silver in the rock and found it, and carried it out" (12). On another level live those miners and merchants "who, when it came into their hands, degraded it by locking it up in a chest, and then it grew diseased and was called *mammon*, and bred all sorts of quarrels" (12). Here, again, MacDonald demonstrates his ability to convey the abstract concretely: the silver can represent belief, faith, spirit, or it can reflect a mere material possession. If Kingsley, as Buckley suggests, arms himself with the material world in his Christian fight, it seems appropriate to align MacDonald with him; *Curdie* depicts a muscular and spiritual poetics in the mountains and the miners – geological evolution becomes a metaphor for spiritual evolution.

These two disparate types of miners – the spiritual and the material – are embodied in the young hero Curdie, who begins to privilege the material over the spiritual: "As Curdie grew, he grew at this time faster in body than in mind – with the usual consequence, that he was getting rather stupid – one of the chief signs of which was that he believed less and less in things he had never seen ... He was gradually changing into a commonplace man" (17). MacDonald concretely presents his theory of evolution/devolution:

There is this difference between the growth of some human beings and that of others: in the one case it is a continuous dying, in the other a continuous resurrection. One of the latter sort comes at length to know at once whether a thing is true the moment it comes before him; one of the former class grows more and more afraid of being taken in, so afraid of it that he takes himself altogether, and comes at length to believe in nothing but his dinner: to be sure of a thing with him is to have it between his teeth. (17–18)

Curdie, unfortunately, seems of the degenerative type, and as he was wounded in the previous novel to symbolize his wounded faith, in *Curdie* he wounds a pigeon to reinforce further how far he has devolved spiritually – he is stronger in body, but weaker in faith. He is muscular, but does not uphold Christian doctrines. As MacDonald writes, "He was becoming more and more a miner, and less and less a man of the upper world where the wind blew" (17).

His destructive act of shooting the bird brings Curdie again to the Grandmother; her lesson to Curdie encapsulates simple theology with worldly realism: "When people don't care to be better they must do everything wrong. I am so glad you shot my bird! ... There is only one way I care for. Do better, and grow better, and be better. And never kill anything without a good reason for it ... There are plenty of bad things that want killing, and a day will come when they [his bow and arrows] will prove useful" (32–3). The Grandmother arms Curdie for a spiritual fight with himself and others, which will eventually entail a physical confrontation.

The central scene in the fairy tale is Curdie's rose-fire baptism by the Grandmother. The baptism into faith (fire) requires, explains the Grandmother to Curdie, "only trust and obedience" (67). "He rushed to the fire, and thrust both of his hands right into the middle of the heap of flaming roses," writes MacDonald. "And it *did* hurt! But he did not draw them back. He held the pain as if it were a thing that would kill him if he let it go – as indeed it would have done. He was in terrible fear lest it should conquer him" (67). The baptism becomes another metaphor for faith that joins the physical and spiritual. After the fire baptism, the Grandmother explains faith scientifically:

Have you ever heard what some philosophers say – that men were all animals once? ... But there is another thing that is of the greatest consequence – this: that all men, if they do not take care, go down the hill to the animals' country; that many men are actually, all their lives, going to the beasts. People knew it once, but it is long since they forgot it. (70)

Alternately drawing on and reversing Darwin through his use of both evolution and devolution, MacDonald also poeticizes Darwinian theory (with a dash of Lamarck) into a Christian metaphor (which echoes Kingsley in *The Water Babies* and *Alton Locke*). Whereas Irene had the magical thread to guide her, now Curdie is armed with his hands; he can tell by touching the hand of another if she or he is going to the beasts or evolving to a higher spiritual plane. Lina, a physically grotesque creature, is an exemplar of the Grandmother's lesson on looking beyond the physical: the beast, Curdie's servant on his quest, has the "hands" of a child. "That paw in your hand now might almost teach you the whole science of natural history – the heavenly sort, I mean" (73), explains the Grandmother. The material and spiritual are again fused in a simple, concrete representation of the potential power of faith.

The remainder of *Curdie* concerns itself with Curdie's journey to the fallen Gwyntystorm and his saving of the ill king (Irene's father) and the city. MacDonald now focuses on the material world as he shows how capitalism, vulgar Social Darwinism, and religion tainted by capitalism are evils that need to be defeated by the strong in faith. With an army of forty-nine Uglies – beasts evolving to spirit

– Curdie journeys to the city, where he finds humans quickly devolving into beasts. Gwyntystorm is a human wasteland, in need of the strong arm of faith: "No man pretended to love his neighbour ... The city was prosperous and rich, and if everybody was not comfortable, everyone else said he ought to be" (95). But Mac-Donald exposes the capitalistic ideology that tempts people into believing that money leads to peace and fulfillment. Jules Zanger argues that in the Curdie books MacDonald portrays "the private nightmares of an England beset from without and within by the forces of social breakdown ... [MacDonald] was fighting nothing less than the Industrial Revolution and the transformations it had wrought upon the face of England" (156).

The illness that capitalism breeds is symbolized by the sick, slowly poisoned king, a kind of fisher king. Curdie soon discovers that the king's men are all beasts, bent on founding "a new dynasty" (136). By helping to restore the king to power, Curdie brings religious order to the kingdom. And MacDonald here becomes didactic: his scathing parody of organized religion demonstrates his perception of devolved spirituality. Chapter 28 – "The Preacher" – describes "Religion day" (188) during which the preacher recites not from the Bible but from *The Book of Nations*; a paraphrased sermon is included:

The main proof of the verity of their religion ... was that things always went well with those who profess it; and its first fundamental principle, grounded in inborn invariable instinct, was, that every One should take care of that One. This was the first duty of Man. If every one would but obey this law, number one, then would every one be perfectly cared for – one being always equal to one ... To be just and friendly was to build the warmest and safest of all nests, and to be kind and loving was to line it with the softest of all furs and feathers, for the one precious, comfort-loving self there to lie, revelling in downiest-bliss. (189)

"Downiest bliss" is far removed from "heavenly bliss," and Prickett contends that in this fairy tale "the suggestion of the passing of Christendom in the self-destructive greed of nineteenth-century commercial society is unmistakable" (*Victorian Fantasy* 188). Gwyntystorm's religion is based on the market, on the material. Early in the fairy tale the Grandmother explains to Curdie's father the difference between being rich and poor: "I am poor as well as rich ... Things come to the poor that can't get in at the door of the rich. Their money somehow blocks it up. It is the great privilege to be poor" (52–3). When religion succumbs to Mammon, MacDonald suggests, then the only hope is the eradication of such religion and unbelief by physical means.

Gwyntystorm is so far lost that a violent battle is needed to restore the city to order, and again we have the Christian soldier Curdie defeating the spiritually weak. MacDonald's depiction of the battle is graphically violent, Grimm-like in its intensity of action; such a physical battle reflects the spiritual battle that must constantly be fought within one's self and outside in the material world. When the king regains power, he becomes an incarnation of the true Old Testament muscular Christian: "Now shall ye be ruled with a rod of iron, that ye may learn what freedom is, and love it and seek it" (215). Curdie and Irene marry, legal and spiritual order is restored, and all should end happily. But MacDonald considered himself a realist: he believed that the battle for belief is never-ending, and once Curdie and Irene (who remain childless) die, the land again becomes spiritually void: "One day at noon, when life was at its highest, the whole city fell with a roaring crash. The cries of men and the shrieks of women went up with its dust, and then there was a great silence ... All around spreads a wilderness of wild deer, and the very name of Gwyntystorm had ceased from the lips of men" (221). The pendulum has swung again, demonstrating that humans have the ability to evolve but remain capable of devolving as well; we must be wary of going to the beasts, of becoming spiritually weak once again.

Thus in the Curdie books MacDonald creates an imaginative space for his tempered version of muscular Christianity, a version at once complementary and antithetic to the Kingsley and Hughes schools of muscularity. Vance's suggestion that the Victorian age reflects various strains of muscular Christianity needs repeating here. And as the variety of the essays in this volume attests, no single definition of muscular Christianity can support the complex positioning of masculinity in the Christian tradition. Colin Manlove, an astute MacDonald critic, contends that "there are arguably two significant writers of Christian fantasy in the Victorian period: George MacDonald and Charles Kingsley" (140); yet he also recognizes the competing Christian visions promoted by the two authors: "All the more striking, then, must be the fact that in nearly every aspect of their art and outlook the two are in fact radically different, so much that together they could be said to form nothing short of a

dualism" (143). Manlove believes Kingsley is a "Victorian," Mac-
Donald a "Romantic"; Kingsley an Aristotelian believing God
works within nature on a horizontal plane, MacDonald a Christian-
Platonist believing God works above nature on a vertical plane. He
concludes: "For MacDonald's fantasy is of the night, and of the
feminine, the mysterious, the interior and the relatively passive;
Kingsley's of the day, of the masculine, the clear, the outdoor, and
the active" (159).

We can adapt Manlove's distinction between Kingsley and Mac-
Donald to critique their versions of a muscularized Christianity:
MacDonald's "muscularity," as we have seen, concerns spirit
(though it is not necessarily passive); archetypally, it could be seen
as feminine. But this is not to suggest that the feminine/masculine
dichotomy presupposes a privileging of one term over the other –
namely, the masculine (active) over the feminine (passive). In
MacDonald's universe, masculinity and femininity can exist sym-
biotically, with no role privileged over the other. Laura Fasick's
overview in this volume of the nineteenth century's paradigm shift
concerning gender roles is illuminating: she posits that men's and
women's roles were no longer placed in a strictly vertical relationship; rather, they were positioned horizontally, suggesting that
"Men and women ... did not compete with each other; they
adapted, entering into a symbiotic relationship that allowed each
sex to benefit from contact with the other." For Kingsley, Fasick
claims, "this version of natural law, in which men and women
defined their gender identities through and against each other,
decreed the proper forms for individual and familial life" (93).
MacDonald, I argue, goes further than Kingsley: he feminizes
muscular Christianity by depicting processes of the integration and
reconciliation rather than polarization and bifurcation of gender
roles, thus making his a more powerful force than Hughes or Kingsley could ever imagine.

Claudia Nelson's recent study, *Boys will be Girls*, provides theoretical support for my reading of MacDonald's feminized muscular
Christianity. Her introductory chapter – "Manliness and the Angel
in the House" – argues that "untainted by nineteenth-century
capitalism, the Angel imaged an alternative society that valued
gentleness, feeling, community, mutual respect, and spiritual
equality" (4), those so-called feminine attributes. "Victorian men
might control money, but Victorian women could control life" (4),

asserts Nelson, and her claim could be applied directly to *Curdie*: Gwyntystorm is literally manned by men who control the market value of the town; they need a fertile woman to "give birth" to the new world order. Masculine materialism is itself sterile. It is only through the Grandmother, a feminized God(dess)-figure, that spirit and life are restored to the city. Gwyntystorm's final destruction results from the continued masculine attempts at mining the mountains for silver and gold, thus weakening the spiritual foundations to such a degree that the entire city implodes. The fantasy or fairy tale, argues Nelson, is a natural form for professing the feminine ideal:

Perhaps more than any other type of children's literature in the nineteenth century, fantasy originated in the idealizing of childhood as a refuge from the excesses of adult masculinity. Postulating a reality impossible by the terms of Victorian (male) science, the genre could adopt ethics impossible within Victorian (male) laissez-faire capitalism. Because fantasy in general – and Victorian fantasy in particular – seeks "that which has been silenced, made invisible, covered over and made 'absent,'" the influence of the Angel [the feminine] resonates through such stories. (148)

To Nelson, MacDonald replaces the Holy Trinity of Father, Son, and Holy Ghost (masculine) with a more feminized trinity that still reflects the spiritual – "Angelic mother, child, poetic truth [found in the imagination]" (157). Indeed, such a trinity exists in the Curdie books as the angelic Grandmother teaches the children Irene and Curdie about spiritual truth in their creative quest to save the kingdom.

In creating a feminine muscular Christianity, MacDonald requires that both the male and female work together to defeat unbelief. Zipes comments that in MacDonald's fairy tales there is "mutual respect and interdependence between men and women" (*Subversion* 108); in *Victorian Fairy Tales* he claims that "in most of MacDonald's tales there is a composite hero, not a single one. That is, a triumph of the self is a union of the masculine and feminine, an erotic display of the utopian drive, that MacDonald allowed himself to express primarily in symbolic form" (176). Claudia Nelson pushes further than Zipes: "Yoked together, feminine virtue and masculine know-how could eradicate the sexual and economic abuses that preoccupied earnest Victorian minds" (173). Discussing Diamond in *At the Back of the North Wind*, Nelson argues that MacDonald, not Kingsley, "creates a more positive version of the quest for androgynous purity; although like Kingsley he accepts Darwin's findings, he

puts them in a moral (and thus un-Darwinian) context. In fiction as in family life holding woman to be the more evolved, MacDonald explores the moral evolution of one child toward physical frailty and spiritual strength" (155). In a sense, then, MacDonald's version of muscular Christianity is radical, transforming those boundaries that seem to define the movement itself – masculinity (body) and femininity (spirit) are blended in Curdie and Irene as they literally marry into a symbolic androgynous union that not only represents MacDonald's version of a spiritualized muscular Christianity, but his own "physical frailty and spiritual strength."

MacDonald's assertive preaching cost him his pulpit, and he was never again to have the power to preach to his own congregation. Only in his sermons (one volume of which was subtitled *Unspoken Sermons*), novels, fantasies, and fairy tales could he preach his gospel of faith, and in doing so was able to poeticize his religious and social beliefs. As Vance says, "It is not surprising that the conventional novel-form gradually collapsed under the weight of the manly Christianity entrusted to it. Dream, myth and fable tend to take over from straightforward realistic narrative" (7). Terry Eagleton argues in *Literary Theory* that the Victorians saw literature as an alternative religion since "literature works primarily by emotion and experience" (26). For MacDonald, his books were his religion. Eagleton lists F. D. Maurice and Charles Kingsley among those Victorians who emphasized "solidarity between the social classes, the cultivation of 'larger sympathies,' the instillation of national pride and the transmission of 'moral' values" (27). We can add George MacDonald's name to this roster of Christian writers who wanted a powerful religion and who fought for both spirit and body, for morality and equality. In his entry dated "December 32" from *Diary of an Old Soul*, MacDonald describes most succinctly his social and religious vision:

> Go, my beloved children, live your life.
> Wounded, faint, bleeding, never yield the strife.
> Stunned, fallen – awake, arise, and fight again.
> Before you victory stands, with shining train
> Of hopes not credible until they *are*.
> Beyond morass and mountain swells the star
> Of perfect love – the home of longing heart and brain.   (132)

WORKS CITED

Altick, Richard, *Victorian People and Ideas*. New York: Norton, 1973.

Buckley, Jerome Hamilton, *The Victorian Temper*. New York: Vintage, 1964.

Carpenter, Humphrey, *Secret Gardens: The Golden Age of Children's Literature*. Boston: Houghton Mifflin, 1985.

Eagleton, Terry, *Literary Theory: An Introduction*. Minneapolis: University of Minnesota Press, 1983.

Hughes, Thomas, *The Manliness of Christ*. Boston: Houghton Mifflin, 1880.

MacDonald, George, *At the Back of the North Wind*. New York: Signet, 1986.

Creation in Christ: The Unspoken Sermons, ed. Rolland Hein. Wheaton, IL: Harold Shaw, 1976.

Diary of an Old Soul. Minneapolis: Augsburg, 1975.

"The Imagination: Its Function and its Culture" in *A Dish of Orts*, pp. 1–42.

A Dish of Orts. Chiefly Papers on the Imagination, and on Shakspere, enlarged edition. London: Sampson Low, 1893.

The Miracles of the Lord, ed. Rolland Hein. Wheaton, IL: Harold Shaw, 1980.

The Princess and Curdie. New York: Puffin, 1980.

The Princess and the Goblin. New York: Puffin, 1984.

"Wordsworth's Poetry" in *A Dish of Orts*, pp. 245–63.

MacDonald, Greville, *George MacDonald and his Wife*. London: George Allen, 1924.

Manlove, C. N., "MacDonald and Kingsley: A Victorian Contrast" in *The Golden Thread*, ed. William Raeper. Edinburgh University Press, 1990, pp. 140–62.

Nelson, Claudia, *Boys will be Girls: The Feminine Ethic and British Children's Fiction, 1857–1917*. New Brunswick: Rutgers University Press, 1991.

Prickett, Stephen, *Romanticism and Religion*. Cambridge University Press, 1976.

Victorian Fantasy. Bloomington: Indiana University Press, 1979.

Vance, Norman, *The Sinews of the Spirit: The Ideal of Christian Manliness in Victorian Literature and Religious Thought*. Cambridge University Press, 1985.

Zanger, Jules, "Goblins, Morlocks, and Weasels: Classic Fantasy and the Industrial Revolution," *Children's Literature in Education* 8 (1977): 154–62.

Zipes, Jack, *Fairy Tales and the Art of Subversion*. New York: Wildman, 1983.

ed., *Victorian Fairy Tales: The Revolt of the Fairies and the Elves*. New York: Methuen, 1987.

CHAPTER 7

"Degenerate effeminacy" and the making of a masculine spirituality in the sermons of Ralph Waldo Emerson

Susan L. Roberson

For a group of writers and ministers in mid-Victorian Britain, Christianity had about it a "muscular" quality, though, perhaps as Charles Kingsley suggests, the adjectives "manly" and "manful" might be more appropriate labels for the version of Christianity that "represented a strategy for commending Christian virtue by linking it with more interesting secular notions of moral and physical prowess" (Vance 1). Indeed, in his Christmas sermon at Cambridge in 1864, Kingsley chaffed against the term "muscular," preferring in its stead "manful": "We have heard much of late about 'Muscular Christianity.' A clever expression . . . For myself, I do not know what it means . . . Its first and better meaning may be simply a healthful and manful Christianity; one which does not exalt the feminine virtues to the exclusion of the masculine" (quoted in Martin, 220). As Norman Vance suggests, that meant infusing Christianity with the "rough and ready tradition of physical sturdiness" (11), social reform, and an insistence on the whole person. A generation earlier and an ocean apart, another minister wrestled with the meaning of a "manful Christianity," fusing secular and Christian traditions and constructing a religion that affirmed the manly or masculine in ways that both foreshadow and diverge from British muscular Christianity, and that allow us to understand better the links between the religious, social, and personal anxieties that pervaded Anglo-American thought during the nineteenth century.

Between the years 1826 and 1832, a young Ralph Waldo Emerson contended with personal and social forces that threatened to cast him into a maelstrom of doubt and anxiety about his position in society and the universe. Like the British Victorian who also would be "deeply troubled with religious doubt, acutely aware of weakness

150

and frustration" (Houghton 216), Emerson and other Americans of his generation felt keenly the anxiety of coming of age in a nation that was shifting from an agrarian to an industrial economic base. And like other young men on both sides of the ocean, Emerson evinced insidious personal doubts about his ability to make his mark in a tumultuous, competitive world. To meet the threat of such emasculating doubt and anxiety, Emerson forged his own Christianity of manliness, masculinity, and power, one that was not completely unlike the muscular Christianity that sprang from Kingsley's pen.

While both men stressed the masculinizing power of the will (as Nietzsche would later in *Beyond Good and Evil* and *The Will to Power*), Emerson and Kingsley differed mainly in their use of the body. Kingsley celebrated a "healthy animalism" (Martin 201) and the inseparability of flesh and spirit, while Emerson, like other American moralists of his time, sought to erase the body even as he thereby inscribed it with meaning. For Emerson, manliness had more to do with the denial of the flesh and its appetites, with the denial of self-indulgence (that for both Emerson and Kingsley represented effeminate disempowerment), than specifically with the robust sport, health, and sexuality of Kingsley's Christianity. Though Emerson would later advocate sport and games for young people, especially after his own children began to arrive, at the crucial time when he was desperately trying to affirm himself, his attitude about the body reflected both his personal reticence about such matters and the distrust of the flesh inherited from his Calvinist forefathers. Emerson's concern, as was the case with his fellow Americans, was with character and the advantages, spiritual and secular, to be had from a disciplined and controlled self, one marked by industry, temperance, and morality. Indeed, it would not be until 1855, in Whitman's "Song of Myself," that an American would proclaim himself to be the poet of the body as well as of the soul.

Even so, Norman Vance, in *The Sinews of the Spirit*, too readily accepts at face value Kingsley's own dismissal of Emerson (79–84, 124). It is true that in *Alton Locke* (1850) Kingsley parodies Emerson in the character of Professor Windrush from America. His sermon, a "wordy abstraction," peddles a convenient transcendentalism meant to appeal to aristocratic intellectuals eager to absolve themselves of sin and responsibility. While Kingsley's spokesman in the

novel criticizes Windrush's lack of "objectives and subjectives"
(196–203), a real sermon by Emerson from early in his career
probably would have sounded less foreign to their ears than does this
version of Emerson's later high-minded philosophy. Indeed, had
Kingsley known the ministerial Emerson, he probably would not
have been as swift to label him Windrush, the professor of "Anythingarianism." Rather he would have found more in common with
Emerson's Christianity and its calls for a stalwart manliness than he
suspected.

After Ralph Waldo Emerson was approbated by the Unitarian
church in 1826, he, like so many of his contemporaries, preached
self-cultivation and the formation of character, a doctrine that
advocated the relentless pursuit of moral perfection. William Ellery
Channing, the spiritual leader of New England Unitarians, defined
self-culture as "the care which every man owes to himself, to the
unfolding and perfecting of his Nature" (226). While the Unitarians
generally stressed human goodness and potential, they also advocated a salvation that finally was unattainable, for it entailed the
on-going process towards perfection, the "developing and unfolding
of a potential inner virtue" (Robinson 13), that was never-ending,
continuing supposedly even in the next life. Emerson, too, preached
that "We shall not have done our duty to ourselves until we have
carried all our powers to the highest perfection those powers can
reach" (No. xxiv).[1] For the young minister, the perfect character
was derived from a conscious effort to shape and master the self.
While God may test the individual with trials meant to strengthen
his character, the final responsibility for moral and spiritual well-
being lay with the individual. As Emerson said, "we are the masters
of our own condition ... We are not feeble, we are not pitiful, any
more than we are vicious, except by our own fault. We are very
powerful beings. We can, as we choose, be trained into angels or
deformed into fiends" (No. xxvii). Indeed, in such a schema, the
individual is responsible for cultivating all areas of life, the intellectual, social, and vocational as well as the spiritual, and advocates
of self-cultivation, whether from behind the pulpit or the podium,
conflated spiritual and secular self-cultivation and self-improvement
as the Christian and American way of life. According to the prevailing myth of success, financial reward accrued only to the moral and
industrious, and the man who could work his way up the corporate

ladder was likely also to work his way to heaven's gate. Daniel Wise, minister and promoter of self-improvement, promised the young reader of his missive, "I will unfold to you the secrets of success and of eminence in this life, and the sure means of winning a crown of glory in the next!" (13–14).

In the young nation, still clearing the woodlands and extending its physical boundaries, still attempting to prove that this experiment in democracy would work, self-cultivation had a practical, utilitarian side. A writer for *The Christian Examiner*, the Unitarian organ, wrote that "We have proved ourselves, confessedly, an active, shrewd, enterprising, and indefatigable people" (4.1 [1832]: 305). As increasing miles of canals, roads, and railroads, and burgeoning towns, cities, and industries were changing the aspect of the landscape and assuring America of progress, the heroes of the early tales of success were equal to the task of building a nation from its raw material. Typically the men behind the inventions and national progress were described as self-made men who, without inherited advantages, shaped their own and their country's fortunes. Edward Everett declared in his 1831 Franklin Lecture, "Our whole country is a great and speaking illustration of what may be done by native force of mind, uneducated, without advantages, but starting up under strong excitement, into new and successful action" (305). The self-made man, the model of American manhood, was promoted in these early decades of the nineteenth century, for he assured his and his nation's success by directing his life into active, useful, and moral service. At the same time, then, that Unitarian ministers were preaching religious self-cultivation, moral and business advisors were advocating self-improvement as the means to success for young men eager to make their mark in the commercial world. As the nation appeared to be self-made, self-generated out of the soil of a new land, so its heroes were those men who, like Benjamin Franklin, owed their success to their own energy and perseverance. From this dream of Americans' potential, there arose the myth that "This is a country of self-made men, than which nothing better could be said about any state of society" (Calvin Colton, quoted in Cawelti, 39). And the definition of America and of its citizens danced around this myth, for both were described as practical, progressive, active, and powerful.

Influenced in part by an organic theory of the self, which located the germs or seeds of character within the self, and by a Lockean notion of the malleability of the self, the apostles of self-culture (to borrow David Robinson's phrase) described life as the growth and training of the developing self. For advocates of self-improvement, character is often described as "a plant which every one may cultivate," requiring constant attention and "great pains-taking" (Todd 58). Although a difficult undertaking, self-cultivation, or at least the idea of self-culture, is nonetheless democratic and positive (if only in theory), for "every one," regardless of inherited position or talent, may gain "dignity and power" (*The Christian Examiner* 4.1 [1830]: 282) from the development of the inner resources of the self. Thus, self-cultivation seems to have derived from trust in the innate nature of the self; indeed, Emerson preached self-trust and urged his congregation to "Know thyself" as an initial step in "the imperative duty to explore our own strength" (No. xxvii). But what seems complicit in the idea of self-cultivation is that without the proper discipline and self-control, the individual will fall easily to self-destruction and become a fiend of sensual indulgence and the perpetrator of his own commercial failure. Because the venture of being is so fraught with moral dangers, the task of self-cultivation or self-improvement is often described as a vigorous, strenuous, and manly undertaking, converting the language of sport into a metaphor for commercial and moral success. To measure up to the cultural and individual expectation of the time, one had to engage in life as if it were a competitive, athletic feat with the prize going to the few gutsy and strong enough to endure to the end.

At the same time that moral advisors in the early decades of the nineteenth century preached human goodness, potential, and perfectability, they knew and warned of men and women's more primitivistic and sinful nature. Although they looked forward to human perfectability, they had a Hawthornian conviction of sin seared on the bosom of the individual. Archibald Alexander told the young men at Nassau Hall that "such is the nature of man, that he has only to follow the current of his own desires, to fall completely into a course of iniquity" (9). The older advisors feared the untamed passions of the younger men, passions that would lead them to drink, sensual indulgence, and to "the strange woman ... whose house is the way to Hell, going down to the chambers of death" (Adams 25). Alarmed no doubt by the lurid scenes of the rapidly industrializing and growing city, Joel Hawes warned the young men of Hartford of the gruesome consequences for those who have not the strength to resist the temptations of life: "they fall in with the mass of corruption around them, and go to swell the monstrous tide of depravity and dissipation, which is rolling, as a mighty desolation, over the cities of our land" (41). Emerson, too, preached of the "gnawing lusts [that] have coiled themselves with a serpent's trail into the place of every noble affection that God set up in the recesses of the soul" (No. 1). He accused not only the indefinable mass of man but himself as well of a proclivity to sin that was likely to ruin his chances for true piety and success. He wrote in his private journal, "I am a lover of indolence, & of the belly. And the good have a right to ask the Neophyte who wears this garment of scarlet sin, why he comes where all are apparelled in white?" (*JMN* II 241).[2] On the one hand, Emerson trusts the "human instinct," the conscience which "prompts us to do good, & refuse evil" (*JMN* II 157), and on the other he knows "There is tremendous sympathy to which we were born by which we do easily enter into the feelings of evil agents" (*JMN* III 67). Forming a dialectic of the self, this twin vision, which sees the self's weakness and yet calls on man to trust himself in the formation of his character, creates a tension in Emerson's thought that informs not only his private musings but the direction of his sermons. Driven to overcome his weaker self, he sketched the parameters of an American spirituality, a "masculine" religion (No. VIII) of virtue and self-reliance. What ensued was a battle of the wills fought not only in the arena of public discourse but in the hearts and private musings of individual citizens, a battle between the will to resist and the will to indulge the appetites of the flesh.

Characteristic of much Western theology, Emerson and other nineteenth-century moral advisors practiced a "dualistic habit of thought" (Christ, *Laughter* 142) which urged the fragmentation of the self and pitted the self against itself. Typically, self-improvement advisors suggested that young men "Form habits of *industry, frugality, and benevolence*" (Winslow 92) as a means of cultivating the resources of the self. At the same time they advised readers to "banish sloth, and an inordinate love of ease; active minds only being fit for employments, and none but the industrious either deserving, or having a possibility to thrive" (*The Young Man's Own Book* 134). Like John Todd, they advised self-control as a corollary of self-cultivation, telling their readers to "govern the appetites . . . govern the tongue . . . govern your thoughts . . . govern your feelings" (Todd 241–56). Indeed, as William Ellery Channing pointed out, "in this country, the chief obstructions [to self-improvement] lie, not in our lot, but in ourselves, not in outward hardships, but in our worldly and sensual propensities" (263). Young men were encouraged to find piety and success in a self marked by contention rather than by integration. Emerson, too, preached self-command and self-control in a reading of human nature that encouraged a split self rather than a whole one; he urged his congregation to diligence, labor, and fortitude and to "temperance & self restraint, that we should have all our appetites & passions under control" (No. xxiv). A young man could not expect to find glory on the basis of an immoral energy; rather, he must constantly strain against his own nature and the world at large in order to make his success. Given the freedom to form the self, "to become *whatsoever [they] will resolve to be*" (Alcott 25), young men were nonetheless urged against the self in a masculinist reading of human nature that preached the dichotomy of mind and body.

Finding the impulses of the natural self to be "swinish" and "unmanning" (No. xxiv), Emerson and other advocates of character formation and success stressed self-denial and abstinence as empowering, masculinizing strategies. Participating in a historically pervasive reading of human nature, these nineteenth-century moralists not only split the self into two contending forces (spirit or mind versus nature, reason versus emotion), but they associated themselves with what they took to be the positive side of the dualism, spirit and reason, and consigned that which they deemed negative and threatening to the feminine. Although these men knew and warned against the passions and appetites, they apparently attempted to deny that these constituted part of their own masculine nature. Instead, they consistently labeled the "weaker" and more sensual impulses "feminine" or "effeminate" and attempted to expurgate them from their definitions of self. As we have noted, Norman Vance explains of British "Christian manliness" that it "represented a strategy for commending Christian virtue by linking it with more interesting secular notions of moral and physical prowess. 'Manliness' in this context," Vance contends, "generously embraced all that was best and most vigorous in man, which might include women as well" (1). But Vance ignores or does not recognize what theologian Carol P. Christ finds pernicious about this very old dualistic habit of mind. She argues that it designed "an alienated paradigm of divine power, a paradigm of domination requiring subjection" (*Laughter* 143) that has participated in the oppression of women. Moreover, this dualistic paradigm has resulted in alienating the self from itself, for the male as well as the female, by instigating the "war" between spirit and flesh, "in which the inferior continually threatens to overwhelm the superior" (*Diving Deep* 25). While Emerson and his fellow moralists did not have the subjugation of woman consciously in mind when they advised against the impulses of the body and labeled those impulses both evil and effeminate, they constructed a definition of the feminine that promoted women's commercial and intellectual failure and required them to read against themselves. Furthermore, the hegemonic male engaged in a one-sided definition of self that excluded "nature, emotion, irrationality, and the body" (*Diving Deep* 25).[3] Nonetheless, Emerson and a long line of religious and moral leaders advised and strove against the body and the natural in order that the mind and spirit might win the war of the self, might transcend the body and nature, and thus masculinize and empower the self. As Emerson put it, "I think that Self Denial is only one form of expression for perfection of the moral character" (*JMN* III 175). At stake in this gambit is power, power over the self, over others, and over the annihilating forces of the universe. Power is the bottom line, what everyone wants and apparently only those manly enough can get. Emerson knew that "the idea of *power* seems to have been every where at the bottom of the theology" (*JMN* I 76), and the idea of power is everywhere at the bottom of his own thought.[4]

Sprinkled, then, throughout this plethora of advice for young men and sermons on self-cultivation is a persistent call to repudiate and control the appetites and impulses of the body, and a consistent regard for those appetites as unmanning, "effeminate and perverted" (*The Christian Examiner*, new series, 22 [1832]: 4). Joel Hawes wrote that pleasure "is utterly inconsistent with all manliness of thought and action" and "forms a character of effeminacy and feebleness ... contempt ... shame ... self-reproach" (69), and Joseph Allen connected the absence of "regular habits of industry and thrift" to "effeminacy and corruption of morals" (10). Even when the feminine is not always described as pernicious, it is regarded by male writers as silly and vain: Orville Dewey, minister at New Bedford and kinsman of Emerson, associated the popular literature of his day with the feminine, and considered both to be "miscellaneous, luxurious, impatient of immediate distinction, covetous of present excitement, and careless of real development of mind or of lasting and solid fame" (*The Evening Gazette*, August 28, 1830). Emerson, too, labels the negative and the weak as effeminate: he contrasts an "effeminate repining" to the act of enduring life's hard knocks with "the nerve of manhood [formed] to athletic strength" by poverty (No. II) and scorns both the "effeminate manhood" of those men raised in grandeur and luxury (No. V) and the "degenerate effeminacy" of those unwilling to attend Sabbath services on any but the sunniest days (No. VII).

Indeed, the pursuit of success through the "process of slow, toilsome self-culture" seemed a task peculiarly fitted for the male, for it required "manly strength of purpose" (Wise 72–3) and perseverance, characteristics unluckily not in the female repertoire, for "they rarely succeed in long works ... their natural training rendering them equally adverse to long doubt and long labour" (*The Evening Gazette*, March 27, 1830). Even when the attributes of success are not explicitly labeled masculine or manly, they are associated with definitions of masculinity. The *OED* lists as synonyms of "masculine," "relative superiority, strength, activity ... virile, vigorous, power," words that form a rhetoric of masculinity and power that runs throughout the literature of self-cultivation. The person who forms his own character does so through "energy of will" (Burnap 65), through "action [that] forms the intellectual constitution to robustness, energy, and strength" (Burnap 22), and through "force" (Channing 224). For Emerson, self-cultivation and salvation are often figured in masculinist terms, describing the "athletic virtue" of the "self existent, self consulting" man as "a tower of strength" (No. LIII) and salvation as a competitive undertaking: "you must go & fetch it. You must search & find it. You must contend & win it" (No. LXXXIII). And, of course, the models of behavior and success are all men – Franklin, Napoleon, Newton, Columbus, Whitney, Fulton, Jesus.

What the inspirationalists accomplished was an implicitly masculine definition of self as "character" that equated character with mind and mind with power. These writers explicitly made this equation, declaring that "Grandeur of character lies wholly in force of soul, ... in the force of thought" (Channing 224), and that "character is power" and "knowledge is power" (Hawes 111, 167). This power paradigm is a masculinist constitution of the self as mind, or its corollary, spirit. By extension, Christianity as preached and practiced by the apostles of culture was also a masculinist construction in which spirituality and power became synonymous. It is in this paradigm that the young Reverend Ralph Waldo Emerson participated, defining himself by it and using it as a model of Christian piety in his early sermons. Indeed, it is a paradigm from which he never escaped, even after he escaped the ready-made institutions of the Church.

Emerson's personal journal testifies to his own battle with the self and demonstrates a dualistic habit of mind that divides him against himself, the frail body against the mind's will, "the man of passion, [against] the man of principle" (*JMN* III 129). As a youngster, though poor and left fatherless at age eight, Emerson belonged to the intellectual elite of Boston. Coming from a long line of New England ministers, he was expected by his family and by himself to distinguish himself in the ministry,[5] one of the few professions open to young men of ambition and talent. But one of the strains that marks the private musings of his early manhood is his disappointment at not yet having distinguished himself and a fear that he never will. He grumbled, "The dreams of my childhood are all fading away & giving place to some very sober & very disgusting views of a quiet mediocrity of talents & condition" (*JMN* III 153). He blamed his apparent inability to meet his ambition on his bodily weakness, a frailty that was both real and reinforced by a Calvinistic reading of human nature. Thus he complained at age twenty-four, "My years are passing away. Infirmities are already stealing on me that may be the deadly enemies that are to dissolve me to dirt and little is yet done to establish my consideration among my contemporaries & less to get a memory when I am gone" (*JMN* III 15). He had a legitimate fear, given his and his family's susceptibility to ill health (three of his brothers were to die of tuberculosis), that he would not live long enough or have the necessary physical strength to make his mark. Just a few months before he left New England in 1826 for the warmer and healthier climate of the South to arrest the tuberculosis that threatened his own lungs, he cried out to his journal, "Health, action, happiness. How they ebb from me!" (*JMN* III 45). The battle against the weakness of the flesh was in that sense very real for young Waldo, for were he to relinquish his guard, the consequences could be quite grim indeed. But there is something more underlying Emerson's conviction of human frailty than fear for his own health, for one inheritance from his Calvinistic forebears was an abiding distrust of the body, which threatens to overcome and unman the higher self of the mind. In his journal for 1823, at a time when he was dissatisfied with the course of his life, he wrote, "it is not Time nor Fate nor the World that is half so much his foe as the demon Indolence within him. A man's enemies are those of his own household ... slothful sensual indulgence is the real unbroken barrier, and that when he has overleaped this, God has set no bound to his progress" (*JMN* II 112). Throughout his journal runs a distrust of the "Belly," the locus of so much "lust" and "bad direction" (*JMN* III 277), and an insistence on temperance and self-denial. He reminded himself "to curtail my dinner & supper sensibly & rise from table each day with an appetite; & so see if it be fact that I can understand more clearly" (*JMN* II 240). As Helena Michie points out in *The Flesh made Word*, women's hunger in Victorian novels disguises through metaphoric deflection the more dangerous appetites of sexuality and power that participated in the mythic Fall. As used in these novels, the hunger metaphor encourages anorexic eating habits in women as a way of denying corporeality and erasing their bodies from texts at the same time that it assures the "ideology of male dominance" (22). Emerson also experimented with anorexia, but whereas for women characters, hunger represents the repression of their desire for sexuality and power, for Emerson it represented both self-mastery and power, as well as his alliance with the dominant ideology. Strength of conviction, will, and mind, then, are entwined in Emerson's thought with self-control: "He to whom appetite is nothing & pleasure nothing & pain nothing before his immutable will, will find not many impossibilities in his way" (*JMN* III 134). In fact, in a bid to master the self and become more spirit-like, he experimented in mastering his appetite by diminishing his own food intake:

28 March my food per diem weighted $14\frac{1}{4}$ oz
29 –   – 13 oz
2 April $12\frac{1}{2}$ (*JMN* IV 6)[6]

As this ledger suggests, Emerson's personal strategy to empower himself was to subordinate the body to the mind, and thereby gain a "higher" state of existence. When, in 1823, he contemplated entering the ministry, he did so in part to regenerate himself, to become manly – a man of the mind and of the soul. In the same entry in which he bemoaned "the demon Indolence," he looked for an

this is also
done throug¹ sport, war, etc
as well as asceticism.

antidote to his "household" enemies in the ministry: "I am hasten-
ing to put on the manly robe" (*JMN* II 112). He hoped that his new
profession would be his "regeneration of mind, manners, inward &
outward estate," and he vowed to devote himself "to the service of
God & the War against Sin" (*JMN* II 241–2).[7]

As a soldier in this "War against Sin," the young reverend
preached a version of spirituality that encouraged the war against
self, the mastering and sublimating of the animalistic and effeminate
self by the mind or spirit. In Sermon No. xxiv, he described the
Christian gentleman as one who directs his own life, through
"action, enterprize, industry," and who commands his life by
"abstinence" from "unmanning intemperance." The true Christian
is he who, tested by the "hard habits" of life, cultivates "the nerve of
manhood to athletic strength [and] brushes aside from the manly
limb the clinging cobwebs of sloth; scours off the rust of sensuality"
and does not stoop to an "effeminate repining" when life is hard
(No. II). Moreover, in the Emersonian text, the Christian's
gentleness is compatible with the "most robust strength & highest
majesty," with "heroic action," and "with the greatest firmness of
character." Not an "effeminacy in ... manners," true Christian
gentleness "goes deeper than [courtesy], & affects the heart as well
as the manners. It teaches a patience that conquers suffering & the
forgiveness of injuries. But it leaves all the sinews of the character in
their original strength, & adds to them the strength (might) of a
divine principle, to make them equal to the whole work of Duty"
(No. xxxiii). Emerson's rhetoric here clearly participates in the
dichotomy of being that equates character with an internal condition of mind or spirit and religiosity with manliness and power.
His rhetoric also equates attention to outer (bodily) appearances
with the frivolous, effeminate, and, finally, dangerous – a "degenerate effeminacy" (No. vii). *The Young Man's Own Book* declares that
"dress is, at best, but a female privilege, and, in man, argues both
levity of mind, and effeminacy of manners" (137), and it appears
that Emerson extends the condemnation of concern for dress to a
condemnation of all outer trappings, both in the passage from
Sermon No. xxxiii and in his later rejection of the Lord's Supper
ritual as a mere shadow or body without life (being). The kind of
religion Emerson preaches is not a showcase of form or ritual, but
derives from the heart, is one of love, benevolence, and sincerity: "It
is cheerful social masculine generous" (No. viii).

The apparent compensation for self-denial, then, is the formation of a muscular, American Christian, a being of manliness, sanctity, and power. Like the self-made man of the American dream, the kind of Christian preached by Emerson and other Unitarians is the product of his own construction. Like the secular self-made man, the Christian character is self-sufficient and independent, relying on no one but himself to determine his own destiny. Free from political restraints to make of himself what he will, he is also free from spiritual determination and is a "Universe [un]to [him]self" (No. XXVII). Since the individual is not born with character, did not "inherit [a] mind stored & expanded," but must develop or cultivate it, the particular decisions of life, to live soberly or riotously, determine the person that one becomes. As Emerson says, "What we are depends on what we do," for "our character is in our own hands" (No. XXIV). By mastering himself, the individual becomes the master *of* himself and assumes the responsibility and power of invention and control often assigned to a higher being; indeed, Emerson's strategy for empowering the individual is to identify him with the divine, with the "Angel & God" (No. LXIII). Just as character is power, so character-making is power-engendering, for, by creating himself, man participates in the power of God, is like the God whose image he reflects.

Free to form his character, the individual is also accountable for the character he makes, for the double edge of freedom includes responsibility for the self one creates. Warning against the "spiritual suicide" of imitation, Emerson declares that "the gospel teaches you to act for yourself, to act as if there was none but yourself in the world to give account of his actions" (No. XXXVIII). While the individual may have only himself to blame for his failures, in accordance with the socially unrealistic belief inherited from the Puritans, the self-made man can also credit himself (with perhaps an obligatory word of thanksgiving to Providence) for his successes. Further, the individual carries within himself his own reward and punishment, for "Riot punishes itself" (No. XXIV) with a life of uselessness and debauchery: "Thus the most degraded sort of man ... when he holds his cup in his hand, knows perfectly well the consequences of his indulgence" (No. LXIII). Likewise, the sober man is rewarded, if not with material comfort, then with a life close to God. Self-denial, Emerson preached, "makes you master of yourself. It brings you nearer alway to God, and every step of your progress makes you stronger and more peaceful and more hopeful, takes away something of mortal infirmity and puts something of immortal enjoyment in its stead." By subordinating "all the lower parts of man's nature, to the higher" (No. LXIII), the self comes not only closer in location to God but closer in being to Him, for like God he becomes a self of the mind – purified and empowered at the same time. No longer a solitary young man shaking his fist defiantly at a God far out in the universe and declaring his independence, as he did in 1823 when he shouted, "I say to the Universe, Mighty One! thou art not my mother; Return to chaos, if thou wilt, I shall still exist" (*JMN* II 190), Emerson now envisions a correspondence, a unity between man (the perfect character) and God that at once maintains the individual's independence and yet makes him a sharer of immortality and thus immures him against the flux of daily life: "We know the style of God by loving him. When the soul joins itself to God, it is at a point of rest. It is no longer a victim to endless agitations. The passions, the appetites no longer warp its judgments. It sees things as they are. It acts with unity & effect" (No. LXXXIV). Self-denial, the means of making a perfect character and of exercising power over the self, creates a being in the likeness of God, a being who participates in the wisdom and power of the Godhead, a being whose sanctity coheres with the masculinist definition of self as mind. By identifying this self-sacrificing individual with God, then, Emerson suggests a masculinist version of God if not a masculine, male God.

But what Emerson finally suggests, and this is what makes his thought daring and unconventional, is an identification between the human and the divine that will locate the spark of divinity within the self and make the self a sharer of the nature of God. When William Ellery Channing delivered his 1828 sermon, "Likeness to God," he told his audience that "true religion consists in proposing, as our great end, a growing likeness to the Supreme Being" (*Selected Writings* 146), the means for which lay organically within the self, "in our essential faculties, unfolded by vigorous and conscientious exertion" to improve the self (157). Channing came close to suggesting what Emerson later would when he said that self-cultivation makes us "more and more partakers of the Divinity" (146). But, for Channing, man remained dependent on the parental God, and he explained that as a child resembles the parent so man has the "likeness of a kindred nature" with God (150). But, where Chan-

ning had softened his "controversial, even heretical" (145) suggestion that man is like God by sounding the familiar rhetoric and
doctrine of self-improvement, Emerson suggests that man does have
the means and power to *create* the self and thus be as God.

Having laid the foundation for his radical thought when he
discovered the power of the indwelling God in the passage from St.
Luke 17:21, "the kingdom of God is within you," Emerson could
declare for the individual of "athletic virtue" in Sermon No. LIII
that:

immortal life consists in the acquisition of virtue; that God is not alone self
existent, but that every mind that he has made which feels the dignity of a
free being and on the ground of its own convictions adopts this law of God's
action, thereby becomes a sharer of his own eternal nature and thus hath
the principles of its own life within itself.

Responsible and accountable for his own character, man is a being
like God, virtuous, "self existent" and free, a being capable of
creating himself from resources within himself, "the principles of
[his] own life." What Emerson means here is something more than
the self-improvement and organic version of the self preached by
more conventional Unitarians and purveyors of the American
dream. Rather than stressing the development of external habits of
conduct, such as industry and temperance, Emerson now advises the
development of the inner man: "a man's improvement is by the
development of his own mind. Our improvement is from within not
from without" (No. XCIII). Progress so far as it is possible, Emerson
tells his congregation in 1830, is measured by a growing likeness to
God and adherence to the truths within the soul, and not by so many
goods accumulated. As Emerson's sight focuses on the inner man, he
finds that authority, power, and generation are all contained within
the self and need only to be realized by close adherence to the oracle
of the God within the self. This is the miracle that Jesus is said to
have accomplished, for more than any other person he was one with
God, with the "Vast Mind" (No. CXXIV) that is the Universe and is
within the self, conforming his thought, action, and character – his
whole being – to the Self within himself. To this extent, then, he
could declare, "I & my Father are one" (No. CIX), and to the extent
that more ordinary men can adhere their being to the oracle of God
so, too, can they declare, "I & my Father are one." The perfect
character in this new schema is a self-created self, for he shapes his
being on the authority of his own soul and from resources that reside

within his own being. Convinced that "God is *in* our soul" (No. CLX), Emerson formulated a new kind of self-sufficiency that tested authority, evidence, and reality against the angle of his own vision.

Although Emerson continued to preach the dichotomy of the flesh and the spirit, as he does in Sermon No. XCIII, still finding that "man hath a spiritual nature superior to his animal life and superior to his intellectual powers," oddly enough he repairs the rent in the human spirit as he locates the "Vast Mind" of God within the carnal self. At once suggesting man's likeness to God, this strategy also gives meaning to the heretofore empty, frivolous, and dangerous external form, the body of man, when it is shaped by the indwelling spirit and corresponds to its higher laws. Of course, this strategy ultimately supercharges the power of the mind, the side of being identified as masculine, for it locates all meaning and reality within the mind of man and the mind of God. Nonetheless, Emerson discovers that a "unity of design" forms a common bond between the physical and the spiritual, the natural and the intellectual, that infuses the physical with sublimity and meaning: "A sublime evidence of his Unity comes up from the strict correspondence of the outward to the intellectual world" (No. CXXVII). Just as nature is a hieroglyphic of the eternal laws, deriving significance for Emerson because it serves as a text by which man can know God, and Jesus is the perfect union of spirit and flesh, the Word made flesh, so, too, the "perfect character," the true Christian, is a living example of the spirit. In the same way, a religion of forms and rituals is empty unless it is infused with morality, righteousness, and belief. In his resignation sermon from Second Church in Boston, Emerson explained his objection to the celebration of the Lord's Supper and his church's insistence that he administer the ritual even though he no longer believed in its efficacy:

I am not engaged to Christianity by decent forms, or saving ordinances; it is not usage, it is not what I do not understand, that binds me to it, – let these be the sandy foundations of falsehoods. What I revere and obey in it is its reality, its boundless charity, its deep interior life, the rest it gives to mind, the echo it returns to my thoughts. (*W* 25–6)[8]

Whatever the significance the Lord's Supper or other rituals may have for Emerson derives not from duty, habit, or gestures – the outer trappings – but from an intensely interior life of the mind. The problem with the old Jewish religion for Emerson is that it "was a religion of forms; it was all body, it had no life" (*W* 27). That appears also to be the problem with modern Christianity and modern man – they have deformed the meaning of religion and success by a one-sided development of external forms of duty, decorum, and habit at the expense of the internal, moral self, where true self-improvement should occur. For Emerson, the mind, the spirit, the moral nature is what counts, and without the informing spirit, the body or ritual is a mere shadow without substance. But when the body and the mind are in harmony, when the mind directs, masters, and commands the body to do its will, then the man and the institution are living representations of the spirit.

This is what made Jesus the perfect man for Emerson; it was not that he was endowed with a divine office, but that he realized more completely than anyone else the unity and oneness of spirit and flesh. Jesus was the "organ of the Allwise & Almighty," the physical means or instrument by which the eternal truths found articulation (No. CIX). He spoke the "words that are felt to be as forcible as actions" and his life was an example of "Unity of character, whose words went with his actions" (No. CXXXIV). In the same way, anyone might become Christlike by developing the interior resources of the self: "It is still at this day as it was at the first, the Word made Flesh, the Word of truth made Flesh or realized in the actions of good men that reconciles man to God" (No. CXXXVIII). The perfect character, like Jesus, "perceives the great truth that God is in him, and that he is no longer his own; as he rids himself of his vices he becomes more and more instinct with life from the Vast Mind that animates and governs the whole Universe" (No. CXXIV). And because this perfect character has surrendered his coarse self to the God within, he is free to act and speak from his heart, the seat of authority for him. He speaks what he thinks and acts as he and "not as others chuse" (No. CXXIV), for "the perfect man is a law unto himself" (No. CXLVI). Indeed, only when the self has plunged into the depths of his own heart, discovering in the Emersonian doctrine the presence of the benevolent God and not the underside of the self, only then is he "conscious of having really thought & acted" (No. CLV). As in the case of Jesus, the perfect character is independent of others and of social institutions because he relies on an internal source of authority and evidence: "By renouncing all other laws & by a devout listening to this oracle, a man shall be guided to truth & duty & to heaven" (No. CLX).

Of course, this is the kind of independence from extraneous codes of thought and conduct that Emerson sought as he worked towards a split from Second Church. Dissatisfied with a life not of his own making, Emerson began to test his will against the larger, cultural expectations and blueprints for the self. He found particularly confining a religion that stressed external sources of authority – social dictum, scripture, and miracle – and rituals that had lost their meaning for him, especially now after he had discovered the true meaning of self-trust. He wrote in his journal of January 10, 1832, the year he would resign his ministerial duties:

It is the best part of the man, I sometimes think, that revolts most against being the minister. His good revolts from official goodness. If he never spoke or acted but with the full consent of his understanding[,] if the whole man acted always, how powerful would be every act & every word. Well then or ill then how much power he sacrifices by conforming himself to say & do in other folks' time instead of in his own. The difficulty is that we do not make a world of our own but fall into institutions already made. (*JMN* III 318)

Clearly Emerson is disgruntled at having to conform his thought and action to other people's perceptions of ministering and religion. Having formulated a theology from the crucible of his own life and thought, Emerson strained against an institution and a vocation that he felt kept him in intellectual bondage. And clearly he longs to realize in his own life the kind of unity of thought and action he had preached. It is no wonder that he used his disagreement with his congregation about the meaning and celebration of the Lord's Supper as the occasion for forcing his personal identity crisis to a head, for his objection to the commemoration parallels his own vocational dilemma.

The closeness of the rhetoric and content of the journal passage with the passages pertaining to Jesus and the perfect character suggests that Emerson identified himself with them and symbolically transferred to himself the powers he had assigned to them. By devising a theology that pronounced self-reliance to be both sanctified and manly, Emerson found a philosophical sanction for his own impulse to "cut & run" (*JMN* III 325). But he also found a way to participate in the power of God as he created his own version of Jesus, invented a fictive character he labeled "perfect" and "genuine," and created himself anew as a "New Man" (No. CLXIV). In a sense, then, Emerson both invents in his sermons the fictive characters of Jesus and the "genuine man" and invents himself from his own text. In his farewell sermon, No. CLXIV, delivered October 21, 1832, Emerson became, for the moment anyway, the character he had preached, demonstrating his personal metamorphosis into a "New Man" who, true to his inner voice, declared his independence from an unmanning conformity as he acted his thought and participated in the "absolute sovereignty" of God.

In this sermon, Emerson turns the myth of the self-made man on its head by announcing that greatness does not consist in winning wars, rearing "grand temples & beautiful palaces," or in sponsoring great art but in the "forming of men[,] true & entire men." The hero of the new age announced by Emerson is not the self-made man of the myth of success who confuses his identity with his dress and money, but a man-made *self* whose self-improvement is internal instead of merely external, whose new identity depends on his unity with the God within. Like Jesus, the "genuine man" "acts always in character because he acts always from his character. He is accustomed to pay implicit respect to the dictates of his own reason & to obey them without asking why. He therefore speaks what he thinks. He acts his thought." And, like Jesus, the genuine man realizes his "likeness to God" (Channing 146) by discovering and making real through word and action the unity between man and God and the unity of his own being.

During the course of his ministry, Emerson had reconstituted the definition of the self and in doing so had reconstituted his own selfhood. Having undergone a personal conversion that made him a new man, "born again" to a "new life" of "balance & energy" and power (No. CLII), Emerson could, on October 21, "speak what he thinks" and act his thought, could declare himself a genuine man by his words and actions, for he had made up his mind to trust himself and to cut his formal ties with Second Church despite objections by his family and his own misgivings about leaving a congregation of friends. He strained at "The yoke of men's opinions" and wrote to his journal:

> I will not live out of me.
> I will not see with others' eyes
>   . . .
> I would be free.   (*JMN* IV, 47)

When he announced his resignation, he spoke from himself and realized in his own person the independence and power concomitant with the unity of word and action that he had so consistently preached in the last year of his ministry.

But even though Emerson redefined the measure by which human success is judged and remade his own character, the equation between masculinity and spirituality remains, for in redefining the essence of man he made firmer the conviction that all that is good and strong in human nature derives from the heart or mind under whose will the body must ever be mastered. Though he preached unity and invented a fictive character who, like the man he perceived Jesus to be, incarnated the spirit in human form, he still persisted in sublimating the body to the soul. Indeed, having located spirituality and reality completely in the mind or soul where the God within dwells, the development of the mind at the expense of the natural self is even more crucial. At the end of his tenure at Second Church he still pronounced what he had at the beginning of his ministry, "Jesus Christ came into the world for this express purpose to teach men to prefer the soul to the body" (No. CLXIV), and spirituality was still equated in his thought with masculinity and power.

Although Charles Kingsley accused Emerson of preaching "Anythingarianism," the sermons testify that Emerson was far from advocating moral or social irresponsiblity. Emerson's insistence on self-control throughout his ministry, indeed throughout his career, belies Kingsley's reading of an easy Transcendentalism. If anything, Emerson's strictures about appetite are more censorious than Kingsley's "healthy animalism" (Martin 201) and confirm Emerson's ties to the Calvinism of another British writer, John Milton. Moreover, the heady, narcissistic spiritualism of which Emerson was so often accused by Kingsley and others has its foundation in a reading of man's intimate relationship to God. Rather than justifying the individual's moral and social inaction, Emerson draws a hero who anticipates those of Kingsley, though, as we have seen, with distinctly American inflections. Taking as his model none other than Jesus of Nazareth, Emerson creates a hero who fuses thought and action, body and soul, and democratically calls on all likewise to experience what Kingsley calls "the divineness of the whole manhood" (quoted in Martin, 219). Concerned with infusing and invigorating Christianity with what they referred to as "manliness," both Kingsley and Emerson hoped to bring about a transformation in religion that would speak more closely to the individual. That both men accomplished their goals, albeit in different ways, testifies to the seductiveness of their ideals during periods of profound personal and social tumult.

NOTES

I wish to thank the American Antiquarian Society for allowing me to use their library and to cite from the following sources: George Burnap, Joel Hawes, Horace Mann, *The Young Man's Own Book*, Winslow Hubbard, John Frost, Archibald Alexander, and Joseph Allen.

1 Emerson's manuscript sermons are housed at the Houghton Library, Harvard University. Although the first three volumes of *Emerson's Complete Sermons*, ed. Albert J. von Frank (1989, 1990), have been published, bringing into print the first 135 sermons, the remaining volume of the series has yet to appear. My citations are to the manuscript text. Emerson's sermons are referred to by number and are so indicated in citations in this essay.

2 *The Journals and Miscellaneous Notebooks of Ralph Waldo Emerson*, eds. William H. Gilman *et al.* (Cambridge, MA: Belknap of Harvard University Press, 1960–1982). Emerson's journal entries are cited in this essay as *JMN* with volume and page numbers.

3 Leland Person Jr. notes that in the nineteenth century "female characters (as well as the female reader, who is encouraged to identify with them and thus against herself) are reduced in male-authored texts to positive or negative signs of male values" (3) and Judith Fetterley argues that what is true of American literature is also true of American sub-literature: "It insists on its universality at the same time that it defines that universality in specifically male terms" (xii).

4 Michael Lopez argues that Emerson's "'philosophy of power' ... seems almost to rival Nietzsche's in its comprehensiveness" and finds that the words "'Power,' 'force,' 'energy' ... seem to recur on every page of Emerson's published works" (122).

5 His family's expectations and his slowness at meeting them are exemplified in a complaint voiced by his father, William Emerson, to a friend when Ralph Waldo was a week shy of his third birthday: "Ralph does not read very well yet" (quoted in McAleer, 16).

6 Richard Grusin discusses Emerson's diet to argue that it represents "temperate eating as the result of clear understanding" about God and temperance (34–5). My contention is that Emerson is trying to become like the spirit that his dead wife has now become. Ellen Tucker Emerson died from tuberculosis on February 8, 1831, at the age of nineteen.

7 Evelyn Barish details Mrs. Emerson's Calvinistic child-rearing practices and surmises that "Food, in fact, and eating seem to have become a crux and symbol of his feeling deprived and unloved" (25).

8 *The Works of Ralph Waldo Emerson: Miscellanies*, ed. J. E. Cabot (Boston: Fireside Edition, 1878–1906). The text for the Lord's Supper Sermon is taken from this edition and is referred to in this essay as *W*.

WORKS CITED

Adams, Jasper, *Laws of Success and Failure in Life: An Address delivered 30th October, 1833, in the Chapel of the College of Charleston before the Euphradian Society*. Charleston: A. E. Miller, 1833.

Alcott, William A., *The Young Man's Guide*, 2nd edn. Boston: Lilly, Wait, Colman and Holden, 1834.

Alexander, Archibald, *A Sermon, preached to the Chapel of Nassau Hall*. Princeton University Press, 1826.

Allen, Joseph, *The Sources of Public Prosperity, A Discourse Delivered in Northborough, April 9, 1829, on the Day of the Public Fast*. Worcester, MA: Griffin and Norrill, 1829.

Barish, Evelyn, *Emerson: The Roots of Prophecy*. Princeton University Press, 1989.

Burnap, George W., *Lectures to Young Men, on the Cultivation of the Mind, the Formation of Character, and the Conduct of Life*. Baltimore: John Murphy, 1840.

Cawelti, John G., *Apostles of the Self-Made Man*. University of Chicago Press, 1965.

Channing, William Ellery, *William Ellery Channing: Selected Writings*, ed. David Robinson. New York: Paulist Press, 1985.

Christ, Carol P., *Diving Deep and Surfacing: Women Writers on Spiritual Quest*, 2nd edn. Boston: Beacon Press, 1980.

  Laughter of Aphrodite: Reflections on a Journey to the Goddess. San Francisco: Harper & Row, 1987.

The Christian Examiner.

Emerson, Ralph Waldo, *The Complete Sermons of Ralph Waldo Emerson*, eds. Albert J. von Frank *et al.* Columbia, MO: University of Missouri Press, 1989– .

  The Journals and Miscellaneous Notebooks of Ralph Waldo Emerson, ed. William H. Gilman. Cambridge, MA: Belknap of Harvard University Press, 1960–82.

  The Works of Ralph Waldo Emerson: Miscellanies, ed. J. E. Cabot. Boston: Fireside Edition, 1878–1906.

The [Boston] Evening Gazette.

Everett, Edward, *Orations and Speeches on Various Occasions*. Boston: American Stationers' Company, 1836.

Fetterley, Judith, *The Resisting Reader: A Feminist Approach to American Fiction*. Bloomington: Indiana University Press, 1978.

Frost, John, *An Oration Delivered at Middlebury, Before the Associated Alumni of the College, on the Evening of Commencement, August 19th, 1829*. Utica: Hastings and Tracy, 1829.

Grusin, Richard A, *Transcendentalist Hermeneutics: Institutional Authority and the Higher Criticism of the Bible*. Durham, NC: Duke University Press, 1991.

Hawes, Joel, *Lectures to Young Men, on the Formation of Character*, 3rd edn. Hartford: Cooke & Co., 1829.

Houghton, Walter, *The Victorian Frame of Mind, 1830–1870*. New Haven: Yale University Press, 1957.

Kingsley, Charles, *Alton Locke: Tailor and Poet. An Autobiography*. New York: Harper & Brothers, 1850.

Lopez, Michael, "Transcendental Failure: 'The Palace of Spiritual Power'" in *Emerson: Prospect and Retrospect*, ed. Joel Porte. Cambridge, MA: Harvard University Press, 1982, pp. 212–54.

McAleer, John, *Ralph Waldo Emerson: Days of Encounter*. Boston: Little, Brown and Co., 1984.

Mann, Horace, *A Few Thoughts for a Young Man: A Lecture Delivered before the Boston Mercantile Library Association on its 29th Anniversary*. Boston: Ticknor, Reed and Fields, 1850.

Martin, Robert Bernard, *The Dust of Combat: A Life of Charles Kingsley*. London: Faber and Faber, 1959.

Michie, Helena, *The Flesh made Word: Female Figures and Women's Bodies*. New York: Oxford University Press, 1987.

Person, Leland S., Jr., *Aesthetic Headaches: Women and a Masculine Poetics in Poe, Melville, & Hawthorne*. Athens, GA: University of Georgia Press, 1988.

Richardson, Richard D., Jr., *Myth and Literature in the American Renaissance*. Bloomington: Indiana University Press, 1978.

Robinson, David, *Apostle of Culture: Emerson as Preacher and Lecturer*. Philadelphia: University of Pennsylvania Press, 1982.

Thorp, Margaret Farrand, *Charles Kingsley, 1819–1875*. New York: Octagon Books, 1969.

Todd, John, *The Young Man, Hints Addressed to the Young Men of the United States*, 2nd edn. Northampton, MA, 1844.

Vance, Norman, *The Sinews of the Spirit: The Ideal of Christian Manliness in Victorian Literature and Religious Thought*. Cambridge University Press, 1985.

Winslow, Hubbard, *The Young Man's Aid to Knowledge, Virtue, and Happiness*, 2nd edn. Boston: Crocker & Brewster, 1839.

Wise, Daniel, *The Young Man's Counsellor: or, Sketches and Illustrations of the Duties and Dangers of Young Men*. New York, 1850.

The Young Man's Own Book. Philadelphia: Key, Mielke and Biddle, 1833.

PART III

Responses to muscular Christianity

The confidence man: empire and the deconstruction of muscular Christianity in "The Mystery of Edwin Drood"

David Faulkner

In 1870 Lord John Russell observed that "[the] time has passed" when Great Britain "could have stood alone"; after conquering and peopling half the world, he urged, "There is no going back" (quoted in Mansergh 1 vi). A less astute imperial spokesman, who appeared that same year in the unfinished pages of Charles Dickens's *The Mystery of Edwin Drood*, did not share Russell's sense of having turned a historical corner. Although Mr. Thomas Sapsea, auctioneer and Mayor-elect of "Cloisterham," has never left England, he confidently claims to "know the world" through the exotic commodities that pass beneath his gavel. He is, nonetheless, "morally satisfied that nothing but himself has grown since he was a baby" (24). What Dickens calls Sapsea's "unspeakable complacency" (26) suggests that the author himself knew better. Indeed, his characterizations are telling here, for an exemplary muscular Christian, the Reverend Septimus Crisparkle, presides over this novel. Norman Vance has argued that the variable cluster of cultural values expressed in "Christian manliness" always reflects "contemporary heroisms and concerns" (1). The portrait of Crisparkle's Christian manliness engages some pressing issues of the late 1860s: the causes and cultural implications of England's accelerated global expansion.

From the outset Septimus Crisparkle, fair and wholesome, appears a pure specimen of the genus "muscular Christian," a cultural ideal of Anglo-Saxon vigor and virtue. Crisparkle's character corresponds to many typical features of the manly Christian spelled out by Vance. In Charles Kingsley's vision, for example, physical manliness was "an index and a condition of psychological, moral and spiritual health" (Vance 110). Thus Crisparkle's mania for exercise indicates soundness of soul:

A fresh and healthy portrait the looking-glass presented of the Reverend Septimus, feinting and dodging with the utmost artfulness, and hitting out from the shoulders with the utmost straightness, while his radiant features teemed with innocence, and soft-hearted benevolence beamed from his boxing-gloves. (38)

Forthrightly opposing both the coercive philanthropy of Honey-thunder (150–52) and the Dean's quietism – "we clergy need do nothing emphatically," says the Dean (146) – Crisparkle partakes of the Kingsleyan tradition of "Christian activism" (Vance 29). Like Kingsley's heroes, Crisparkle counsels reticence and exertion against the emotional excesses of "morbid introspection" (Vance 93). His inner life is so undramatic, he avers, that his diary requires "A line for a day, nothing more" (86).

This strong, silent type emerges out of the "romantic Teutonism" which Vance sees as a "historical and racial underpinning for the ideal of sturdy Protestant manliness" (76). Indeed, Dickens introduces Crisparkle's home life by evoking the turbulent pre-Norman history of Cloisterham: "Swaggering fighting men had had their centuries of ramping and raving about Minor Canon Corner" (39). Crisparkle is clearly drawn as a modern liberal avatar of these combative virtues, but he also appears as a representative Englishman. The cultural climate surrounding his portrait held the supposedly inherent racial characteristics of the Anglo-Saxon – and his English descendants – "in high favour" (Vance 100).[1] *The Mystery of Edwin Drood* conflates muscular Christianity and Englishness as such. If the putatively timeless "manly Christian" ideal of chivalry and gentility appealed to many in a time of social and economic upheaval (Vance 17), then Crisparkle's wholehearted innocence seems wishfully to represent, for Dickens, a cultural still-point in a turning world.

For *Edwin Drood*, uniquely in Dickens's canon, inflects a world that was changing very rapidly indeed. In a typical Dickens novel, the little-known colonial world exists stubbornly at the distant margins of the story – the West Indies in *Dombey and Son*, Australia in *David Copperfield*, Borioboola-Gha in *Bleak House*. Nearly all of his novels feature characters tied to the non-European world, such as Magwitch or Micawber, Mrs. Jellyby or Walter Gay. The books of Dickens and his contemporaries reproduce an increasingly well-articulated imperial structure of hierarchical asymmetry, with the metropolis at the center, and colonies or other supplementary

in the name of geography, culture, or psychology.[7] Such a reading generally shows how the transparent, self-evident values of pastoral England – embodied and enforced by Crisparkle as muscular Christian – would, had Dickens only lived longer, triumphantly redeem their own dark, parasitical cosmopolitan opposites. In other words, amid wedding bells, Crisparkle would bring Jasper to justice for Edwin's murder.

Of course, the interpretive gesture made by such readings – enhancing a discrete boundary between the novel's hemispheres – is intermittently solicited by the text. Dickens may well have intended this comic resolution. Still, the unfinished manuscript, Dickens's contradictory reticence about the *dénouement*, and his nagging difficulties with the plot (Cardwell xxv–xxvii) make that question ultimately undecidable. Shelves full of "solutions" to the "mystery" proclaim the irresistible temptation to seal our borders once and for all. We can, however, read this novel with a difference: having smuggled the exotic East into the tranquil English center of Cloisterham itself, under the sign of opium and in the person of John Jasper, Dickens liberates forces that can displace his whole novelistic practice, moving his last novel away from the same representational conventions he had helped to shape.

These two ways of reading correspond broadly to England's two "native policy" alternatives for its new imperial situation, emblematized by Froude's authoritarianism and Colenso's relativism: English culture imposed from above, or the permission of more spontaneous hybrid cultural formations.[8] *Edwin Drood* projects both competing cultural visions. To put it another way, we might read this milieu of cultural confrontation filtered through *Edwin Drood* as an irreconcilable tension between two emergent narrative paradigms – between the inexorable teleology of the detective plot and the seductive convolutions of Jasper's case history. The detective plot – which Crisparkle governs – drives towards a lustrative closure that ratifies the dominant culture by scapegoating the "Orientalized" other, as Rosa Bud seeks to "cleanse" herself from "the stain of [Jasper's] impurity by appealing against it to the honest and true [that is, Crisparkle]" (176). Yet Dickens's hypnotic focus on Jasper's cultural schizophrenia stalls this teleology and briefly clears a new kind of cultural space. In that space, mediated by the liminal opium den, we glimpse the critical possibility that the metropolitan self and culture may be inhabited, indeed constituted, by heterogeneous otherness. In *Edwin Drood*, the gulf between home and abroad is always already bridged.

Two broad areas of textual evidence support this view: Dickens's use of (1) psychological doubling between characters, and (2) another form of teeming repetition in which elements from either sphere uncannily parody the other. Instances of the first type include those characters having doubled initials (John Jasper, Dick Datchery, the Princess Puffer), or the Landless twins, or the identically matched "china shepherdesses," Crisparkle's mother and aunt (42).[9] The extensive pairing between Jasper and Crisparkle, however, with its showdown between muscular Christianity and cosmopolitanism, provides the most obviously fruitful example of the first type of doubling.

The two characters correspond at nearly every point. The name "Crisparkle" suggests only a less opaque form of the crystal evoked by "Jasper." Their first full descriptions appear on the same page: Crisparkle is "fair and rosy" as opposed to Jasper's "dark" coloring; Crisparkle is "boy-like," while Jasper "looks older than he is"; the one is "cheerful," while the other "sombre," and so forth (6–7). Yet even within this apparently polarized distribution, they converge on certain points. Like the choirmaster, Crisparkle is also "musical" (6), and habitually sits up late "very softly touching his piano" (60), rather unsettlingly like Jasper's custom, while accompanying Rosa, of "carefully and softly hinting the key-note from time to time" (51). Crisparkle's eyesight – "he had the eyes of a microscope and a telescope combined" (40) – rivals the concentrated intensity of Jasper's mesmeric gaze. Although Jasper's involuntary opium flashbacks sometimes throw a "film" over his vision (10), Crisparkle willingly impairs his own sight with unnecessary spectacles in order to flatter his mother (40). As foils, the two men appear quite often together, but occasionally there is little to distinguish them, as when Neville Landless finds both conspiring against him as "central figures" of the group pursuing him (133).

The apparently straightforward apportionment of opposed traits gets increasingly slippery. Just before Edwin's murder, Jasper tells Crisparkle, "You had but little reason to assume that I should become more like yourself. You are always training yourself to be, mind and body, as clear as crystal, and you always are, and never change, whereas I am a muddy, solitary, moping weed" (129). The ironies here are heavy. Jasper's luminous confidence bears the influence, not of divine music, but of opium (we later learn that he has visited the Princess Puffer this d. y [210]). He imitates his honest counterpart by having pledged to obstruct justice, by destroying his potentially self-incriminating journal: "I shall burn the evidence of my case," he says, "and begin the next volume with a clearer vision" (129). Finally, a surreptitious biblical allusion (Jacobsen 132) links the two more closely than Crisparkle might care to know: in Revelation 21:11, the New Jerusalem has a radiance "like unto jasper stone, clear as crystal." The cumulative effect of this convergence of Crisparkle's and Jasper's traits and behavior is ultimately not to consolidate but to erode their supposed moral polarity. Crisparkle's "purity" as a muscular Christian ideal is never unadulterated. It requires only the slightest turn of the screw for the pugilistic Crisparkle, sparring aggressively with his reflection, to evert unexpectedly into Jasper vowing the destruction of Edwin's murderer (146) – himself – somewhat as Jasper mockingly urges Sapsea to "turn inside out" the "character" of Durdles "with a few skilful touches" (101).

The second type of repetition operates in different tonal registers, from the humorous to the uncanny. Thematic elements, character motifs, words, or phrases from one pole of the novel echo through the other, transgressing or fragmenting the implicit cultural boundary. Miss Twinkleton's watchfulness over Edwin and Rosa (18), for example, comically anticipates Jasper's sinister surveillance. Playful instances of male impersonation at the Nun's House School (18, 66) may nominate Helena Landless, who also has a history of cross-dressing in Ceylon (49), as a candidate for the detective Datchery.[10] Less cozily, Rosa's craving for Turkish Lumps-of-Delight (20) mirrors Jasper's addiction. Mr. Grewgious's picture of the state of mind of "the true lover," who lives "at once a doubled life and a halved life" (95), and Miss Twinkleton's "two states of consciousness which never clash, but each of which pursues its separate course as though it were continuous instead of broken" (15), resonate in a more psychotic key with Jasper's schizophrenia. (This is the novel's persistent cultural dilemma writ small: are cultures whole and continuous, or "broken"?) As these repetitions and lateral slippages multiply like computer viruses, they perforate the assumption that this novel presents some homogeneous cultural norm of English Christian manliness, whose opposite is a parasitic declension. Neither sphere can, with any confidence, claim to be pure, self-consistent, or internally constituted. As Jasper insinuates, "There is said to be a hidden skeleton in every house" (11).

The novel plays obsessively on a range of concepts clustered about the word "confidence," in its many senses: "belief in," "trust and openness," "something imparted and held secretly," with a general sense of frank immediacy and unqualified wholeheartedness – in short, "mutual friendship." Crisparkle presides over this array. Onomastics leads us to expect that Crisparkle's quintessential Englishness represents transparent confidence as against Jasper's exquisitely "Oriental" extremes of self-division and deceit. Indeed, to the bitter end, one of the novel's voices insists on the gulf between them:

> It is not likely that they ever met, though so often, without a sensation on the part of each that the other was a perplexing secret to him ... [They] must at least have stood sufficiently in opposition, to have speculated with keen interest each on the steadiness and next direction of the other's designs. But neither ever broached the theme.
>
> False pretence not being in the Minor Canon's nature, he doubtless displayed openly that he would at any time have revived the subject, and even desired to discuss it. The determined reticence of Mr. Jasper, however, was not to be so approached. (202–3)

Each man seems opaque to his counterpart's understanding because each reads the other from his own book. Jasper cannot fathom plain dealing, while Crisparkle balks at the hint of duplicity: "Mr. Crisparkle continuing to observe [Jasper's face], found it even more perplexing than before, inasmuch as it seemed to denote (which could hardly be) some close internal calculation" (86).

Translated into the broad cultural framework invited by his status as a representative muscular Englishman, Crisparkle's claim to "transparency" presumes a seamless, unproblematic relation of the individual to culture – a state of affairs in which a culture is organically whole and thoroughly transparent to itself, without any blind spots or *aporia*. Jasper would then embody self-division, *anomie*, a broken or discontinuous relation to culture. Indeed, total transparency is what Crisparkle demands above all, from himself and his charges. He admonishes Neville to forgive Edwin without the slightest trace of reserve:

> What may be in your heart when you give him your hand, can only be known to the Searcher of all hearts; but it will never go well with you, if there be any treachery there ... So much the more weight shall I attach to the pledge I require from you, when it is unreservedly given. (83–4)

Crisparkle rings changes on this theme throughout the novel. And yet even he is not above deception. Perhaps we should not be surprised by now that Jasper has parodied Crisparkle's disciplinary strictures two chapters earlier, appearing to pacify Neville and Edwin when it is his deeper purpose to antagonize them:

"Perhaps," says Jasper, in a smoothing manner, "we had better not qualify our good understanding. We had better not say anything having the appearance of a remonstrance or condition ... Frankly and freely, you see there is no anger in Ned. Frankly and freely, there is no anger in you, Mr. Neville?" (57)

I have already alluded to Crisparkle's having, for his mother's benefit, "invented the pretence" (40) of nearsightedness; he is certainly reluctant to confide other things to his mother, such as Neville's quarrel with Edwin, except that Jasper kindly informs her of it (77). Nor does he hesitate to "feign to be looking out of window in a contemplative state of mind when a servant [enters]" (39), when he has just been engaged in the somewhat unclerical art of shadow-boxing. The novel's contention that "false pretence" is foreign to Crisparkle's nature inevitably invites its own skepticism.

Crisparkle falls prey to the contradiction that his own draconian muscular Christian standard makes virtually inevitable, when he "gives Neville a bright nod and a cheerful goodbye: expressing (not without intention) absolute confidence and ease" (122). "Absolute confidence," even as a cultural ideal of transparent immediacy, seems ineluctably undermined by calculatedness, traversed by parenthetical reservation, opacity, and duplicity. The novel everywhere insists upon this point. Even after Edwin and Rosa reach the serenity of mutual friendship by agreeing to part, they maintain "a reservation on each side" – she silently resolves to quit Jasper's musical tuition, while he speculates on Helena Landless's affections (119). In the midst of her contented confidence in Helena's protection, Rosa recognizes that "her latest friendship had a blank place in it of which she could not fail to be sensible" (113). That this "blank space" is the name of Edwin Drood – of the novel at hand – should not be lost on us. No culture, it seems, can be confidently transparent to itself.[11]

Another brief contrast with *Dombey and Son* illustrates how these displacements realign the poetics of the imperial novel. Not culture, but class, fractures the doubling of Edith Dombey and Alice Marwood, and the lower-class subplot clearly supplements, without putting into question, the upper-class main plot: "Were this miserable mother, and this miserable daughter, only the reduction to their lowest grade, of certain social vices sometimes prevailing higher up?" (*Dombey* 477). In *Drood*, however, the doubled relationship is no longer the asymmetrical one of main plot and reinforcing subplot, or main hero and secondary alter ego. The colonial presence here is neither a subordinated theme nor exotic grace-note, but a transformative historical and psychological *pressure*, a paradigm-shift legible in the deep structure of the novel. On Christmas Eve, Cloisterham's shops boast of luxurious, Oriental excess: "Lavish profusion is in the shops: particularly in the articles of currants, raisins, spices, candied peel, and moist sugar" (120). And even what might claim to be the moral center of this novel, the fictional space most opposed to the opium den, from which pure sweetness and light ought to radiate – Mrs. Crisparkle's closet – proves to have a skeleton of its own:

It was a most wonderful closet, worthy of Cloisterham and of Minor Canon Corner ... The upper slide, on being pulled down (leaving the lower a double mystery), revealed deep shelves of pickle-jars, jam-pots, tin canisters, *spice-boxes, and agreeably outlandish vessels of blue and white, the luscious lodgings of preserved tamarind and ginger ... the lower slide ascending, oranges were revealed, attended by a mighty japanned sugar-box, to temper their acerbity if unripe.* (79, my emphasis)

Crisparkle's Other already inhabits his presiding genius. The cultural difference lies not between but within.[12]

Edwin Drood presents many instances of this hybridized or impure culture-concept. Perhaps the irrepressible, even intrusive motif of "unfinishedness" – Rosa's portrait (7), Durdles's house and works (29, 37, 103), Grewgious's features (66, 68), to name only a few examples – bespeaks Dickens's narrative problems with the kind of ideological closure typically required by the imperial novel. This resistance to closure extends even to such a basic generic constituent of the Victorian novel as "character," or what D. H. Lawrence called "the old stable ego." If Jasper figures a discontinuous or duplicitous relation to culture, then it seems important to consider his status as a "character." From the outset, Jasper is split at the root, and his "scattered consciousness" can only "fantastically [piece] itself together" (1) at discontinuous intervals. His body itself threatens to deliquesce instantly under Grewgious's accusing gaze: "Mr Grewgious heard a terrible shriek, and saw ... nothing but a heap of torn and miry clothes upon the floor" (138). Jasper's life moots the possibility that characters and cultures, like Miss Twinkleton's two states of consciousness, pursue their separate courses *as though* they were continuous instead of "broken." Only the catastrophically obtuse Sapsea could conclude of Jasper that "that young man ... is sound, sir, at the core" (100). *Edwin Drood's* incompleteness – its "unfinishableness," even if Dickens had lived longer – is built into its structure as the conflicting claims of two incompatible yet interdependent narrative projects.

Thus we quit *Edwin Drood* feeling suspended between two competing worldviews – a sensation somewhat like Edwin's disorientation at Mr. Grewgious's indecipherable "compromise between an unqualified assent and a qualified dissent" (92). Crisparkle believes that his muscular regime of self-discipline produces "the composition of a fine character": to Neville he adduces Helena as an example of one who "govern[s]" and "dominate[s]" and "bend[s] her pride into a grand composure that is ... a sustained *confidence* in you and in the truth" (155, my emphasis). But Neville knows better that "a strong hand," paradoxically, has deprived him of anything like a stable purchase on cultural identity, producing self-division and unspeakable *anomie* instead:

This has made me secret and revengeful ... This has driven me, in my weakness, to the resource of being false and mean. I have been stinted of education, liberty, money, dress, the very necessaries of life, the commonest pleasure of childhood, the commonest possessions of youth. This has caused me to be utterly wanting in I don't know what emotions, or remembrances, or good instincts – I have not even a name for the thing, you see! (49)

Of *Drood's* two competing visions of culture, one is fluid, multicultural, pieced together – almost like Colenso rewritten by postmodern anthropology – and the other is rigidly autocratic, like Sapsea's Froudean slips. Sapsea's favorite songs exhort him

to reduce to a smashed condition all other islands but this island, and all continents, peninsulas, isthmuses, promontories, and other geographical forms of land soever ... In short, he rendered it pretty clear that Providence made a distinct mistake in originating so small a nation of oaks, and so many other verminous peoples. (100)

Despite the obvious satire directed against Sapsea's nascent jingoism, however, a well-known celebration of English pastoralism near the end of the fragment draws upon its cultural assumptions.

The Dickensian passage is justly famous, and it often functions as

the pivot of "comic" solutions to the mystery. It homogenizes
Englishness by evoking the island as a single integrated garden:

A brilliant morning shines on the old city ... Changes of glorious light from
moving boughs, songs of birds, scents from gardens, woods, and fields – or,
rather, from the one great garden of the whole cultivated island in its
yielding time – penetrate into the Cathedral, subdue its earthly odour, and
preach the Resurrection and the Life. (215)

The canonical status of two literary antecedents, Shakespeare and
Wordsworth, invests some much-needed cultural capital in this
venture. John of Gaunt's dying invocation of England in *Richard II*
lurks in the background:

> This fortress built by Nature for herself
> Against infection and the hand of war,
> This happy breed of men, this little world,
> This precious stone set in the silver sea,
> Which serves it in the office of a wall,
> Or as a moat defensive to a house,
> Against the envy of less happier lands;
> This blessed plot, this earth, this realm, this England.
>
> (II.i.43–50)

An even closer echo reverberates from Wordsworth's 1802 sonnet
"Composed in the Valley near Dover, on the Day of Landing":

> Here, on our native soil, we breathe once more.
> The cock that crows, the smoke that curls, that sound
> Of Bells; – those boys who in yon meadow-ground
> In white-sleeved shirts are playing; and the roar
> Of the waves breaking on the chalky shore; –
> All, all are English. (lines 1–6)

Marlon Ross, on this sonnet, writes: "The all-inclusiveness of
Englishness – nothing in England can be alien to him or to England
itself ... serves as totalizing harmony for the pastoral union of people
and land" (61). Dickens similarly identifies Englishness with the
salvific quality of the pastoral itself, collapsing land and culture into
a seamless unity.

His celebration thus reinscribes England's topographical boundaries as transhistorical cultural essences, as natural fortresses against
racial infection, in the uncertain world of 1870. Crisparkle, muscular Christian, masquerades as global policeman, guarding Anglo-
Saxon virgins and casting out foreign devils. Cumulatively,

however, the displacements afforded by Dickens's fascinated identification with Jasper's self-divided artistic genius ultimately allow us to glimpse England itself as a colonizable, indeed a colonized space. English culture appears highly permeable, pieced together from difference and otherness:

Cloisterham ... was once possibly known to the Druids by another name, and certainly to the Romans by another, and to the Normans by another, and one name more or less in the course of many centuries can be of little moment to its dusty chronicles. (14)

Midway through the fragmentary novel, Jasper eavesdrops on the broken conversation of Crisparkle and Neville, in which "The word 'confidence,' shattered by the echoes, but still capable of being pieced together, is uttered by Mr. Crisparkle" (104–5). Jasper then hears his own name, and bursts into a puzzling fit of laughter. Dickens may have come to suspect that Crisparkle's cultural "confidence" is, from one point of view, only what the novel elsewhere calls "a piecing together of falsehood in the place of truth" (141). Perhaps this novel of Minor Canon Corner should no longer be exiled to a corner of Dickens's minor canon.

NOTES

1 See, for example, Faverty, especially pp. 13–40.
2 Dickens's personal position is pertinent here. Emigration – and its dark double, transportation – engaged his attention throughout his adult life: his philanthropy was broad enough to endorse the Ragged Schools' policy of training leading to emigration (Kaplan 149), and on behalf of Angela Burdett Coutts and Urania Cottage, he "supervised arrangements to send promising residents to Cape Town or Australia" (Kaplan 229). Only two of his sons remained in England during his lifetime; all the other Dickens boys had imperial careers. Dickens's anxieties about his chronically impecunious sons lingered throughout the 1860s. As for so many middle-class sons, empire seemed the natural alternative: "Since opportunities at home were limited, there were seas to sail and continents to conquer. Frustration at home could be overcome by imperial challenges abroad. Whatever the mixture of motives, after 1858 [Dickens] promoted [his sons'] early departure, even when it pained him to see them leave" (Kaplan 427). Frustrated ambition and empire-as-outlet form a significant part of *Edwin Drood*'s structure of feeling, certainly more visibly than in earlier works. Jasper, envious of Edwin's engineering future in Egypt, admits that "even a poor monotonous chorister and grinder of music ... may be troubled with some sort

of stray ambition, aspiration, restlessness, dissatisfaction, what shall we call it?" (12).

3 I have explored elsewhere the ramifications of the emergence of a new global conceptual space for the Victorian "culture-concept." See Faulkner, "The Birth of Culture from the Spirit of Cartography."

4 Wendy Jacobsen claims that in *Edwin Drood*, "Dickens's juxtaposition of the Christian church in Cloisterham with the exotic East and the demonic in man (represented by the passionate nature of the Land-lesses) reflects this new relativism" (86–7).

5 For these reasons, I cannot finally accept Eve Sedgwick's otherwise brilliant reading of *Edwin Drood* in *Between Men* (180–200). The power of that and similar anti-imperialist or antihomophobic interpretations often depends on maintaining the very boundaries that they purport to criticize: "the novel in many ways connives in a view of Englishness, of culture and race, or simply of 'psychology,' that insulates Jasper's experience from that of the novel's wholesome and blond characters" (Sedgwick 198). I am suggesting that the volatile cultural milieu of the 1860s undermined even these "insulating" structures, before a more concerted and self-conscious imperialism allowed them to retrench. At least equal forces were working in the opposite direction, even though they seem muted in retrospect. In my view, Sedgwick reads backwards from her later examples of Kipling's *Kim* and T. E. Lawrence's *Seven Pillars of Wisdom*, without paying enough attention to the specific economic, political, and cultural moment of *Drood*.

6 See also Brantlinger: "In the middle of the most serious domestic concerns, often in the most unlikely texts, the Empire may intrude as a shadowy realm of escape, renewal, banishment, or return for characters who for one reason or another need to enter or exit from scenes of domestic conflict" (12). I owe to Edward Said the broad outlines of this brief account of the poetics of imperial fictions. What I hope to add is a degree of specificity at (what is for me) a crucial historical juncture for the British Empire, a moment of structural change which throws this framework into crisis.

7 In this sense, Sedgwick's reading participates in the same geographical divisions that characterize the most traditional and moralized readings of *Edwin Drood*.

8 Froude is not the villain, nor Colenso the hero, of this piece. I suggest that the two contradictory yet mutually inclusive possibilities were generated by the new structural shifts in the empire, not that one or the other was more desirable. Lately, *Edwin Drood* has been invoked frequently as an exemplary "bad" text of racist, imperialist, or homophobic ideologies (see, for example, Sedgwick and Nunokawa). The whole story is a good deal more complicated than that. Moreover, I use these two opposed models of "'native policy' alternatives" heuristically, to represent broad categories of cultural response, without advancing any specific claims about the actual cultural projects of Froude or Colenso.

For a brief survey of the range of British cultural policy, see Porter 17–24, 178–88.

9 Indeed, in a perhaps unexpected sense, not separate identity but *repetition* characterizes the Crisparkle family. Its genetic history of twins, as well as Crisparkle's Christian name, suggests not the splendidly self-constituted individuality of the muscular Christian, but serial interchangeability: "Septimus, because six little brother Crisparkles before him went out, one by one, as they were born, like six weak little rushlights, as they were lighted" (30). Moreover, Dickens inserted this clause about naming as an afterthought in the manuscript (38n), and only settled on the name "Septimus" in what became the sixth chapter, the first chapter of the second monthly number. Such revision supports the intuition that what Dickens originally may have conceived as a stable moral opposition broke down under the pressure of imagining Jasper's criminal and artistic genius.

10 The first scene of such transvestism at the Nun's House – Rosa's schoolmates pretending to be one another's brothers and fiancés – was added by Dickens after the manuscript stage (18n, 19n), suggesting that this sort of corrosive cross-referencing between the novel's hemispheres was, to some degree, a matter of conscious revision.

11 In fact, Jasper himself unwittingly acknowledges that the novel itself could not exist without such a "contamination" of confidence by secrecy. When Jasper recovers from Grewgious's disclosure that Edwin and Rosa had already broken their engagement (thus scuttling Jasper's motive for murder), he reasons, "your disclosure, ... showing me that my own dear boy had a great disappointing reservation from men ... kindles hope within me" (140). Reservations within confidences – secrets within disclosures – generate hope, suspense, mystery, and narrative desire. The engine of the mystery-plot is the necessarily mutual inclusiveness of the novel's twinned regimes of transparency and opacity.

12 I have found my intuitions about *Edwin Drood*'s cultural problematic corroborated by Jacques Derrida's recent assertion of an "axiom" of culture: "*what is proper to a culture is to not be identical with itself*... There is no culture or cultural identity without this difference *with itself*" (90, original emphasis).

WORKS CITED

Arac, Jonathan and Harriet Ritvo, eds., *Macropolitics of Nineteenth-Century Literature: Nationalism, Exoticism, Imperialism*. Philadelphia: University of Pennsylvania Press, 1990.

Berridge, Virginia, "East End Opium Dens and Narcotic Use in Britain," *London Journal* 4 (1978): 3–38.

"Victorian Opium-Eating: Responses to Opiate Use in Nineteenth-Century England," *Victorian Studies* 21 (1978): 437–62.

Berridge, Virginia and Griffith Edwards, *Opium and the People: Opiate Use in Nineteenth-Century England*. London: Allen Lane, 1981.

Bodelsen, C. A., *Studies in Mid-Victorian Imperialism*, revised edn. London: Heinemann, 1960.

Brantlinger, Patrick, *Rule of Darkness: British Literature and Imperialism 1830–1914*. Ithaca: Cornell University Press, 1988.

Cardwell, Margaret, "Introduction" to *The Mystery of Edwin Drood*. Oxford: Clarendon, 1972.

Derrida, Jacques, "The Other Heading: Memories, Responses, and Responsibilities," *PMLA* 108 (1993): 89–93.

Dickens, Charles, *Dombey and Son* (1848), ed. Alan Horsman. Oxford: Clarendon, 1974.

  The Mystery of Edwin Drood (1870), ed. Margaret Cardwell. Oxford: Clarendon, 1972.

Dilke, Charles Wentworth, *Greater Britain: A Record of Travel in English-Speaking Countries during 1866 and 1867*. 2 vols. London: Macmillan, 1868.

Faulkner, David, "The Birth of Culture from the Spirit of Cartography," *Victorian Newsletter* 81 (Spring 1992): 45–7.

Faverty, Frederic E., *Matthew Arnold the Ethnologist*. Evanston, IL: Northwestern University Press, 1951.

Haight, Gordon S., ed., *The Portable Victorian Reader*. Kingsport, TN: Viking, 1972.

Harding, Geoffrey, *Opiate Addiction, Morality and Medicine: From Moral Illness to Pathological Disease*. New York: St. Martin's, 1988.

Hobsbawm, Eric, *The Age of Capital 1848–1875*. Scarborough, ONT: New American Library, 1984.

  The Age of Empire 1875–1914. New York: Pantheon, 1987.

Jacobsen, Wendy, *A Companion to "The Mystery of Edwin Drood"*. London: Allen & Unwin, 1986.

Kaplan, Fred, *Dickens: A Biography*. New York: William Morrow, 1988.

Mansergh, Nicholas, *The Commonwealth Experience*. 2 vols. University of Toronto Press, 1982.

Morris, James, *Heaven's Command: An Imperial Process*. New York: Harcourt, 1973.

Nunokawa, Jeff, "For Your Eyes Only: Private Property and the Oriental Body in *Dombey and Son*" in Arac and Ritvo, eds., *Macropolitics of Nineteenth-Century Literature*, pp. 138–58.

Parssinen, Terry, *Secret Passions, Secret Remedies: Narcotic Drugs in British Society 1820–1930*. University of Manchester Press, 1983.

Porter, Bernard, *The Lion's Share: A Short History of British Imperialism 1850–1983*. 2nd edn. London: Longman, 1984.

Ross, Marlon, "Romancing the Nation-State: The Poetics of Romantic Nationalism" in Arac and Ritvo, eds., *Macropolitics of Nineteenth-Century Literature*, pp. 56–85.

Sedgwick, Eve Kosofsky, *Between Men: English Literature and Male Homosocial Desire*. New York: Columbia University Press, 1985.

Thompson, Thomas W., *James Anthony Froude on Nation and Empire: A Study in Victorian Radicalism*. New York: Garland, 1987.

Vance, Norman, *The Sinews of the Spirit: The Ideal of Christian Manliness in Victorian Literature and Religious Thought*. Cambridge University Press, 1985.

CHAPTER 9

The re-subjection of "Lucas Malet": Charles Kingsley's daughter and the response to muscular Christianity

Patricia Srebrnik

> But what prison? Where am I cloistered? I see nothing con-
> fining me. The prison is within myself, and it is I who am its
> captive.
>> Luce Irigaray, "And the one doesn't stir without the other" (60)

> How can this object of transaction claim a right to pleasure
> without removing her/itself from established commerce?
>> Luce Irigaray, *This Sex which is not One* (32)

In 1902, Charles Kingsley's second daughter, Mary St. Leger
Kingsley Harrison (1852–1931), became a convert to Roman
Catholicism. Mrs. Harrison was already a public figure, well-known
for the essays and fiction she wrote under the pen name of "Lucas
Malet"; according to one contemporary critic, "the library public
clamoured" for the half-dozen novels she published in the 1880s and
1890s (Courtney, "A Novelist of the 'Nineties," 231). In interviews
granted to newspapers and magazines, Mrs. Harrison simultaneously asserted her personal affection for her father and her deviation
from his values and philosophy. Certainly her conversion came as no
surprise to her friends, for "Lucas" – as she insisted they call her –
had long been a rebel against "muscular Christianity." As I will
demonstrate, this rebellion is encoded in her most famous novel, *The
History of Sir Richard Calmady* (1901).

Charles Kingsley was known, of course, for his belief in the
sanctity of heterosexual married love; for his emphasis on "manly"
strength and chivalry, particularly when exercised on behalf of
women; and for his uncompromising hostility to the Church of
Rome. In her youth, Mary Kingsley was a dutiful daughter.
Although she studied painting at the Slade School of Fine Art, she
gave up her plans to become a professional painter when Kingsley

194

insisted she become engaged to his close friend and assistant curate, William Harrison, who was thirteen years older than his bride. The couple married within months of Kingsley's death in January 1876. Soon after, Harrison accepted the living of Clovelly, Devonshire, where Mary's paternal grandfather had been the rector, and where Charles Kingsley had spent his boyhood.[1]

The "exchange" of women to strengthen personal and familial ties between men has been analyzed by Claude Lévi-Strauss and by many feminist theorists.[2] But as Freud has noted, even the dutiful daughter may resist "the oedipalization of desire," either by turning her back on sexuality altogether, or by pretending that she is actually a man.[3] Mary Harrison apparently made no secret of her desire to escape from her marriage and home: according to one friend, the parsonage at Clovelly was no better than "a prison-house to her adventurous soul" (Courtney, *The Women of my Time*, 42). The Harrisons had no children, and Mary came increasingly to treat herself as an invalid, a role which entailed frequent trips to the Continent without her husband. William Harrison's stipend was insufficient to pay for these journeys, and so, ostensibly for the sole purpose of supplementing their income, his wife began to write fiction.

Critics found much to praise in her early novels, which included *Mrs. Lorimer: A Sketch in Black and White* (1882), *Colonel Enderby's Wife* (1885), and *A Counsel of Perfection* (1888). The novels were described as being similar in tone and sentiment to the fiction of George Eliot, and "Lucas Malet" was extolled as one of the major novelists of the period.[4] But, invariably, the critics remarked that Malet was a daughter of Charles Kingsley; frequently they devoted considerable space to demonstrating that her literary talent, her style, and even her ideas were a natural inheritance from her father.

In *The Madwoman in the Attic*, Sandra M. Gilbert and Susan Gubar describe the anxiety of the woman writer "enclosed in the architecture of an overwhelmingly male-dominated society" (xi). How much more severe the anxiety must be for the woman author whose actual biological father is widely acclaimed as one of the primary architects of the ideological and literary structures which confine her. By becoming a writer herself, Malet rebelled against her father's plans for her, and also against what Christine Froula has described as "the hysterical cultural script ... that dictates to males and females alike the necessity of silencing the woman's speech when it threatens the father's power" (112). Again, the theories of Gilbert and Gubar assist us in understanding the strategies deployed by Malet in this rebellion. In *No Man's Land*, Gilbert and Gubar make use of Freud's model of female psychosexual development to argue that the female artist may develop in ways that parallel female submission or resistance to the law of the father. The female author may oscillate between allegiance to literary fathers and longing for literary mothers; either "affiliation" will result in ambivalence, as she experiences desire and defiance, exuberance and anxiety (168–70). Lucas Malet declared repeatedly that she was not indebted to Charles Kingsley for her literary ability; rather, she insisted that she, her father, her uncle Henry Kingsley, and her cousin Mary Kingsley, the African explorer, had all inherited "whatever brains we happen to have" from female forebears (Dolman 149). Her ambivalence concerning these "literary mothers" is evident, however, in the fact that she searched for them in the paternal rather than the maternal line. Despite the masculine resonances of her pen name, it was chosen to honor her paternal grandmother, whose maiden name was Lucas, and the grandmother's aunt, a Miss Malet (Halsey 69). Whenever possible, Charles Kingsley's daughter did her own literary work at a writing-table inherited from her father's mother.

Malet also struggled to develop a set of aesthetic and religious beliefs that diverged dramatically from the tenets of "muscular Christianity" or, to use the term her father had preferred, "Christian manliness." For example, in one of her first published essays, "The Youngest of the Saints" (*Fortnightly Review*, September 1885), Malet discusses the career of General Charles George Gordon (1835–85). As Malet describes Gordon, his was a character that Charles Kingsley would simultaneously have admired and deplored: although Gordon was a military hero who died in battle at Khartoum, he was also an ascetic and a celibate who had no interest in "intimate family or social relations" (407). One of the puzzling aspects of the essay is that Malet provides few clues concerning her own opinion of Gordon. She remarks without comment that Gordon regarded women as "inferior creatures" (405–6). She does seem, however, to endorse Gordon's association of the body with Satan, an association that Kingsley had attributed to Catholicism and done his best to combat. Thus it is significant that in this essay, Malet compares Protestantism and Catholicism: according to Malet, "the genius of Protestantism must obviously be somewhat of the battering-ram" (400). In describing Protestantism as aggressive and combative, Malet implicitly associates it with masculinity. "Catholicism, in contrast" is said to emphasize "unqualified submission to the will of God," that is, to endorse values conventionally associated with femaleness (400). The point here is that Malet, like her father before her, thought of religion in gendered terms. Taken to its logical conclusion, her argument implies that although Protestantism may be suitable for the manly, Catholicism is better suited for individuals inclined to feminine "submission."

It is evident that Malet, like so many other artists and authors of the time, was strongly attracted to Catholicism: in "The Other Side of the Moon" (*Fortnightly Review*, April 1886), Malet contrasts "the lean and arid piety of a defunct Calvinism" to "the charmed and glorified, the rich and magical atmosphere of Catholic thought" (628). Yet in "The Progress of Woman in Literature" (*Universal Review*, 1888), Malet urges women authors to practice an aesthetics not of submission, but of rebellion against "the Squaw and Toy superstition" that would relegate women to either folly or servitude (295). Malet pays homage to the great women authors of the early and mid-nineteenth century: Jane Austen, Charlotte Brontë, Mrs. Gaskell, and above all George Eliot, who is deemed the greatest and most "modern" of women authors due to the "democratic" and "scientific" nature of her thought (298). Malet also praises many of her contemporaries, including Anne Thackeray Ritchie, Mary Elizabeth Braddon, Eliza Lynn Linton, "Ouida," and Margaret Oliphant. And yet, Malet asserts, the advance of woman in literature has not been equal to her advance since mid-century in politics, medicine, education, music, painting, or sculpture. Malet urges women to become greater writers, not by imitating "that inferior being ... the average Englishman" (297, 301), but by exercising "our high and daring temper. Amazons, perhaps it is best to call us ... Amazons fighting the battle of progress ... in new, self-invented armour of salvation" (297). The essay concludes with Malet's dream of "the coming of some new greater writer among us," one who would combine the realism of Fielding, the humanity of Dickens, and the science of George Eliot (301).

This last passage perhaps indicates what Malet aspired to achieve in her next novel, *The Wages of Sin* (1891). The hero of this novel, James Colthurst, is a "passionate," "sensuous," "ambitious," and "sensitive" painter who rebels against the Calvinistic creed in which he has been raised because of "its fierce refusal to accept the artistic and intellectual inheritance bequeathed to us by centuries of human imagination" (36, 51). Colthurst takes "a rather morbid enjoyment of all that is strange, jarring, unexpected, abnormal." The narrator remarks that, "Some persons, indeed, have gone so far as to accuse him of a love of actual physical deformity and a relish of horror for mere horror's sake." The narrator, however, defends Colthurst, in terms more appropriate to describe the work of a novelist than the work of a painter:

No doubt his power of appreciation was widely catholic, his view of beauty an original one. Yet he invariably, as far as I could see, rejected that which was unnatural or unsavoury, unless the presentation of it formed so essential a part of his subject that to omit it was to spoil the point of the story. If it was a necessary part of the drama, he portrayed it with an honest and fearless hand. And that he enjoyed doing so I am not prepared to deny. (33)

Colthurst's personal life is equally unorthodox: he has an illegitimate child with his model, but refuses to marry her, in part because she once saved him from starvation with money she earned as a prostitute. In the melodramatic conclusion, Colthurst is murdered by his mistress's father.

Despite the fact that Colthurst is punished for his sins, many critics were alarmed to find sexual passion described at such length and in such occasionally graphic detail in a novel written by a woman. They were distressed also by the possibility that Lucas Malet might share the aesthetic philosophy of her painter-hero. The *Contemporary Review*, for example, devoted eighteen pages to demonstrating the error of Colthurst's rebellion against "Calvinistic" and "Puritanical" constraints upon art and literature. This article, entitled "Morality in Fiction," concluded that although Malet's novel "makes for righteousness ... we may have too much of the pathology of evil": "It is possible to give honest praise to Lucas Malet's last novel, while hoping that she may have no feeble imitators in a style of fiction which requires purity of heart and delicate tact to prevent it from degenerating, as French fiction has so largely degenerated, into a morbid and bastard realism" (MacColl 252). Nonetheless, critics hailed *The Wages of Sin* as Malet's most impressive achievement to date. It was termed "the most striking of recent novels" and "the book of the season" (Oldham 163).

The great commercial and critical success of *The Wages of Sin* was one of a series of events that would transform Malet's life. In 1892, when their mother Frances Grenfell Kingsley died, Malet and her unmarried sister Rose inherited the still considerable income from the copyrights to their father's books.[5] The increase in her earnings enabled Malet to spend most of her time in France, Switzerland, or Italy; the death of William Harrison in 1897 made it unnecessary for Malet ever to return to the parsonage at Clovelly. The deaths of her mother and husband may also have liberated Malet to speak out even more candidly against "muscular Christianity" in general, and her father's celebration of heterosexual married love in particular. In one interview, Malet recalled Kingsley's "kind delicacy," but remarked that her father would have objected to her career as a novelist: "He held the old-fashioned and chivalrous notion that women should be treated *en princesse*, should be provided for, worked for, not permitted to struggle with the world at first hand" (Dolman 147). In the same interview, Malet discussed at length her interest in French fiction, claiming Balzac as an influence on her own writing.

By insisting that her literary talent was inherited from female ancestors, and by affiliating herself with French rather than English literary traditions, Malet repudiated the influence of her father. But as Gilbert and Gubar remark, the process of affiliation is similar to a literal adoption in that, although it may disrupt "the inexorable lineage of the biological family," it also allows for "possibilities of both choice and continuity" (*No Man's Land* 171). Since at least the mid-1880s, Malet had turned for emotional gratification, not to her husband, but to close women friends. Within a few years of Harrison's death, Malet adopted her second cousin, Gabrielle Vallings (b. 1886), a grand-niece of Charles Kingsley who was a teenager at the time of the adoption, and who lived with Malet until Malet's death in 1931. The precise nature of their relationship remains unclear, in large part because Vallings destroyed the bulk of Malet's personal papers. It is apparent, however, that the relationship with Vallings was the most significant of Malet's later life, and that Malet encouraged Vallings to develop precisely those creative abilities that Kingsley believed women should suppress. At Malet's urging and expense, Vallings trained her voice and became an opera singer. In 1916, Vallings published the first of a dozen novels, several of them advocating socialism.[6] It must have been while Vallings was at work on her novel that Malet revised and completed

The Tutor's Story (1916), a novel based on an unfinished manuscript discovered by Malet in her father's papers. Malet explained in the "Prefatory Note" to *The Tutor's Story* that she had tried "to maintain ... the rather pathetic charm of a 'day that is dead'" even though "I, personally, hold no brief for that day either in its literary, social, or political methods" (vii). Fifteen years later, Vallings would complete Malet's last, posthumous novel, *The Private Life of Mr. Justice Syme* (1932).

But doesn't her whole existence amount to an "accident"? An accident of reproduction? A genetic monstrosity? For [if] a human life takes its form only from its father ... *how can a girl be conceived*? (Luce Irigaray, *Speculum of the Other Woman* 167)

Meanwhile, Malet was hard at work on the novel she intended to be her masterpiece. *The History of Sir Richard Calmady* was not published until 1901, although it is evident that Malet had its plot clearly in mind for many years before this: Honoria, one of the main characters in the later novel, makes a cameo appearance in *The Wages of Sin*. As I will demonstrate, *The History of Sir Richard Calmady* can be read as an account of what the late Victorians referred to as "inverted" sexual behavior. Thus it is significant that after Malet's death, a critic who knew her personally suggested that Malet delayed publication of *The History of Sir Richard Calmady* because she was waiting out "the decadent Beardsley 'Yellow-Book' period, followed by the violent revulsion of 1895 after the Oscar Wilde scandal" (Courtney, "A Novelist of the 'Nineties'" 237). I suggest that the novel should also be read as a metaphorical retelling of Malet's own life and desires: the claustrophobic confinement within conventional ideals of womanhood which she experienced in childhood and youth, the unsatisfactory engagement and marriage, and the eventual relationship with Gabrielle Vallings. Above all, *The History of Sir Richard Calmady* constitutes a protest against the crippling constraints imposed upon women in a patriarchal, "Puritanical" society, by means of the rhetorical strategy which Luce Irigaray has described as "mimicry" or "mimesis."

The novel commences with a reference to the "blighting shadow" cast by "the fanatic zeal of Puritanism" (1). One of the most sympathetic characters is Julius March, an Anglican priest who regards himself as a disciple of John Henry Newman: "At Oxford he had lived exclusively among men, while the Tractarian Movement had offered a sufficient outlet to all his emotion" (23). Although March loves the Anglican Church too deeply to follow his conscience to Rome, he does impose upon himself a vow of chastity, in order "to bring the flesh into subjection to the spirit" (20). March finds it all the more necessary to make such a vow because he is secretly in love with Katherine, Lady Calmady, the widowed but perpetually beautiful mother of Sir Richard. Reviewers praised this character as the ideal woman (Gwynn 485; "Fiction. *The History of Sir Richard Calmady*" 261). In fact, Katherine Calmady embodies a powerful, preoedipal fantasy: that of a devoted and highly desirable woman-mother who is able to understand and fulfill her child's every need.[7]

The bulk of the novel, however, is concerned with the adventures of the title character. Sir Richard Calmady is an aristocrat who is born grossly deformed: in fulfillment of a centuries-old family curse resulting from an ancestor's cruelty to his cast-off mistress and illegitimate child, Sir Richard's feet grow directly out of his knees. Even as an adult he must be carried about by his servants like a helpless child. Other characters in the novel repeatedly describe Sir Richard as "a monster ... monstrous." Readers of *The Water Babies* will recall that in this novel, which was written for his children, Charles Kingsley implied that physical deformity is a sign of moral degeneration. In *The History of Sir Richard Calmady* there is a character who, "like all sound and heathy-minded men, ... had an inherent suspicion of the abnormal. He could not but fear that persons unusually constituted in body must be the victims of some corresponding crookedness of spirit" (101).

But Sir Richard is only a monster from the waist down: the godlike beauty of his head and torso provoke other characters to describe him as "half angel, half monster" (61) – a description which recalls the ambivalent feelings many Victorians entertained regarding women's bodies. In other ways as well Sir Richard seems more like a woman than a man. As a result of his deformity he is isolated from the public world of masculine activity, confined to the domestic realm as surely as if he had been born a woman. "Captive, maimed, imprisoned, perpetually striving, perpetually frustrated in the effort to escape" (511), Sir Richard spends most of his time in a suite of rooms equipped with furniture specially designed for him. His closest relationship is with his mother; together, mother and son pass their days in luxurious inactivity.

"Dickie," as the mother calls him, relies upon her to arrange a marriage for him, and soon he is engaged to a young, naïve girl of noble family. But the fiancée humiliates him by eloping with another man, and despite his deformity, Sir Richard undertakes a sexually scandalous "rake's progress" across Europe. Even in debauchery, however, Sir Richard is passive: he is seduced and "ravished" by his cousin, the sinister but beautiful Helen de Vallorbes, who is said to have "fine aesthetic appreciations ... The artist was at least as present in her as the whore" (452). Like James Colthurst, the painter-hero of *The Wages of Sin*, Helen is fascinated by the abnormal; thus she is perversely attracted by Sir Richard's deformity. When Sir Richard ends their affair, Helen retaliates by urging another of her lovers – a French symbolist poet – to beat Sir Richard nearly to death.

Helen de Vallorbes is, then, the incarnation of decadent feminine sexuality. Her virginal counterpart within the novel is another cousin of Sir Richard's, the "boyish" and "unusually tall" Honoria Quentin. Honoria's costume is a mixture of the feminine and the masculine: she combines a matador's hat and a tailored jacket with a skirt, but no crinoline (177). Honoria enjoys athletics, and is fond of asserting that although she is hopeless with a needle, she "can meet men pretty well on their own ground," that is, shooting, fishing, billiards, and riding. She claims she does not envy men because she has not allowed herself to be "shut out" of their sphere (498). But she is not attracted to men sexually. She plans to embrace celibacy and use her wealth "to espouse the cause of womanhood at large" (247); towards women, in fact, she feels "knight-errancy" and "chivalry":

A burning compassion animated Honoria for all feminine as against all masculine creatures; for the bitter patience demanded of the passive, as against the large latitude permitted the active principle; for the perpetual humiliation of the subjective and spiritual under the heavy yoke of the objective and practical; for the brief joy and long barrenness of all those who are condemned to obey and to wait, merely, as against those who are born to command and to create. (413)

When they meet as adults, Honoria is repelled by Sir Richard's body, but she comes to love him despite his deformity. Although she has already declared she is "not what you call a marrying man" (410), eventually it is she who proposes marriage to Sir Richard, remarking as she does so that she is "man enough" to risk rejection

(610). As one contemporary critic commented, Honoria claims for herself "the right to speak and to think as a man ... the woman in her is kept ... locked up in a back attic" (Gwynn 481).

I suggest that the gender reversals that are evident in the characterization of Sir Richard and Honoria, and that make their relationship possible, would have reminded contemporary readers of the theories of Havelock Ellis and other "sexologists" who in the 1890s were attempting to develop a scientific explanation of homosexuality and lesbianism. Many of these researchers retained conventional assumptions concerning masculinity and femininity. The term "sexual inversion" was used, not just to denote sexual preference, but to indicate a total reversal of one's sex role (Chauncey 119). Ellis believed that homosexuality resulted when, by some congenital freak, body and soul had been mismatched: homosexual men had female souls in male bodies, and homosexual women had male souls in female bodies. In *Sexual Inversion: Studies in the Psychology of Sex*, Ellis described lesbians in terms that recall the descriptions of Honoria in Malet's novel:

> When they still retain female garments, these usually show some traits of masculine simplicity ... there are all sorts of instinctive gestures and habits which may suggest ... that such a person "ought to have been a man" ... The direct speech, the inflexions of voice, the masculine straightforwardness and sense of honour, and especially the attitude towards men, free from any suggestion either of shyness or audacity, will often suggest the underlying psychic abnormality to a keen observer ... There is also a dislike and sometimes incapacity for needlework and other domestic occupations, while there is often some capacity for athletics. (250)[8]

Honoria's physical vigor is certainly a contrast to the physical helplessness of Sir Richard. But Honoria and Sir Richard are alike in sharing a deep concern for the welfare of those less well off materially than themselves, a concern that each of them explicitly connects with Sir Richard's deformity: as Honoria considers the miserable lot of factory workers, she reflects that Sir Richard's "family" is a large one, for "the age of human sacrifice" is not yet over (575–6). Sir Richard muses that "by the fact of his deformity he was emancipated from the delusions of his class; was made one, in right of the suffering and humiliation of it, with the dull-coloured multitudes" (546). Such passages prompted some reviewers in the periodical press to recall that Charles Kingsley, also, was vitally concerned with the welfare of the lower classes.

Twentieth-century feminist critics have suggested other ways in which to interpret the numerous "monsters" who populate fiction written by women. Many have noted that Freud discussed the female body in terms of lack or error or as an inverted reproduction of the masculine; thus woman is equivalent to a genetic accident or monstrosity. Gilbert and Gubar argue that monsters should be regarded as a projection of the anxiety of the woman author; they explain that the woman author may be influenced by the traditional association between creative women and monsters and thus imagine herself as somehow deformed (*Madwoman* 79). In the context of these ideas it becomes evident that *The History of Sir Richard Calmady* should be regarded as a radical manifesto not only against the injuries of class, but also against the injuries of gender, that is, against the limitations imposed upon all those members of the human "family" who are regarded at birth as "deformed" because, like Sir Richard, their bodies lack a simple physical endowment. When we read Malet's novel as a protest against patriarchal definitions of the female, we can better appreciate Sir Richard's desire to be delivered "from that hideous apprehension of universal mutilation, of maimed purposes, maimed happenings, of a world peopled by beings maimed as he was himself, but after a more subtle and intimate fashion – a fashion intellectual or moral rather than merely physical" (458).

The contemporary critical response to *The History of Sir Richard Calmady* was even more ambivalent than the response to *The Wages of Sin* ten years earlier. Malet's new novel was denounced as "unsavoury" (*Saturday Review*, October 19, 1901, 501), "morbid" (*Academy*, September 28, 1901, 261), and "gruesome to the point of repulsiveness" (*Contemporary Review*, October 1901, 601). Although one critic described it as "the best novel since *Middlemarch* written by a woman" (Gwynn 480), *The History of Sir Richard Calmady* was more frequently compared, not to the novels of George Eliot, but to the more explicit treatments of sexuality to be found in Meredith and Hardy (Courtney, "Lucas Malet's Novels", 535). Critics complained that the novel was "in no sense a woman's work" (Courtney, "A Novelist of the 'Nineties'", 231); the reviewer in the *Times* described it as "an offence against good taste and good manners," and then proceeded to refer to Malet's "masculine audacity" (September 16, 1901). Nearly every critic found it necessary to comment, not only on Malet's sex, but upon her parentage: the *Literary Digest* entitled its review, "A Great Work by the Daughter of Charles

Kingsley"; the *Outlook* suggested that the story of Sir Richard would have offended Kingsley's "common sense" and "muscular Christianity."[9]

In terms of the argument I have been developing concerning Malet's attempts to overcome the limitations of gender by rejecting, or at least revising, the tenets of "muscular Christianity," the most perceptive discussion of *The History of Sir Richard Calmady* was that by Stephen Gwynn in the *New Liberal Review*. Gwynn commences by remarking that, "'Lucas Malet' is a woman, and the daughter of Charles Kingsley" (480). Unlike other reviewers, Gwynn declines to reverence Kingsley's memory: "Charles Kingsley is a writer to whom the world very justly refused the title of great. He was ... essentially of his own time," especially in "his portraiture of women as ... creatures secluded and set apart" (481). Nonetheless, Gwynn describes Malet's novel as an attempt to apply the philosophy of Charles Kingsley, "from a woman's standpoint." Gwynn notes that Sir Richard's cravings for "sport and exercise" and "to take his place as a man in the regard of women" are " at every turn denied and thwarted" (488). Thus Malet is said to depict, in this account of "the moral effect of deformity upon the deformed" (483), "the ideal figure not of a man but of a woman, disciplined by suffering, acquiescent, but not broken, a true pattern of human nobleness" (487).

Stephen Gwynn was a personal friend of Malet's cousin, Mary Kingsley, the African explorer, and it is possible that when he wrote this review, he was aware that Malet's conversion to Catholicism was imminent.[10] At any rate, his comments concerning Sir Richard's cravings for sport and exercise suggest that he would have explained Malet's conversion in much the same way as did the journalist Janet Courtney, who suggested, soon after the conversion, that

Kingsley's daughter, quite apart from her own idiosyncrasies of temperament, must almost have been born an adherent of the flesh-and-blood school of robust religious thinking. She ought also to have been born a Protestant, but perhaps muscular Christianity, when it takes feminine shape and indulges in less open-air exercise and combativeness, is apt to seek satisfaction in a religion which makes other appeals to the senses. ("Lucas Malet's Novels" 535)[11]

I have already quoted from essays written by Malet in the 1880s, essays that indicate that even then, like many of the literary figures associated in the public mind with "aestheticism" and sexual inversion, Malet was beginning to feel the appeal of the Catholic faith. As we have seen, Malet's religious beliefs were intertwined with her aesthetic theories and with her attempts to come to terms with the gender ideology of muscular Christianity. When we recall that Malet associated Protestantism with masculinity and Catholicism with femininity, that she referred to "the charmed and glorified, the rich and magical atmosphere of Catholic thought," we may well conclude that by converting to Catholicism, Malet was seeking consolation for what I have termed the injuries of gender.

But because, as Luce Irigaray argues, there is no position "outside" phallocentric discourse from which the woman writer can express her protest, she must make use of subversive rhetorical strategies from within. Irigaray proposes the strategy of "mimicry" or "mimesis": by consciously assuming traditionally feminine roles, woman may "try to rediscover the locus of her exploitation by discourse." Thus if women appear to men in such images as the ideal mother, the seductive sensualist, the virgin, the genetic monstrosity, women should take those images and reflect them back to men in magnified proportions, in order to undo the effects of phallocentric discourse by overdoing them. I suggest that Malet attempts such "mimesis" in the characters of Katherine, Helen, Honoria, and Sir Richard, and that she was "play[ing] with mimesis" herself when she converted to Catholicism. But as Irigaray notes, there is an inherent danger in the strategy of mimesis: the woman who mimes miming must thereby "resubmit herself ... to ideas about herself that are elaborated in/by a masculine logic" (*This Sex* 76). As a result, the woman who practices mimesis may freeze rather than subvert patriarchal notions of the feminine, thereby reinforcing her confinement within the structures of phallocentric discourse.[12]

Would it not involve a new prison, a new cloister, built of their own accord? (Irigaray, *This Sex which is not One* 33)
In *This Sex which is not One*, Irigaray equates the phallus with "the contemporary figure of a god jealous of his prerogatives; we might suspect it of claiming ... to be the ultimate meaning of all discourse, the standard of truth and propriety ... in addition to continuing, as emblem and agent of the patriarchal system, to shore up the name of the father (Father)" (67). According to Irigaray, the God projected by man has no love for woman; thus, woman must imagine a female god in order to achieve "self-affection" independent of masculine

approval, and in order to represent herself as different from the male. In *Speculum of the Other Woman*, Irigaray describes the hysteric as one who expresses in somatic terms woman's relegation to the role of commodity and object, and the mystic as one who expresses herself in a discourse where masculine consciousness is no longer master. But as many commentators on Irigaray have remarked, within a symbolic system regulated by "the law of the Father," it is impossible for the hysteric or mystic to communicate her self-knowledge; indeed, the incoherence of the hysteric or mystic is likely to be regarded as madness.[13]

Many Victorian women did dare to imagine a female god, or at least a female savior who would serve also as muse to the woman writer. In *Cassandra*, Florence Nightingale hoped that "the next Christ will perhaps be a female Christ" (53). Margaret Fuller concluded *Woman in the Nineteenth Century* by asking, "will not she soon appear – the woman who shall vindicate their birthright for all women; who shall teach them what to claim, and how to use what they obtain?" (177).

For reasons that I will analyze in a moment, Malet was apparently unable to imagine a female god. But as we have seen, Malet did anticipate the coming of a new, great (female) author in her 1888 essay on "The Progress of Woman in Literature." In an interview granted in the spring of 1902, Malet implied that her conversion to Catholicism was motivated at least in part by the desire to become a greater writer herself. Malet contrasted Catholicism to the set of religious and aesthetic beliefs that she labeled "Puritanism," but that she attributed to Protestantism as a whole. According to Malet, a novel should hold a mirror up to nature; it should show "life as a whole." But the typical English novelist, raised in an atmosphere of "Puritanism," has great difficulty in writing honestly:

Puritanism is so stupidly afraid of the lessons of life as a whole, and so resolute never to learn them, that it insists on our wearing, or pretending to wear, blinkers, so as to see nothing that is inconsistent with its preconceived moral scheme. Think of the weakness, the unphilosophic quality of Puritanism, compared with Catholicism, as a basis or background for art! (Archer 220)

Malet went on to refer to the "warping and stunting influence of Puritanism upon art" (223), metaphors which recall the deformity of Richard Calmady. Malet explained also that she took her own inspiration from the great French novelists, such as Balzac, who could never have adapted themselves to the "Puritanism" of British publishers, readers, and reviewers. Malet did not distinguish between the problems of the male author and the problems of the woman author. But as reviews of her own novels amply illustrate, English critics were far more likely to chastise a woman than a man for tearing off the blinkers of "Puritanism." By becoming a Catholic, Malet repudiated the authority of "Puritan" aesthetics. She also indicated her determination to write as candidly and as openly as a (French) man of letters.

Unfortunately for Malet's career as an author, the conversion did not have the desired effect. It is possible, of course, that under any circumstances she would have been unable to surpass the achievement of *The Wages of Sin* or *The History of Sir Richard Calmady*, but critics suspected that the ten novels she wrote after 1902, including *The Far Horizon* (1906) and *Adrian Savage* (1911), were weakened by her evident desire to portray Catholic dogma sympathetically, or at least to refrain from offending the Church. For example, in *The Far Horizon*, Malet tells the story of Dominic Iglesias, who as an adult returns to the Catholic faith of his ancestors. Iglesias dismisses "modern Protestantism" as a utilitarian religion, devoid of spirituality or philosophy or art, a religion inhospitable to "the making of saints" (246–7). He is equally hostile to those "neo-mystics" who celebrate "hysteria" and "the sub-conscious self": "to the madhouse ... Iglesias had not the very smallest desire to go" (247–8). Iglesias regards the Roman Catholic Church as the "appointed warden" of the law of God. Thus, although "it is no light matter to subject attitude of mind and daily habit to distinct rule" (250), he accepts the Church's message "of conquest, of iron self-mastery and self-restraint" (204). The critics remarked that Malet herself "wrote in fetters," and their suspicions were confirmed when Malet reissued *The History of Sir Richard Calmady* with considerable omissions (Courtney, "A Novelist of the 'Nineties" 240).

The conversion to Catholicism seems also, paradoxically, to have ended Malet's efforts to extricate herself from the gender ideology of muscular Christianity. Indeed, precisely because she continued to think about religion and aesthetics in gendered terms, Malet was compelled, despite her earlier rebellion, to reassert many of her father's assumptions concerning appropriate gender roles for women.

This contradiction within her thought became apparent when in 1905 she contributed to the *Fortnightly Review* an essay entitled "The Threatened Re-Subjection of Woman." Early in the essay, Malet appeals to "right reason and common-sense" (807) to explain her concern over the fact that so many *feministes* and "New Women" are choosing a life of economic independence and sexual celibacy. By the end of the essay, however, it becomes apparent that she is actually motivated by her Catholic faith: she expresses her conviction that under the "mysterious influences" of "a power unseen but absolute," women will reassume their proper roles as wives and mothers; for, "in the department of religion, the unostentatious yet steady advance of the great mother church of Christendom ... forces recognition that not only the logic of history is with her, but the even more convincing logic of the needs and aspirations of the human heart" (816–17). Malet is perhaps thinking of her own younger self when she makes an exception for "the woman of genius" (817–18). But Malet claims not to envy such a woman, whom she describes as a creature of ambiguous gender:

For to possess the dual nature – a man's brain and ambitions, and woman's capacity of loving and suffering along with that most intricate and capricious piece of mechanism, a woman's body – is, indeed, to dwell in a city divided against itself and to be unevenly yoked with an unbeliever. (818)

Malet concludes "The Threatened Re-Subjection of Woman" with a remark that indicates her ultimate inability to move beyond the constraints of a gender-based ideology: she asserts that it is "among the constant characteristics of the feminine mind" that "complete liberty to act in a given manner" takes away all desire to rebel. By rejecting muscular Christianity, Malet had seized the liberty to pursue her personal and professional ambitions; she sought to exercise what she apparently regarded at one time as "a man's brain" in "a woman's body." But this stage of her rebellion ended when, in her effort to escape muscular Christianity by converting to Catholicism, she came to believe in the essential femininity of her own mind.

Malet's story can be seen, then, as that of a woman writer whose attempts to subvert the phallocentric images of woman served merely to confirm her imprisonment within the symbolic constructs of the father. And yet it would be a mistake to assume that in the last thirty years of her life, Malet again became the dutiful daughter she had been in her youth.

In "The Female Subject: (What) Does Woman Want?" Jerry
Aline Flieger suggests that women may escape the totalizing structures of phallocentric discourse and yet retain the capacity for
coherent speech by taking up the position of the prodigal daughter:

She is a daughter still, who acknowledges her heritage: or rather, like the
prodigal child of the Biblical account – who is of course a son in the original
parable – she goes beyond the fold of restrictive paternal law, only to
return. But unlike the prodigal son of legend, who returns repentant, she
returns enriched – for she is "prodigal" in a second sense of the term as well
... To be prodigal in this sense is to alter the law, to enlarge its parameters
and recast its meaning ... Thus the law to which the prodigal daughter
accedes – yes, in the name of ethics and responsibility, however phallic one
may consider these terms – is an altered ethics; her subjectivity is indeed
"hers," rather than a deficient version of his. (59–60)

In *Adrian Savage*, there are several passages that suggest that Malet
remained a prodigal daughter in the sense proposed by Flieger.
Savage, the hero of the novel, is a half-English, half-French,
devoutly Catholic man of letters. I suggest that he serves also as a
mask or persona for Malet, especially when he asserts that
Englishwomen "have an excuse for revolt": according to Savage,
English fathers, husbands, and brothers "crave to exercise power"
over their female relatives (144). As a result, the typical Englishwoman is "snubbed, depressed, depreciated, grumbled at, scolded,
made to think meanly of herself." We have seen that Malet was
unable to imagine a female god; but she causes Savage to argue that
because Luther, Calvin, and Henry VIII "conspired to depose Our
Blessed Lady from her rightful throne in heaven," the "modern,
non-Catholic woman" has "no Eternal, Universal Mother whose
aid and patronage she can invoke" against "the tedious tyrannies of
arrogant, sullen, selfish, slow-witted, birch-rod-wielding, pedagogic
man" (146). Furthermore, although in *The Far Horizon* Malet
rejected "mysticism," "hysteria," and "the sub-conscious" as
sources of feminine self-knowledge, there is evidence within this later
novel that her relationship to Gabrielle Vallings did enable her to
achieve and express some degree of love for the feminine "same":
Adrian Savage courts the impossibly beautiful, charming, and
devout Gabrielle St. Leger. St. Leger was of course Malet's own
middle name, and the novel is dedicated "as a love-token" to
Gabrielle Vallings.

NOTES

Much of my preliminary research on "Lucas Malet" was done while I was a participant in the 1988 National Endowment for the Humanities Institute on Victorian Culture and Society at the Yale Center for British Art. I am grateful also to the Calgary Institute for the Humanities and to the Social Sciences and Humanities Research Council of Canada, which have provided the time and resources for additional research.

1 For details of Malet's life, see Archer, Battiscombe, Courtney (*The Women of my Time*), Dolman, Halsey, Hichens, and Smith.

2 See, for example, Irigaray, *This Sex which is not One*; and Gayle Rubin, "The Traffic in Women: Notes on the 'Political Economy' of Sex."

3 See the discussion of Freud's theories in Gilbert and Gubar, *No Man's Land*, pp. 167–72.

4 See, for example, the review of *Colonel Enderby's Wife* in *The Spectator* 58 (1885): 710; the review of *A Counsel of Perfection* in *Universal Review* 1 (1888): 306; and the review by Malcolm MacColl of *The Wages of Sin* in *Contemporary Review* 60 (1891): 252.

5 Malet's and Rose's letters to the Macmillans, publishers of Charles Kingsley's books, are in the British Library (Additional Manuscripts 54911, 54914, 54916). This correspondence indicates that the royalties from Kingsley's books declined dramatically in the late 1890s.

6 I am indebted to Mrs. Angela Covey-Crump and Miss Brenda Hudson-Perramon, nieces of Gabrielle Vallings, who generously shared with me family stories and personal recollections concerning Lucas Malet and Gabrielle Vallings. In addition, I am grateful to Mrs. Covey-Crump for access to the surviving letters and papers. Both Mrs. Covey-Crump and Miss Hudson-Perramon believe that Malet found heterosexual relationships to be distasteful. Miss Hudson-Perramon believes that Malet persuaded Vallings to remain single. Indeed, it is tempting to suspect that the plot of Vallings's first novel, *Bindweed*, is based at least in part on Vallings's own experiences: the singer-heroine, Eugenie, lives first with an aunt so jealous that she murders a man suspected of being Eugenie's suitor; then Eugenie is cared for by a retired opera singer who trains Eugenie's voice, and who also attempts to prevent Eugenie from marrying (see Daims and Grimes 583).

7 According to Freud, the child addresses its love to the mother until the child perceives that the mother, far from being all-powerful, is "castrated" and thus subordinate to the father. At this point, in the case of the female child in particular, "the motives for hostility, which have long been accumulating, gain the upper hand" (see Irigaray's account of Freud's thought in *Speculum of the Other Woman*, 63, 68). Because Sir Richard is a posthumous child, his relationship with the mother is not disrupted by the father. Sir Richard becomes aware that his mother's powers are limited, however, when she is unable to secure for him the

wife he requests of her, and his subsequent debauchery does seem to constitute a rebellion against Katherine.

8 For this quotation from Ellis I am indebted to George Chauncey Jr., "From Sexual Inversion to Homosexuality," pp. 120–21. In *Sexual Anarchy*, Elaine Showalter notes that by the mid-1880s, sexologists were devoting their attention to lesbianism, which they regarded as morbid and masculine, and which they associated with feminism (23).

9 It is unlikely that Malet was offended by references to her "masculine audacity": she was fond of asserting that she wrote "like the man of science" (Courtney, "A Novelist of the 'Nineties" 238). Gilbert and Gubar note that many nineteenth-century women authors insisted that as writers they *were* men; this tactic sometimes led the "male impersona-tor" to regard herself as "freakish" (69). Critics who interviewed Malet in person frequently remarked that she was "tall and large" and resembled her father physically (see, for example, Halsey 68). Given the implicit link between masculine women authors and monsters, it is significant that Janet Courtney, a writer herself, regarded Malet as somewhat freakish when they met in 1902: "It was my first sight of her, and I was unprepared for her rather excessive use of *maquillage* ... She was a tall, commanding figure, with considerable presence, and she wore a blouse of a somewhat bizarre shade of pink" ("A Novelist of the 'Nineties," 238–9).

10 Gwynn refers to Mary Kingsley in his review of *The History of Sir Richard Calmady*. Their correspondence is in the National Library of Ireland; Gwynn's *Life of Mary Kingsley* was published in 1933. Kingsley was present at William Harrison's funeral and described with some disgust, in a letter dated May 1, 1897, the "atmosphere of weird emotionalism with little or no real feeling under it ... I have no mind to be mixed up in the gossip [Mary Harrison and Rose Kingsley] surround themselves with" (Mary Kingsley to Miss Hatty Johnson, the Kingsley Collection, South African Library, Cape Town).

11 Compare the belief of Edward Carpenter, a homosexual who wrote extensively on gender questions, that women want a free life "far more in the open air, with real bodily exercise and development, some amount of regular manual work, a knowledge of health and physiology, an altogether wider mental outlook, and greater self-reliance and nature-hardihood" (Sime 66).

12 For more extensive discussions of Irigaray's notion of "mimesis," see Elliot and Whitford.

13 For more extensive discussions of Irigaray's theories concerning hys-teria, mysticism, and the need for a female god, see Elliot, Grosz, and Whitford.

WORKS CITED

Archer, William, *Real Conversations*. London: Heinemann, 1904.

tations on Greece strikingly converge with Kingsley's celebration of the male body as the focal point of a muscular ethos.

That these affiliations seem surprising testifies to the enduring power of a gender ideology in which Pater and Kingsley define virtually antithetical models of masculinity. Even Norman Vance, who in *The Sinews of the Spirit* notes "a possible meeting-point" between Pater and Kingsleyan manliness in the moralized Hellenism of much late-Victorian thought (185), goes on to obscure that important conjunction by reaffirming a profound division between the two writers in gendered terms – the familiar opposition between, crudely speaking, the robust, bluff heterosexual and the timid, furtive homoeroticist. The distinction as thus figured typically incorporates two closely related rhetorical oppositions. First, Pater's writings define a spectatorship that contrasts markedly with Kingsley's stress on active, strenuous participation: for Pater, muscularity figures principally as spectacle rather than as activity to emulate. The sense of voyeurism in such spectatorship seems to have been the principal incitement to contemporary (and more recent) attacks on the "effeminacy" of his criticism. Yet Kingsley's muscularity also at once incorporates and animates a profoundly erotic appreciation of the virile body. Pater's writings, conversely, approach Kingsleyan muscularity as they envision male beauty and energy as the incarnation of *askesis*, a discipline at once physical and intellectual: hence the powerful allure of Sparta as a cultural model in his late writings. The gendered distinction between spectatorship and participation is linked to a second antagonism that opposes Pater's oblique, highly nuanced, muted rhetoric to the slashing, blunt, eminently "manly" style of Kingsley. But here, too, Pater lays claim to a more conventional "manliness" by appropriating the rhetoric of Victorian earnestness in order to insist that the very shadings and hesitations of his style incarnate a strenuous intellectual discipline. Throughout his later works, Pater suggests that the muscularity he so admires in Spartan discipline has a counterpart in his own spectatorship, which he presents not as the passive self-indulgence so roundly decried by his critics, but as the incarnation of a sustained intellectual rigor and ethical program. Pater's ability to take over what might seem the wholly alien rhetoric of earnestness underscores not only the powerfully ascetic strain so often overlooked in his writings, but also his indebtedness to a Carlylean psychological economy – another sur-

Battiscombe, Georgina, "Harrison, Mary St. Leger" in *Dictionary of National Biography* (1931–1940).

Bell, Florence, "Sir Richard Calmady," *Fortnightly Review* n.s. 70 (1901): 894–901.

Chauncey, George, Jr., "From Sexual Inversion to Homosexuality: Medicine and the Changing Conceptualization of Female Deviance," *Salmagundi* 58–9 (1982–3): 114–46.

Courtney, Janet, "A Novelist of the 'Nineties," *Fortnightly Review* n.s. 131 (1932): 230–41.

[Janet E. Hogarth], "Lucas Malet's Novels," *Fortnightly Review* n.s. 71 (1902): 532–40.

The Women of my Time. London: J. Dickson, 1934.

Daims, Diva and Janet Grimes, *Novels in English by Women, 1891–1920. A Preliminary Checklist.* New York: Garland, 1981.

"The Deformed Reformed," *Outlook*, October 12, 1901: 342.

Dolman, Frederick, "'Lucas Malet' at Home: A Chat with the Daughter of Charles Kingsley," *The Young Woman: A Monthly Journal and Review* 4 (1896): 145–9.

Elliot, Patricia, *From Mastery to Analysis: Theories of Gender in Psychoanalytic Feminism.* Ithaca: Cornell University Press, 1991.

Ellis, Havelock, *Sexual Inversion*, 3rd rev. edn. in *Studies in the Psychology of Sex*, vol. II. Philadelphia: F. A. Davis, 1915 (first published 1897).

"Fiction. *The History of Sir Richard Calmady*," *Academy*, September 28, 1901: 261.

Flieger, Jerry Aline, "The Female Subject: (What) Does Woman Want?" in *Psychoanalysis and . . .* , eds. Richard Feldstein and Henry Sussman. New York: Routledge, 1990, pp. 54–63.

Froula, Christine, "The Daughter's Seduction: Sexual Violence and Literary History" in *Daughters and Fathers*, eds. Lynda E. Boose and Betty S. Flowers. Baltimore: Johns Hopkins University Press, 1989, pp. 111–35.

Fuller, Margaret, *Woman in the Nineteenth Century.* Boston: Jewett, 1855. Reprinted New York: Norton, 1971.

Gallup, Jane, *Feminism and Psychoanalysis: The Daughter's Seduction.* London: Macmillan, 1982.

Gilbert, Sandra M. and Susan Gubar, *The Madwoman in the Attic.* New Haven: Yale University Press, 1979.

No Man's Land: The Place of the Woman Writer in the Twentieth Century, vol. I: *The War of the Words.* New Haven: Yale University Press, 1988.

Grosz, Elizabeth, *Jacques Lacan: A Feminist Introduction.* London: Routledge, 1990.

Gwynn, Stephen, "Sir Richard Calmady," *New Liberal Review* 2 (1901): 480–88.

Halsey, Francis Whiting, ed., *Women Authors of our Day in their Homes. Personal Descriptions and Interviews.* New York: James Pott, 1903.

Hichens, Robert, *Yesterday.* London: Cassell, 1947.

"The History of Sir Richard Calmady," *Saturday Review*, October 19, 1901: 501.

Irigaray, Luce, *Ce sexe qui n'en est pas un*. Paris: Minuit, 1977. Tr. as *This Sex which is not One*, tr. Catherine Porter with Carolyn Burke. Ithaca: Cornell University Press, 1985.

    Et l'une ne bouge pas sans l'autre. Paris: Minuit, 1979. Tr. as "And the one doesn't stir without the other," tr. Hélène Vivienne Wenzel. *Signs* 7 (1981): 60–67.

    Speculum de l'autre femme. Paris: Minuit, 1974. Tr. as *Speculum of the Other Woman*, tr. Gillian C. Gill. Ithaca: Cornell University Press, 1985.

MacColl, Malcolm, "Morality in Fiction," *Contemporary Review* 60 (1891): 234–52.

Malet, Lucas, *Adrian Savage*. London: Hutchinson, 1911.

    The Far Horizon. London: Hutchinson, 1906.

    The History of Sir Richard Calmady: A Romance. London: Methuen, 1901.

    "The Other Side of the Moon," *Fortnightly Review* n.s. 39 (1886): 615–32.

    "Prefatory Note" to *The Tutor's Story: An Unpublished Novel by the Late Charles Kingsley. Revised and Completed by His Daughter Lucas Malet (Mrs. Mary St. Leger Harrison)*. London: Smith, Elder, 1916.

    "The Progress of Woman in Literature," *Universal Review* 2 (1888): 295–301.

    "The Threatened Re-Subjection of Woman," *Fortnightly Review* n.s. 77 (1905): 806–19.

    The Wages of Sin. London: Swan Sonnenschein, 1891.

    "The Youngest of the Saints," *Fortnightly Review* n.s. 38 (1885): 395–412.

Nightingale, Florence, *Cassandra*, ed. Myra Stark. Old Westbury, NY: Feminist Press, 1979.

"Notable Books of the Day. A Great Work by the Daughter of Charles Kingsley" (New York), *Literary Digest*, November 9, 1901: 580.

Oldham, C. E., "Two Novels on One Theme," *Newbery House Magazine: A Monthly Review for Churchmen and Churchwomen* 7 (1892): 161–9.

"Recent Novels," *The Times*, September 16, 1901: 12b.

Rubin, Gayle, "The Traffic in Women: Notes on the 'Political Economy' of Sex" in *Toward an Anthropology of Women*, ed. Rayna R. Reiter. New York: Monthly Review Press, 1975, pp. 157–210.

Showalter, Elaine, *Sexual Anarchy: Gender and Culture at the Fin de Siècle*. New York: Viking, 1990.

Sime, A. H. Moncur, *Edward Carpenter: His Ideas and Ideals*. London: Kegan Paul, Trench, Trubner, 1916.

Smith, Laura Alex, "Lucas Malet (Mrs. Harrison)," *The Western Weekly News*, January 29, 1898.

"Some Notable Books of the Month. The History of Sir Richard Calmady," *Review of Reviews* 24 (1901): 421–2.

"Some Recent Books," *The Contemporary Review* 80 (1901): 599–608.

Whitford, Margaret, *Luce Irigaray: Philosophy in the Feminine*. New York: Routledge, 1991.

CHAPTER 10

Pater's muscular aestheticism

James Eli Adams

> I could wish I were an Apollo for His sake! Strange idea,
> seems so harmonious to me!
>
> Charles Kin[

My title gestures towards a conjunction of two writers, Kingsley and Walter Pater, that to most readers will proba[ ] an implausible pairing, save as an exercise in parody. What[ ] more remote from Kingsley's muscular Christian than the [ ] aesthete? Yet the two figures arise out of a common proj[ ] reclamation of the body from the antagonisms of an or[ ] ascetic morality. What was at issue in Kingsley's quarr[ ] Newman, as many scholars have pointed out, was not so [ ] mendacity as sexuality. Newman's "Manichaeism" was a sta[ ] affront to Kingsley's insistence on the sanctity of the flesh – di[ ] ing precisely because it challenged the hard-won and preca[ ] resolution of Kingsley's struggles with his own sexuality.[2] Pater[ ] begins his career by decrying the war between flesh and spirit[ ] first and most famous work, *The Renaissance* (1873), takes a[ ] subject the historical period that marks, as Pater put it, m[ ] "reassertion of himself, that rehabilitation of human nature, [ ] body, the senses, the heart, the intelligence" in opposition t[ ] medieval tendency "to depreciate man's nature ... to make[ ] ashamed of itself" (31). Pater's most vivid emblem of this "rehab[ ] tation" is the recovery of Greek sculpture, an achievement to whi[ ] he returns throughout his writings in celebrations of the male bod[ ] Over the course of his career, these celebrations increasingly dra[ ] on the rhetoric of Victorian athleticism as Pater comes to explai[ ] "the Hellenic ideal" not simply in the Hegelian formulations of *Th[ ]Renaissance*, but as the product of a consummate physical discipline.[ ] In a trio of late works, "Lacedaemon" (1892), "Emerald Uthwart" [ ] (1892), and "The Age of Athletic Prizemen" (1894), Pater's medi-

prising but profound affiliation between his aestheticism and Kingsley's muscular Christianity.

In contemporary controversy over Roman Catholicism, Kingsley wrote in a letter of 1851, "the whole question is an anthropological one," in which the first challenge must be, "Define a human being" (*Life and Works* II 265). The "popular Manichaeism or Gnosticism" of his adversaries, Kingsley objected, envisioned man as "a spirit accidentally connected with and burdened by an animal" (II 267), whereas "the Creed of the Bible," he insisted, envisioned man as "a spirit embodied in flesh and blood," "a spirit embodied in an animal" (II 266). The stress on *embodiment*, on the sanctity of the human body and its "animal" aspects as a manifestation of spirit, is the central axiom of Kingsley's faith. On this rock Kingsley founded not only his private sexual happiness but his fictional celebrations of physical vitality and un-self-conscious belief, as well as his furious, obsessive attacks on celibacy and "aristocratic" forms of belief, most notoriously in his controversy with Newman. In short, it is the sanctity of the body that impels that feature of Kingsley's writings that early reviewers seized upon: "the vigor with which he contends for ... the great importance and value of animal spirits, physical strength, and hearty enjoyment of all pursuits and accomplishments which are connected with them" (Newsome 198–9).[3]

Kingsley finds a ready and resonant emblem of these concerns in one of the central icons of Victorian intellectual and moral authority: Greek sculpture. The prominence of that achievement in Victorian discourse reflected the widespread belief, derived ultimately from German Hellenism, that the ancient Greeks had achieved a perfect harmony of physical and intellectual excellence.[4] But Kingsley's appropriation tellingly gives most weight to the perfection of physical vitality. In a lecture on sanitary reform, entitled "The Science of Health," for example, he offers the achievements of Greek sculptors as an incitement to concern for public health: we must be stirred, he urges, by attending to

those precious heirlooms of the human race, the statues of the old Greeks; to their tender grandeur, their chaste healthfulness, their unconscious, because perfect, might; and say – There; these are tokens to you, and to all generations yet unborn, of what man could be once; of what he can be again. (*Health and Education* 22)

"Nausicaa in London: Or, The Lower Education of Women" opens similarly, by invoking "the Marbles of the British Museum" as "forms of men and women whose every limb and attitude betokened perfect health, and grace, and power, and a self-possession and self-restraint so habitual that it had become unconscious," attributes which make those forms "a perpetual sermon to rich and poor" (*Health and Education* 69). Greek sculpture, in short, is a standing incitement to the pursuit of a "health" that expresses mental soundness in superb physical vigor: "harmony and sympathy, proportion and grace, in every faculty of mind and body" (*Health and Education* 70).

As Kingsley was exhorting audiences to attend to the "sermon" embodied in Greek sculpture, Pater was forming a critical program that also looked to Greek sculpture as an ideal at once aesthetic and moral. In "Winckelmann" (1867), which has been called "the first rallying cry ... of the new aesthetic hellenism" (Jenkyns 222), he instances the Panathenaic frieze as the epitome of "that Hellenic ideal, in which man is at unity with himself, with his physical nature, with the outward world," because he had not yet begun to pursue "a perfection that makes the blood turbid, and frets the flesh, and discredits the actual world about us" (*Renaissance* 177). Here is an ideal of health closely akin to Kingsley's: a vitality that emanates from an "unperplexed" mind, which has not been baffled and enervated by the quest for an ascetic "perfection" that would denigrate the body. Of course, as Bruce Haley has demonstrated, in its outlines this ideal was a widely shared tenet of a great variety of Victorian writing. But whereas Kingsley's conception seems most importantly indebted to Carlyle's identification of health, both intellectual and physical, with unconscious vigor, Pater's account of the Greek mind as "unperplexed" derives most immediately from Hegel's *Aesthetik.* "Winckelmann" bears surprisingly close affinities to Carlyle, however, inasmuch as the essay, in effect, historicizes the German Romanticism that Carlyle so influentially popularized in England, by going back to the wellsprings of the tradition – through Hegel and Goethe to Winckelmann, and thence to "the Hellenic ideal" in its earliest incarnations in Greek sculpture. While Pater constructs an intellectual genealogy that seems to exclude Carlyle, that patriarchal figure is ever-present as the mediator of Goethe's example – a mediation tellingly signalled when Pater perpetuates Carlyle's influential misquotation of Goethe's account of culture,

"Im Ganzen, Guten, Wahren" (*Renaissance* 182).[5] In this light, Pater's celebration of the "unperplexed" Hellenic ideal, and of Winckelmann's ability "to escape from abstract theory to intuition, to the exercise of sight and touch" (*Renaissance* 147), shares with Kingsley's ideal of health a crucial shaping influence as well as similar aspirations.

One strand of Pater's argument in "Winckelmann," however, evokes Winckelmann's conception of ancient Greece only to reject it, in accordance with Pater's broadly Hegelian logic, as an intellectual state from which we are irrevocably estranged; Greek sculpture endures as an emblem of our distance from Greece, not as an ideal for the present. Yet on this point "Winckelmann" betrays a divided allegiance that characterizes the whole of Pater's career, and which underscores Pater's affiliation with Kingsley. "Winckelmann" outwardly endorses Hegel's consummately Romantic teleology: Greek art declined, Pater explains, because "it was necessary that a conflict should come, that some sharper note should grieve the existing harmony, and the spirit chafed by it beat out at last only a larger and profounder music" (*Renaissance* 178). This scheme informs Pater's contention that Winckelmann is a splendid anachronism, and that Goethe's example was necessary to confirm the authority of the Hellenic ideal in the modern world. Yet Pater's construction of an authoritative critical "character" in his earliest surviving essay, "Diaphaneite" (1864), so closely anticipates his account of both Winckelmann and Greek sculpture that "Winckelmann" incorporates verbatim a number of phrases from the earlier essay (*Renaissance* 418, 424, 434–5). Greek art likewise merges with a modern critical ideal in the ideal of culture that Pater derives (again, via Carlyle) from Goethe: "For Goethe, possessing all modern interests, ready to be lost in the perplexed currents of modern thought, he defines, in clearest outlines, the eternal problem of culture – balance, unity with oneself, consummate Greek modelling" (*Renaissance* 182). In this context, "consummate Greek modelling" reaffirms Pater's Hegelian contention that the Hellenic ideal defines "*the* standard of taste" throughout the history of European art (*Renaissance* 159, my emphasis), but also departs from Hegel's claim that the modern mind has, in effect, outgrown that achievement. For Pater, that is, the modern pursuit of culture emulates the formal triumph of Greek sculpture as a perfect embodiment of the Greek mind: in Pater's usage Hegel's *Allgemeinheit* and

Heiterkeit, breadth and repose, are simultaneously physical and psychological attributes, not only in Greek sculpture but in Winckelmann himself. This two-fold triumph is more subtly evoked in the ambiguity of "he," who "defines the eternal problem of culture" for Goethe: the pronoun most immediately refers to Winckelmann, but it equally applies to any male form in classical sculpture. That ambiguity is pushed towards identity in the central metaphor of the essay, which presents Winckelmann's temperament as "a relic of classical antiquity," whose appearance, like the previous excavation of literal relics of Greek art, at once confirms and extends the enduring authority of "the Hellenic tradition." The trope urges us to envision Winckelmann not merely as an intellect but as a body, a being who uncannily resembles those bodies in Greek sculpture that so triumphantly incarnate mind in material form.

This early formulation of "culture" delineates a recurrent division in Pater's writings. "The Hellenic Ideal" is the product of what he calls "the delicate pause in Greek reflexion," which under his Hegelian logic is irrecoverable (*Renaissance* 165). Unlike Hegel, however, Pater yearns to recapture some equivalent of that "happy limit" to self-consciousness embodied in Greek sculpture – even as he savors the appeal of the turbulent, brooding "inwardness" of Romantic art.[6] Of course this divided allegiance is a familiar Romantic structure, which is powerfully articulated in Carlylean aspiration: the Paterian observer struggles through the cultivation of self-consciousness to escape from the burdens of self-consciousness.[7] Kingsley's muscular Christianity represents (among other things) an effort to cut this Gordian knot of belatedness by celebrating a willed truncation of consciousness, which tends to a glorification of impulsive action. Thus, for example, Aben-Ezra in *Hypatia*, at "the bottom of the abyss" in speculation, puts himself on the road to "a faith past arguments" when he impulsively intervenes to rescue the Christian Victoria (*Life and Works* IX 185; X 5). Amyas Leigh embodies a similar assurance in *Westward Ho!*, where Kingsley stresses the scheming and tortured apologetics of the Jesuits in order to celebrate by contrast Amyas's vigorous habit of "just doing the right thing without thinking about it" (V 65). Pater, on the other hand, cultivates the tension of opposing ideals, which are anatomized in the incessant dualisms of his writings – pagan and medieval, classical and Romantic, Dorian and Ionian, centrifugal and centripetal – and embodied in his various *Imaginary Portraits*, the protagonists of which are typically torn by the claims of "rival religions," as the conflict is phrased in *Marius the Epicurean*. Far more than Kingsley, Pater dramatizes the fascination of Carlyle's "abyss" of self-scrutiny as an allurement at once exhilarating and treacherous. Nonetheless, the longing to recover some latter-day equivalent of the "happy limit" of Greek thought is a recurrent structure in his writing. Indeed, even the "Conclusion" to *The Renaissance* can be usefully read as the mapping of a Carlylean strategy, in which Pater deploys a mastery of "modern thought" in order to destroy the authority of that thought, to insist on the emptiness of "theories" as anything more than stimuli to an ideal of "success in life" which leaves them behind. That "success," moreover, recapitulates the economy of Carlylean work inasmuch as it offers labor as its own reward. For Paterean observation is indeed a labor: "To burn always with a hard gem-like flame," which is how Pater defines "success in life," is the goal of a remarkably strenuous hedonism, which owes as much to Carlyle's example as to the "modern thought" of contemporary science (*Renaissance* 188–9). "See, for the night cometh, wherein no man may see" – thus Pater's "Conclusion" in effect rewrites the injunction of John 9:4, which energized so much of Carlyle's social gospel and thereby became perhaps the fundamental imperative of high Victorian moral earnestness.[8]

I am suggesting, then, that in both rhetoric and psychological economy the ethical program of Pater's aestheticism develops out of the structures of Carlylean earnestness, a genealogy which it shares with Kingsley's muscular Christianity. From the very outset of his career, Pater, like Kingsley, follows Carlyle's lead in resisting abstract and metaphysical questions as, at best, "unprofitable" to an ideal of "success in life" for which self-delighting experience is its own reward. If we have overlooked this affiliation, it is principally because we have been blinded by the power of gender ideology, within which Pater and Kingsley seem to stand as virtually antithetical models of masculinity. Or, to adapt a crudeness that befits traditional accounts of the period, Kingsley is the quintessence of "manliness," while Pater evokes all that is "unmanly" and "effeminate." Anyone wishing to enforce the contrast can find ample material merely in the two writers' differing responses to Greek sculpture. Whereas Pater emphasizes the delicacy and grace of its figures, Kingsley stresses their incarnation of physical power, and that distinction in turn informs a more specifically erotic contrast:

Kingsley is careful to stress "the awful yet tender beauty of the maiden figures from the Parthenon and its kindred temples" (*Health and Education* 69–70) whereas Pater clearly endorses Winckelmann's views that the supreme beauty of Greek art "is rather male than female," and as such can only be fully appreciated by those who share Winckelmann's "enthusiasm" – enthusiasm "in the broad Platonic sense of the *Phaedrus*" (*Renaissance* 152).

Pater's is certainly the more canny appropriation of Greek sculpture, particularly in the relative deliberation and explicitness with which he insinuates its erotic – which is to say, homoerotic – appeal. But there remains a powerful shared impulse in the two writers' responses, which should complicate our understanding not merely of Kingsley and Pater, but of the gender ideology in which they are so often opposed. Pater's depictions of the recovery of Greek sculpture clearly enact his imaginative identification with an escape from baffled self-consciousness:

Filled as our culture is with the classical spirit, we can hardly imagine how deeply the human mind was moved, when, at the Renaissance, in the midst of a frozen world, the buried fire of ancient art rose up from under the soil. Winckelmann here reproduces for us the earlier sentiment of the Renaissance. On a sudden the imagination feels itself free. How facile and direct, it seems to say, is this life of the senses and the understanding, when once we have apprehended it! Here, surely, is that more liberal mode of life we have been seeking for so long, so near to us all the while. How mistaken and roundabout have been our efforts to reach it by mystic passion, and monastic reverie; how they have deflowered the flesh; how little have they really emancipated us! Hermione melts from her stony posture, and the lost proportions of life right themselves. (*Renaissance* 146–7)

"Suddenly the imagination feels itself free": that exclamation is charged with both exhilaration and pathos, particularly in light of what Billie Andrew Inman has recently discovered about the scandal that nearly destroyed Pater's career at Oxford in the 1870s. Here, nearly a decade earlier, Pater daringly insinuated the subversive power of an erotic liberation in likening the recovery of buried Greek relics to the opening of "an ancient plague-pit" from which "all the world took the contagion of life and of the senses" (180). The phrasing seems to cast a gibe not only at medieval Christianity, but at contemporary constructions of a moral hygiene that identified sexual discipline with effective sanitation, and hence might find the erotic freedom of Greek art "unhealthy" (Mort

19–64). Of course Kingsley himself was one of the leading participants in such constructions – his invocations of Greek sculpture
frequently appear in his writings on sanitation – and he anticipates
objections to Greek sculpture when he insists on its paradoxical
conjunction of freedom and discipline: "a self-possession and self-
restraint so habitual and complete that it had become unconscious,
and undistinguishable from the native freedom of the savage"
(*Health and Education* 69). Yet such responses are at one with Pater's
in vividly suggesting how powerful a vehicle of sublimation Greek
sculpture was to the middle-class Victorian spectator. It is a measure
of Kingsley's erotic investment in those forms that he so frequently
conjoins them with modern "savages": they are produced by:

a people of rare physical beauty, of acutest eye for proportion and grace,
with opportunities for studying the human figure such as exist nowhere
now, save among tropic savages, and gifted, moreover, in that as in all
other matters, with that innate diligence, of which Mr. Carlyle has said,
"that genius is only an infinite capacity of taking pains ... " (*Lectures* 24)

Ostensible opposites, Greek art and modern "savagery" converge in
Kingsley's mind as the two realms in which nakedness is available to
a contemporary public gaze. But "savage" nudity unsettles Kingsley because he construes it as the mark of a sexuality unrestrained by
self-discipline; Greek sculpture, by contrast, enables Kingsley – as it
does Pater – to regard the human form in all its erotic attraction as a
triumphant intellectual achievement. Pater anatomizes the shared
appeal quite closely: the goal is to recover a perspective that "does
not fever the conscience," like the "sensuousness" that Winckelmann realizes when "he fingers those pagan marbles with unsinged
hands" (*Renaissance* 177). In Greek art Pater finds a perfect sublimation of desire in aesthetic form, or in Kingsley's terms a body at
once free and disciplined, naked and restrained.

In the quest for such satisfaction, Kingsley's rhetoric of disciplined muscularity articulates a powerfully homoerotic gaze, which
is enthralled by the spectacle of virility. Consider, for example, the
fascinating scene in *Alton Locke* when Kingsley's hero first visits the
Dulwich Gallery. Recalling his puritanical mother's iconoclasm –
all pictures were in her eyes "the rags of the scarlet woman no less
than the surplice itself" – Locke enters the gallery "in a fever of
expectation," like the fever which Pater so deftly analyzes in
"Winckelmann." Yet when he enters the gallery – where "the rich
sombre light of the rooms, the rich heavy warmth of the stove-heated

air, the brilliant and varied colouring and gilded frames" underscore the strange, novel sensuousness of the world of art – what arrests Locke's gaze is not the scarlet woman, or indeed any woman:

> my attention was in a moment concentrated on one figure opposite me at the furthest end. I hurried straight towards it. When I had got half-way up the gallery I looked round for my cousin. He had turned aside to some picture of a Venus which caught my eye also, but which, I remember now, only raised in me then a shudder and a blush, and a fancy that the clergymen must be really as bad as my mother had taught me to believe, if they would allow in their galleries pictures of undressed women. I have learnt to view things differently now, thank God. I have learnt that to the pure all things are pure. I have learnt the meaning of that great saying – the foundation of all art, as well as all modesty, all love, which tells us how "the man and his wife were both naked, and not ashamed" ...
> Timidly, but eagerly, I went up to the picture, and stood entranced before it. It was Guido's St. Sebastian. (*Life and Works* VII 180–81)

In its retrospective conclusion that "to the pure all things are pure," the passage obviously re-enacts Kingsley's reconciliation with his own sexuality, which, as David Rosen explores in an essay appearing in this volume, is rehearsed in early letters from Kingsley to his wife. But the prohibition of graven images curiously exempts the male form: Locke's gaze is regulated not by strictures against art as such, but by gendered desire. The retrospective invocation of purity is redundant when it comes to the mesmerizing image of St. Sebastian, which so powerfully embodies Kingsley's own sense of erotic martyrdom as a young man in the torments of unfulfilled desire:

> those manly limbs, so grand and yet so delicate, standing out against the background of lurid light, the helplessness of the bound arms, the arrow quivering in the shrinking side, the upturned brow, the eye in whose dark depths enthusiastic faith seemed conquering agony and shame, the parted lips, which seemed to ask, like the martyrs in the Revelations, reproachful, half-resigned, "O Lord how long?" – Gazing at that picture since, I have understood how the idolatry of painted saints could arise in the minds even of the most educated, who were not disciplined by that strength of regard for fact which is – or ought to be – the strength of Englishmen. I have understood the heart of that Italian girl, whom some such picture of Saint Sebastian, perhaps this very one, excited, as the Praxiteles the Grecian boy, to hopeless love, madness, and death. (V 181–2)

So enraptured is the gaze – "my eyes seemed bursting from my head with the intensity of my gaze" – that the sway of "discipline" can be exerted only retrospectively, through interjected understandings of "the pure" and "that strength of regard for fact" and "what I have understood" that were realized only later. But of course another discipline is already incarnated in the painting itself, where the tortuous constraint of Sebastian becomes a powerfully erotic spectacle in its own right – recalling the sado-masochistic images of the martyred Saint Elizabeth of Hungary that Kingsley composed for his wife-to-be during their divided courtship. The passage eroticizes discipline itself, as inhibitions are conquered and sensuous appetites fulsomely indulged, only to be repeatedly checked by further interventions of discipline in new forms, which in turn generate new pleasures. Tellingly, at this very moment in the novel, Locke is awakened from his erotic "trance" and catches sight of Lillian, who will become the great passion of his life. Having cast aside the Puritanism of his mother by entering the gallery, Locke experiences the enraptured "idolatry" of the novice; that erotic passion is abruptly constrained by appeals to a subsequent experience of art, but the rapture is nonetheless prolonged in the fictional present – albeit now transferred to the alter-ego of "Italian girl" or "Grecian boy" – until the appeal of art itself is undermined by the intrusion of a form, "Beautiful, beautiful, beautiful, beyond all statue, picture, or poet's dream." "My newfound Venus Victrix," as Locke thinks of Lillian, arrests at once the appeal of art and the homoerotic desire called out by the torments of Saint Sebastian, which is now almost ritualistically cast out in favor of the Venus from which he had just previously turned away. Locke, in short, repudiates the idolatry of art and the male form on behalf of a living, female idol – an idol whom he will ultimately cast out in turn as unworthy of his passion.

A more thorough-going scrutiny of Kingsley's writings would reveal how profoundly they are structured by what Eve Kosofsky Sedgwick has called "homosocial desire", which sustains a powerful continuum between normative and transgressive sexualities. Here I simply want to begin to break down traditional characterizations that would oppose Pater and Kingsley as radically divergent forms of masculinity. As they distort the complex and shifting structures of gender in Victorian discourse, such oppositions also lead to caricatures of the particular writers in question. Consider, for example, Richard Jenkyns's recent sneering characterization of Pater in *The Victorians and Ancient Greece*, as "a middle-aged gentleman loitering wistfully at the edge of the playing fields" (225). Some might indeed elicit that impression from a reverie over the image of Socrates at

Salamis, where, "then sixteen years of age, the loveliest and most cultivated lad in Athens, undraped like a faun, with lyre in hand, was leading the chorus of Athenian youths ..." But these are not Pater's words, they are Kingsley's, from his late essay "The Stage as It Was Once" (*Lectures* 26).[9] That they could be confused so easily should remind us that Kingsley, too, frequently engages in a virtually pagan exultation over the spectacle of the virile body. The gentleman at the edge of the playing-fields, after all, was frequently a man who had been, or perhaps continued to be, an immensely vigorous, "manly" participant in games.

Of course the powerful homoerotic dimension in Kingsley's writings failed to incite the sort of suspicion that greeted Pater's works. An immense array of factors entered into this difference in reception, but one crucial distinction is the absence in Pater's work of any overt structure of traditional ethical discipline in his spectatorship – a discipline that would have (among other things) outwardly regulated the erotic pleasures of spectatorship in a manner akin to Kingsley's strategy in *Alton Locke*. Instead, Pater's "culture" is a standing affront to an ethos that associates both morality and masculinity with aggressive, concerted action in the public realm – an ethos that was similarly antagonized by Arnold's "culture," which was likewise denounced as effeminate. Over against Kingsleyan calls to strenuous physical activity and exercise, Pater seemed to offer only detached, passive contemplation, "the exercise of sight and touch" evoked in "Winckelmann." That enterprise, moreover, was presented through a rhetoric of secret wisdom and cultic experience that was further provocation to a Kingsleyan rhetoric of open, democratic "manliness." Yet in so far as Pater presents his own "exercise" as the refinement of a Carlylean earnestness, he is able to appropriate something of the rhetoric of earnestness. In the process, he defends himself against contemporary suspicion by presenting aesthetic contemplation as a strenuous discipline, akin to, perhaps precisely congruent with, that discipline which shaped both the subjects and techniques of Greek art.

A hint of this rhetoric appears in "Winckelmann," in Pater's account of both Greek sculpture and "the eternal problem of culture" – which are in effect the same achievement. The "generality" of Greek sculpture, Pater urges, "has nothing in common with the lax observation, the unlearned thought, the flaccid execution" of some art denoted "general" (he is evidently thinking of Rossetti's criticism of "Sir Sloshua" Reynolds) but arises instead from a culture "minute, severe, constantly renewed, rectifying and concentrating its impressions" (*Renaissance* 170). That discipline is to be emulated by those in the modern world who seek Goethe's life *im Ganzen*: the aspiring intellect must rigorously grapple with "every divided form of culture" in the construction of a perfectly disinterested vitality: "It struggles with these forms till its secret is won from each, and then lets each fall back into its place, in the supreme, artistic view of life. With a kind of passionate coldness, such natures rejoice to be away from and past their former selves" (183). "Passionate coldness" neatly distills the disciplined vitality that both Pater and Kingsley discover in Greek sculpture, as well as the qualities evoked in the capacity "to burn with a hard, gem-like flame." In his later writings Pater increasingly locates a model for such discipline in Greek *askesis*, a concept which suggestively unites physical and mental exercise in a discipline which, like Kingsleyan muscularity, is also erotically charged.[10] But Pater's development of the rhetoric of ascesis assumes an emphatically gendered character only after the publication of *The Renaissance*, when accusations of "effeminate desires" in his writings, in conjunction with private scandal at Oxford, became increasingly threatening.[11]

Paterian ascesis takes on a more recognizably contemporary bearing in *Marius the Epicurean*, Pater's most sustained and explicit response to the outcry provoked by *The Renaissance*. In a footnote added to the third edition of *The Renaissance* (1888), Pater explained that he had omitted the "Conclusion" in the second edition "as I conceived that it might possibly mislead some of those young men into whose hands it might fall," but is now restoring it, "since I have dealt more fully in *Marius the Epicurean* with the thoughts suggested by it" (186). The unsettling reception of *The Renaissance* quite pointedly informs the narrator's insistence that Marius's skepticism is *not* "a languid, enervating, consumptive nihilism, a precept of 'renunciation,' which would touch and handle and deal with nothing" (I 135). Tellingly, Pater envisions his adversary in precisely the language of Kingsley's attacks on Tractarian "Manichaeism." Marius's "New Cyrenaicism," Pater responds, is "not so properly the utterance of the 'jaded Epicurean' as of the strong young man in all the freshness of thought and feeling," who pursues "that clear-eyed intellectual consistency, which is like spotless bodily cleanliness, or scrupulous personal honor" (II 16). The hyperbolic insistence on purity and vigor suggests the rigors of mid-Victorian – and specifically Kingsleyan – gender surveillance. Moreover, Marius's intellectual pilgrimage confirms the most cherished virtues of Victorian moral earnestness. Despite his skepticism, Marius evinces "a genuine virility," "vigorous intelligence," "a cold austerity of mind," "the honest action of his own untroubled, unassisted intelligence" (1 124–5); even when he embraces the daring views of Heraclitus, Marius finds there "many precepts towards a strenuous self-consciousness in all we think and do, that loyalty to cool and candid reason, which makes strict attentiveness of mind a kind of religious service" (1 130).

Virile, vigorous, austere, honest, untroubled, strenuous, loyal, candid, strict, religious: these are adjectives far more readily associated with Kingsley's characters than with Pater's. But their prominence in *Marius* not only reflects the apologetic design of the novel; they are in keeping with the dynamic of ascesis throughout his writings, although they recast that dynamic in a form that readily appropriates the vocabulary of Victorian moral earnestness, which still carried immense authority in 1885. In *Marius* and indeed throughout Pater's later writings, the dialectical structures within which ascesis operates become still more emphatically gendered, as the rhetoric of earnestness is supplemented by appeal to the ancient dichotomy of masculine reason and feminine matter. *Plato and Platonism* makes this formulation especially central, setting forth a conception of "manliness in art" as the type and basis of a comprehensive masculine ethos:

Manliness in art, what can it be, as distinct from that which in opposition to it must be called the feminine quality there, – what but a full consciousness of what one does, of art itself in the work of art, tenacity of intuition and consequent purpose, the spirit of construction as opposed to what is literally incoherent or ready to fall to pieces, and, in opposition to what is hysteric or works at random, the maintenance of a standard. (*Plato* 280–81)

Not surprisingly, Pater's association of exacting prose with ancient norms of masculinity has found a sympathetic audience among male readers. Indeed, in an unwitting tribute to the success of Pater's rhetorical self-construction, the anthropologist David Gilmore has recently quoted this description of "manliness in art" as the epitome of a trans-cultural norm of "manhood" understood as "a mythic confabulation that sanctifies male constructivity" (113, 226). But in historical context, Gilmore's quotation of Pater as a spokesman for

manhood is rich in irony: Pater's account of "manliness" is formulated in tacit response to suspicions about his own masculinity, and
that of his aestheticism; it is offered in a volume devoted to Plato,
whose writings were for Pater and late-Victorian culture a central
locus of transgressive male sexuality; and Pater defines this norm in
terms that his own early writings seem to confound. "The maintenance of a standard" is precisely what Pater seems to renounce in his
early writings, inasmuch as the phrase suggests an evaluation of art
in accordance with some specific set of aesthetic norms, rather than
a self-delighting surrender to "experience." Yet the discipline of
such a limiting, shaping, ascetic standard is already at work in the
"Conclusion," I've suggested, as a *psychological* program for organizing one's life into "a hard gem-like flame." This disciplinary impulse
becomes foregrounded in Pater's later writings, both in presen-
tations of the writer's craft as a strenuous, exacting search for the
Flaubertian *mot juste* – most notably in "Style" – and in the sustained
project of self-fashioning that occupies Marius in his skeptical pilgrimage. Indeed, even the pronounced reserve of Pater's characters,
which is so marked a departure from the bluff self-assertiveness of
Kingsleyan heroes, is offered as the mark of a strenuous self-
discipline: reserve embodies one's power of self-control, incorporat-
ing what Pater elsewhere calls Plato's "intellectual astringency," for
example, "enhancing the sense of power in oneself, and its effect
upon others, by a certain crafty reserve in its exercise" (*Plato*
280–81).

With the cultivation of this disciplined reserve, however, Pater's
characters bring to appropriately veiled light the strains in late-
Victorian discourse of manliness. Tractarian reserve, after all, had
called forth widespread denunciations of an effeminate, deceiving
treachery, which violated every canon of forthright, plain-spoken
English manhood. At the same time, however, such reserve exercised an undeniable, albeit profoundly unsettling, fascination:
witness Kingsley's own obsessive preoccupation with Newman and
his associates. I have argued elsewhere that Pater's rhetoric appeals
to such fascination through a calculated appropriation of the
Tractarian reserve that transgressed normative "manliness"
("Gentleman, Dandy, Priest"). In his late writings, Pater gives a
different slant to this tension by situating reserve within normative
programs of masculine discipline that appealed centrally to the cult
of late-Victorian athleticism. Thus in "Lacedaemon" (1892),

reprinted in *Plato and Platonism*, Pater looks to Spartan discipline as a
fundamentally aesthetic exercise, precisely congruent in its mental
regime with the self-discipline sustained by the Paterian beholder.
"Why this loyalty to a system, so costly to you individually?" is the
question Pater poses to the Spartan ephebe. The question is
enforced by the "Conclusion" to *The Renaissance*, where Pater had
urged that *any* "theory or idea or system which requires of us the
sacrifice of any part of" the world of experience "in consideration of
some interest into which we cannot enter ... has no real claim upon
us" (189). In "Lacedaemon," however, Pater has discovered a
profound congruence between the late-Victorian cult of athleticism
and his own enterprise: his imaginary Spartan ephebe responds,
"To the end that I myself may be a perfect work of art" (*Plato* 232).
In the rigors of Spartan discipline, Pater can find a technology of the
self, in Foucault's phrase, that confirms a gratifying sense of authority through the aesthetic discipline of one's mind and body. As
Linda Dowling points out, Pater in "Lacedaemon" thereby deftly
"appropriate[s] the language of cultural legitimation in such a way
as to authenticate the proscribed" (5) – namely, the unnamed
pederasty that centrally structures Spartan discipline – by couching
it in a rhetoric absolutely fitted to the most "manly" Victorian
schoolmaster. Spartan discipline, in Pater's account, "ethically ...
aimed at the reality, aesthetically at the expression, of reserved
power, and from the first set its subject on the thought of his personal
dignity, of self-command, in the artistic way of a good musician, a
good soldier" (221) – or a Paterian writer, one might add, for the
discipline thus evoked is not only that of Marius, but of Pater's own
program of "manliness in art" as it is set forth in "Style."

   To be sure, Pater's sympathy with the Spartan project is characteristically hedged: the essay concludes by stressing the mystery of
the motives underlying "that exacting discipline of character." But
Pater returns to just such a discipline in "Emerald Uthwart" (1892;
republished in *Miscellaneous Studies*), an imaginary portrait that
readers have long recognized as a companion piece to "Lacedaemon." In "Lacedaemon," Pater repeatedly draws analogies
between Spartan training and a Victorian public school education;
in "Emerald Uthwart," Pater depicts a contemporary English
schoolboy who seems the almost wholly passive recipient of "influences," shaped like the young Spartans in perfect compliance to
"the lightest touch, of the finger of law" (*Plato* 79). At school,

Uthwart is "the plain tablet, for the influences of the place to inscribe" (*Miscellaneous* 179); through such inscription he is impressed with a "sense of responsibility to the place" (185) that reproduces the young Marius's "sense of responsibility ... to the world of men and things" (1 18), just as the fascination of young Marius's reserve is echoed in the young Uthwart's "soldier-like, impassible self-command" (184), which arrests the gaze of all around him. Here, however, Pater more obviously locates the model of his ephebe's fashioning in the Hellenic ideal embodied in Greek sculpture. Even as the influences of his school shape the "unmeaningly handsome facial type" in a more complex expressiveness, Uthwart retains a seemingly perfect psychic equilibrium: all these influences leave "the firm, unconscious simplicity of the boyish nature still unperplexed." Here is the world of Greek sculpture uncannily reconstituted in the modern world as the apparent goal of Paterian discipline. "It would misrepresent Uthwart's wholly unconscious humility to say that he felt the beauty of the *askesis* ... to which ... as under a fascination he submissively yields himself" (182). Yet the achievement is destroyed in a moment when, with the exuberant daring of a young soldier, Uthwart violates military law – "almost the sole irregular or undisciplined act of Uthwart's life" (139). Within the program of Paterian discipline, what could otherwise seem merely a wayward irruption of desire re-enacts the transgression of the Greek mind's "happy limit" – a curtailment that Pater at once longs to recover and at the same time suggests is an impossible, self-destructive repression. As William Shuter has noted, the very aesthetic perfection Uthwart embodies also makes him a sacrificial victim.

"Young Apollo," Uthwart is called; but, the narrator objects, he "was more like a real portrait of a real young Greek, like Trypho, son of Eutychos" (191). That model refers us once again to the critical authority of Greek sculpture, which in "Emerald Uthwart" as in "Lacedaemon" seems perpetuated in the rhapsodies of Victorian athleticism. In "The Age of Athletic Prizemen" (1894; subsequently reprinted in *Greek Studies*) the fusion of these two discourses seems complete: for Pater as for Kingsley the heroic athletes of Greek art are superbly reincarnated as cricketers on the banks of the Thames. Like Kingsley, Pater looks to the celebration of the body in both English youth and Greek art as an aesthetic triumph that affirms a consoling theology. "Man with them was divine, inasmuch as he could perceive beauty and be beautiful himself," as Kingsley phrases it in "The Stage as It Was Once" (*Lectures* 52), and the "work" of the Greeks in every sphere was to assert "the dignity of man." Pater initially finds in heroic sculpture a more specific triumph: its celebration of youth, he urges, is "a sign that essential mastery has been achieved by the artist ... For such youth, in its very essence, is a matter properly within the limits of the visible, the empirical world; and in the presentment of it there will be no place for symbolic hint" (*Greek* 282). But what might seem a narrowly technical achievement encapsulates the governing impulse of Pater's aestheticism: from his earliest writings Pater presents his vocation as a programmatic extension of empiricism, which would confine and focus the mind's activity "within the limits of the visible, the empirical world." Hence the seeming paradox that Pater's acutely self-conscious discipline could find not merely a stimulating beauty but an emblem of its largest aspirations in the perfectly unconscious perfection of the Discobolus, which embodies "all one has ever fancied or seen, in old Greece or on Thames' side, of the unspoiled body of youth, thus delighting itself and others, at the perfect, because unconscious, point of good fortune, as it moves and rests just there for a moment, between the animal and spiritual worlds" (288). One could hardly find a more eloquent contribution to the late-Victorian celebration of athleticism – even, curiously, to the pronounced current of anti-intellectualism that animates it: "It is of the essence of the athletic prizemen ... not to give expression to mind, in any antagonism to, or invasion of, the body; to mind as anything more than a function of the body, whose healthful balance of functions it may so easily perturb; – to disavow that insidious enemy of the fairness of the bodily soul as such" (286).

Of course, one might see Pater's description as a quiet parody of Kingsleyan muscularity, inasmuch as it evacuates any hint of mind in fetishizing the athletic body – removing the *mens sana* from the *corpore sano*. Pater is in league with the "insidious enemy," after all, inasmuch as his description will not allow us to forget the mind that the sculpture – like youth itself – excludes. But what he is constructing here is yet another representation of the Greek mind's "happy limit," which like the achievement of the athlete is a delicate, precarious poise "just there for a moment, between the animal and spiritual worlds." In fact, the sculpture embodies at least three time schemes: the brief moment of stasis in the athlete's motion, the point of equilibrium between youth and maturity, between "the animal and spiritual worlds," and "the delicate pause in Greek reflection" that marks the Greek mind's happy limit in the history of human consciousness. By presenting the psychic equilibrium of the Hellenic ideal in such emphatically temporal terms, Pater seems to renounce any possibility of recovering it, to ironize the nostalgia informing his rapturous gaze. Once again, however, Pater's response to Greek sculpture reproduces the divided aspirations of his own vocation. In the very moment of his success, the athlete may be unconscious, yet his achievement in all its significance, Pater reminds us, is the product of a sustained, concerted discipline. "The athletic life certainly breathes of abstinence, of rule, of the keeping under of oneself. And here in the Diadumenus, we have one of its priests, a priest of the religion whose central motive was what has been called 'the worship of the body'" (295). Such discipline is obviously reproduced in the ascetic discipline of those who commemorate it, the sculptor and Pater himself, who consistently presents his vocation as an assertion of rule dedicated to the worship of the body, as the focal point of a delight in the visible, sensuous world. The Discobolus, Pater notes, is full of "learned involution," yet that quality is entirely "subordinated to the proper purpose of the Discobolus as a work of art, a thing to be looked at rather than to think about" (306). Once again the refinement of self-consciousness is deployed to the aim of arresting reflection, and such is the aspiration of Pater's own criticism. The notion that art is "a thing to be looked at rather than to think about" may seem incongruous with Pater's own practice in *The Renaissance*, yet it echoes the premise of "The School of Giorgione," that art "is always striving to be independent of the mere intelligence, to become a matter of pure perception" (108). Even in his famous reverie on the *Mona Lisa*, Pater seeks to evoke hidden depths of intention and meaning in order ultimately to return us to the surfaces of an image with an enriched appreciation for its immediate, primary appeal as "a thing for the eye." If the Diadumenus is a priest in the worship of the body, so, too, is Pater: "the Hellenic tradition" invoked in "Winckelmann," after all, is an apostolic succession in which Pater himself figures as but the most recent in a long series of disciples. In this regard not merely the discipline but the crowning achievement of the athletic prizemen is reproduced by the sculptor's labors, and by those of the critic who re-creates and extends the example of both in subsequent generations.

The cricketer or quoits-player "under the eternal form of art" thus becomes at once the object and emblem of Paterian longing. Only in recognizing this significance can we appreciate the extraordinary valedictory with which Pater closes "The Age of Athletic Prizemen":

Take him, to lead you forth out of the narrow limits of the Greek world. You have pure humanity there, with a glowing, yet restrained joy and delight in itself, but without vanity; and it *is* pure. There is nothing certainly supersensual in that fair, round head, anymore than in the long, agile limbs; but also no impediment, natural or acquired. To have achieved just that, was the Greek's truest claim for furtherance in the main line of human development. He had been faithful, we cannot help saying, as we pass from that youthful company, in what comparatively is perhaps little – in the culture, the administration, of the visible world; and he merited, so we might go on to say – he merited Revelation, something which should solace his heart in the inevitable fading of that. We are reminded of those strange prophetic words of the Wisdom, the *Logos*, by whom God made the world ... "I was by him, as one brought up with him; rejoicing in the habitable parts of the earth. My delights were with the sons of men." (*Greek* 318)

In one sense, this emphatic historical framing is a mode of distancing Pater from the achievement he celebrates; certainly the invocation of Christianity seems to hedge Pater's allegiance to the Hellenic ideal in a way that is remote from "Winckelmann." But it is not so much the Greek ideal that has been revalued as Christianity – with the result that Pater's meditation on Greece, despite its characteristically wistful and hesitant rhetoric, startlingly recalls Kingsley's liberal and muscular Christianity. The satisfactions of "pure humanity" incarnated in the athletic body, satisfactions defined through renunciation of the "supersensual," are sanctified, becoming the vehicle of a grace that will redeem those who have proven their worthiness simply through a devotion to "the visible world." In Pater's reverie, the Greek athlete has realized the youthful Kingsley's "strange idea": he has become "an Apollo for His sake."

This is of course a decidedly partial account of its subject, which is content to elicit unexpected affinities – in particular, the striking congruences between two outwardly antithetical disciplines that are in fact affiliated by a shared reliance on the structures of Victorian earnestness and a delight in the spectacle of virility. In an effort to disturb traditional categories of masculinity, I have neglected the many ways in which Pater remains intractably opposed to Kingsley's muscularity. Ultimately, in its great suspicion of spontaneity and cultivation of reserve, the discipline of the Paterian aesthete is more indebted to the example of Thomas Arnold's Christian gentleman, and even to Newman's ascetic priest, than to Kingsley's muscular Christian. But neither of those models had a place for the body and its pleasures except as an adversary to be conquered. Kingsley, perhaps more than any other middle-class Victorian writer, placed the male body into widespread circulation as an object of celebration and desire.[12] In this light, it might well be argued that Kingsley's muscular Christianity was an essential precedent for Pater's aestheticism. A strange idea, perhaps, but the contours of Victorian masculinity offer many unexpected vistas.

NOTES

1 Letter to Fanny Grenfell, June 1842, *Life and Works*, I, 87–8.
2 For accounts of Kingsley's struggles with his sexuality, particularly as they shaped his reaction to Newman and "Manichaeism," see Vance, 31–40 and 78–103; Chitty, 53–63; and Chadwick, 126–31. Critics of Kingsley's fiction tend to focus on the specifically theological and social stances shaped by these struggles; only Vance's work has really taken note of how his narratives might incorporate unresolved sexual tensions, the conflicts of a man, in Chadwick's words, "whom the physical troubled, who worried over the physical, who did not take the body for granted" (129).
3 This is from the *Edinburgh Review* of January 1858, which the *OED* cites in defining "muscular Christianity." However one defines the phrase, the contemporary usage surveyed in Newsome, 195–239, makes clear that contemporaries identified it first and foremost with the cult of athleticism, and it is in this context that I refer to Pater's "muscular aestheticism."
4 A thorough exploration of the representations of Greek sculpture in Victorian culture would be an extremely valuable study. Jenkyns, 133–54, offers a witty but relentlessly patronizing survey of the obvious but deeply troubled erotic investments in late-Victorian responses; Haley's fine study repeatedly notes Victorian appeals to ancient Greece as the norm of "health," but gives no sustained attention to Greek sculpture.
5 As Donald Hill points out in his invaluable edition (439–40), Goethe's words are "Im Ganzen, Guten, Schönen/Resolut zu leben" ("Generalbeichte"); Pater follows Carlyle's immensely telling substitution, in both "Schiller" and "Death of Goethe," of "Wahren" for "Schönen."

6 DeLaura, 202–22, offers a careful account of the tensions in Pater's argument in "Winckelmann," although I would argue he gives too much weight to the influence of Arnold.

7 See Hartman, "Romanticism and Anti-Self-Consciousness," in *After Formalism*, 298–310, for a general account of this structure in Romantic literature.

8 Houghton, 218–62, remains the best survey of Victorian ideals of earnestness. Pater's indebtedness to Carlyle, though frequently noted in passing, has not been studied at length, although Dellamora, 62–7, offers a suggestive account of "Diaphaneite" that stresses Pater's revision of Carlylean masculine anxiety.

9 Ironically, Jenkyns quotes J. A. Symonds's more dryly expository account of the same episode, in *Studies of the Greek Poets*, in order to elicit a specifically "homosexual" preoccupation from the fact that Symonds "dwell[s] so much upon the poet's adolescence" (217). Kingsley's tribute to fawn-like male beauty might be more profitably pondered in light of Linda Dowling's more careful and incisive speculations about the construction of a "homosexual" code of allusion among writers connected with Oxford in the 1860s and 1870s, including Pater. The central term in that code, Dowling suggests, is the Greek *poikilos*, "dappled" or "pied," which is the term habitually applied to the skin of a fawn, particularly as it is part of the regalia of Bacchus (5–6). Although it is doubtful that Kingsley consciously participated in this community as Dowling defines it, the conjunction reminds us of the ways in which a shared classical education (in every sense of the term) gave middle-class men both experience of and a ready language for vicarious homoerotic pleasure, however consciously articulated.

10 Geoffrey Galt Harpham offers a suggestive account of asceticism as "essentially a meditation on, even an enactment of desire" in contemplating "the relation between human life and aesthetic form" (45 xiv).

11 The rhetorical strategies of Paterian ascesis addressed in the next three paragraphs are discussed more fully in Adams, "Gentleman, Dandy, Priest."

12 Gagnier, *Subjectivities*, 55–98, is a salutary reminder that the separation of mind and body in canonical Victorian discourse is a class-bound distinction responsive to material conditions; working-class memoirs, recounting lives in which physical labor had a much more central place, naturally give much more, and less anxious, place to representations of the body.

WORKS CITED

Adams, James Eli, "Gentleman, Dandy, Priest: Manliness and Social Authority in Pater's Aestheticism," *ELH* 59 (1992): 269–94.

Chadwick, Owen, *The Spirit of the Oxford Movement*. Oxford: Clarendon, 1990.

Chitty, Susan, *The Beast and the Monk: A Life of Charles Kingsley*. London: Hodder and Stoughton, 1975.

DeLaura, David J., *Hebrew and Hellene in Victorian England: Newman, Arnold, Pater*. Austin: University of Texas Press, 1969.

Dellamora, Richard, *Masculine Desire: The Sexual Politics of Victorian Aestheticism*. Chapel Hill: University of North Carolina Press, 1990.

Dowling, Linda, "Ruskin's Pied Beauty and the Constitution of a 'Homosexual' Code," *Victorian Newsletter* 75 (1989): 1–7.

Gagnier, Regenia, *Subjectivities: A History of Self-Representation in Britain, 1832–1920*. Oxford University Press, 1991.

Gilmore, David D., *Manhood in the Making: Cultural Concepts of Masculinity*. New Haven: Yale University Press, 1990.

Haley, Bruce, *The Healthy Body and Victorian Culture*. Cambridge, MA: Harvard University Press, 1978.

Harpham, Geoffrey Galt, *The Ascetic Imperative in Culture and Criticism*. University of Chicago Press, 1987.

Hartman, Geoffrey, "Romanticism and Anti-Self-Consciousness" in *After Formalism*. New Haven: Yale University Press, 1970, pp. 298–310.

Houghton, Walter, *The Victorian Frame of Mind 1830–1870*. New Haven: Yale University Press, 1954.

Inman, Billie Andrew, "Estrangement and Connection: Walter Pater, Benjamin Jowett, and William M. Hardinge" in *Pater in the 1990s*, eds. Laurel Brake and Ian Small. Greensboro, NC: ELT Press, 1990, pp. 1–20.

Jenkyns, Richard, *The Victorians and Ancient Greece*. Cambridge, MA: Harvard University Press, 1981.

Kingsley, Charles, *Health and Education*. New York: Appleton, 1893.
Lectures Delivered in America in 1874. London: Longman, Green & Co., 1875.
The Life and Works of Charles Kingsley, 19 vols. London: Macmillan, 1901.

Mangan, J. A., *Athleticism in the Victorian and Edwardian Public School*. London: Farmer Press, 1986.

Mort, Frank, *Dangerous Sexualities: Medico-Moral Politics in England Since 1830*. London: Routledge & Kegan Paul, 1987.

Newsome, David, *Godliness and Good Learning: Four Studies on a Victorian Ideal*. London: Cassell, 1961.

Pater, Walter, *Greek Studies*. London: Macmillan, 1910.
Marius the Epicurean, 2 vols. London: Macmillan, 1910.
Miscellaneous Studies. London: Macmillan, 1910.
Plato and Platonism. London: Macmillan, 1910.
The Renaissance: Studies in Art and Poetry, ed. Donald L. Hill. Berkeley: University of California Press, 1980.

Sedgwick, Eve Kosofsky, *Between Men: English Literature and Male Homosocial Desire*. New York: Columbia University Press, 1985.

Shuter, William F., "The Arrested Narrative of 'Emerald Uthwart'," *Nineteenth-Century Literature* 45.1 (1990): 1–25.

Vance, Norman, *The Sinews of the Spirit: The Ideal of Christian Manliness in Victorian Literature and Religious Thought.* Cambridge University Press, 1985.

Index